CRIMINOLOGICAL ETHNOGRAPHY

AN INTRODUCTION

CRIMINOLOGICAL ETHNOGRAPHY

AN INTRODUCTION

JAMES TREADWELL

Los Angeles | London | New Delhi
Singapore | Washington DC | Melbourne

Los Angeles | London | New Delhi
Singapore | Washington DC | Melbourne

SAGE Publications Ltd
1 Oliver's Yard
55 City Road
London EC1Y 1SP

SAGE Publications Inc.
2455 Teller Road
Thousand Oaks, California 91320

SAGE Publications India Pvt Ltd
B 1/I 1 Mohan Cooperative Industrial Area
Mathura Road
New Delhi 110 044

SAGE Publications Asia-Pacific Pte Ltd
3 Church Street
#10-04 Samsung Hub
Singapore 049483

Editor: Natalie Aguilera
Editorial assistant: Eve Williams
Production editor: Sarah Cooke
Marketing manager: George Kimble
Cover design: Stephanie Guyaz
Typeset by: C&M Digitals (P) Ltd, Chennai, India
Printed in the UK

Library of Congress Control Number: 2018967948

British Library Cataloguing in Publication data

A catalogue record for this book is available from
the British Library

ISBN 978-1-4739-7570-5
ISBN 978-1-4739-7571-2 (pbk)

At SAGE we take sustainability seriously. Most of our products are printed in the UK using responsibly sourced
papers and boards. When we print overseas we ensure sustainable papers are used as measured by the PREPS
grading system. We undertake an annual audit to monitor our sustainability.

CONTENTS

ACKNOWLEDGEMENTS

This book has been a long time coming, and it would not have happened without a lot of input and learning from others, such is the way of the ethnographer.

I would like to thank Dr Steve Wakeman. The project began with him and would not have happened without him, however he would not take any credit. I would also like to thank those amongst the Critical Criminology group of the BSC and colleagues and students in and of Criminology interested in ethnography, some of whom I have the pleasure of working with and alongside, many more I have learned from and with. My colleagues at Staffordshire University and in Law, Policing and Forensics, and all those involved in the BSC at BCU in 2018. There are too many criminologists to mention, and lots appear in the book. I hope I didn't miss anyone out.

However, most of these people only work with me. It's living with an ethnographer that is really difficult. In that respect I want to thank Abi and Evie, who put up with many of the negatives that come with living with a long term ethnographer. I love you both and this is dedicated to you.

PART ONE
BACKGROUND

1

WHY CRIMINOLOGICAL ETHNOGRAPHY?

LEARNING OBJECTIVES

This chapter seeks to introduce the reader to the basics of 'criminological ethnography'. It will introduce the basics and fundamentals of social scientific research, the background of which is essential to learn before becoming practised in the application of the approach and methods of ethnography. It will explore the research process and the fundamental conceptual components of undertaking social research, and the core elements of various research approaches. By reading it, you will gain an understanding of the positivist and interpretivist paradigm, as well as more complex ideas that frame all social research. By the end of this chapter you should have a better understanding of:

* what criminological ethnography is
* the basics of criminological research
* what I mean by the terms ontology and epistemology
* the positivist and interpretivist research paradigms
* what is meant by terms such as reliability, validity, generalisability and credibility.

INTRODUCTION

You have been told to go grubbing in the library, thereby accumulating a mass of notes and liberal coating of grime. You have been told to choose problems wherever you can find musty stacks of routine records based on trivial schedules prepared by tired bureaucrats and filled out by reluctant applicants for fussy do-gooders or indifferent clerks. This is called 'getting your hands dirty in real research'. Those who counsel you are wise and honorable; the reasons they offer are of great value. But one more thing is needful: first hand observation. Go and sit in the lounges of the luxury hotels and on the doorsteps of flophouses; sit on the Gold Coast settees and the slum shakedowns; sit in

Orchestra Hall and in the Star and Garter burlesk [sic]. In short, gentlemen, go get the seat of your pants dirty in real research.[1]

Criminological ethnography has entered a Dark Ages of legal constraint and institutional disrespect ... Ethnographic studies are seldom found in mainstream books or journals of crime and deviance ... Such studies are routinely overlooked ... and they receive only scant attention in many textbooks. (Ferrell and Hamm, 1998: 268)

Before I begin it is perhaps useful to briefly say something about the book and its intended aims. This is a book on 'criminological ethnography', an approach which for me has long been a central strand of criminological inquiry. From the outset, I have preferred to try and talk of 'criminological ethnography' as an approach, rather than a methodology, because for me, ethnography is not purely a research method (a data collection technique) or a methodology (a philosophical framework). Rather, I would suggest that it is a research strategy and more than that, a sensibility, that is, a sense of the lived expectations, complexities, contradictions, possibilities and ground of any given cultural group in a setting at a given point. Why ethnography matters where crime and its control are concerned is because it is a way of critical thinking, a way of being and a way of gaining better understanding.

Ethnography is a research strategy that involves spending time within a setting in order to study it. Unlike other qualitative research methods, it tends to be participant focused and driven. Traditionally, it often involved a larger time commitment (though the traditions of longstanding immersion in a setting are perhaps now not as significant as once they were). Almost all ethnographic studies take place within natural settings relating to the participants, as opposed to an artificial setting that is created in research interactions such as interviews. Yet stripped down, the basic ethnographic approach is that of watching, listening, thinking and writing. It is amazing how much there is to see and learn if we just watch, listen and think.

In criminology there is a long history of ethnographic study that dates back to Thrasher's book, *The Gang* (1927), Klockars' work on deviant subculture (1974), and Howard Becker's seminal book *Outsiders* (1963), Polsky's (1967) work on hustlers, Young's book *The Drugtakers* (1971) and Stan Cohen's study of *Folk Devils and Moral Panics* (1972). Much of criminology's most fundamental work has emerged from ethnographic research that some have dismissed as idiosyncratic, impressionistic and marginal. This book is my personal attempt to make it more mainstream.

---

[1] An unpublished statement made by Robert Park, recorded by Howard Becker while a graduate student in the 1920s, and first published in McKinney, 1966: 71.

This book seeks to introduce readers to the varied methodological, practical and ethical challenges involved in doing ethnography on crime and control. It also aims to ensure those working in the field of criminology could become versed in ethnography relevant to the subject, from the simplest fundamentals of the practice to more complex theoretical debates connected with it. To that end, you will find that this book seeks to be a mix between textbook, guide and introduction to the topic, and specifically to that end, the book seeks to be an interesting starting point for those new to the subject, but also, to engage in more complex debates about the nature and character of the ethnographic approach and sensibility as specific to criminology.

WHAT IS 'CRIMINOLOGICAL ETHNOGRAPHY'?

While I am happy to talk of 'criminological ethnography', I recognise that the title might strike some readers as a little odd. The central claim, that there is a strand of the ethnographic endeavour that is specifically 'criminological', or that 'criminological ethnography' is a thing that exists in its own right as a specialism or a subject might, may not convince everyone. However, it would seem to me that rather than being a somewhat niche or specialist research practice used by only a few committed researchers (a caricature that perhaps accurately captures the situation encountered with ethnography and criminology the 1980s and 1990s), the social sciences more broadly, and criminology quite specifically, have increasingly embraced an ethnographic sensibility.

It would seem now that talk of ethnographic criminology or criminological ethnography is becoming established in criminology. Rather than being a marginal or maverick research strategy, ethnography in criminology has become increasingly mainstream and, I would argue, worthy of a book. In 2015 and 2016 I attended symposiums at the University of Leicester and University of Birmingham on 'ethnography on crime and control', and the topic seems to hold a growing interest for students in the UK and the USA. Moreover, I have watched the popular and sometimes controversial reception of texts such as Sudhir Venkatesh's *Gang Leader for a Day* (2009) and Alice Goffman's *On the Run* (2014) and the increasing mainstream appetite for such 'real' research. Criminological ethnography has featured heavily in the nominees in all the major categories of the British Society of Criminology book prizes in recent years, and several recent winners of main book prizes have been for ethnographic work (Fleetwood, 2014; Fraser, 2015) while ethnography has also done well in the critical criminology prize categories in the UK and USA (Ellis, 2016; Briggs and Monge Gamero, 2017). In the UK, the popular BBC Radio 4 programme *Thinking Allowed* has even instituted an annual award for ethnography, and there seems to be growing receptiveness to the method in official quarters. In many ways in criminology, and in the social sciences generally, it seems that ethnography is in the ascendency, moving out of the Dark Ages.

The title of this book was chosen partly out of convenience, and yet I understood there were many other ways I might have framed the focus of this text. I could have stressed the links between ethnography and criminal justice, or ethnography and the study of deviance (and the sociology of deviance). However, I quite like 'criminological ethnography' as the title also reflects the growth of criminology as a subject.

Criminology as an academic subject has gone through something of a meteoric growth, from the first small degrees just a few years ago and its status as largely a postgraduate subject, and has emerged from the periphery of social science to become its success story. In the UK at least, the growth of criminology has come as something of a challenge to sociology, and hence, while many students will take modules on social research or criminological research methods, I am struck by the fact that this often sees ethnography on criminology degrees reduced to just a single teaching session or a textbook chapter. Yet as I hope to show here and in the coming pages, criminological ethnography is sufficiently broad and complex to merit so much more. It is a fantastic subject on which to have real world debates, and to critically reflect on and analyse the state of the discipline of criminology, and the academic enterprise more generally. I would suggest that criminological ethnography then is deserving of more extensive coverage.

It is not my intent to simply produce a textbook that instructs readers how to conduct ethnography of crime and punishment, or use the methods associated with the approach to study crime, criminals and forms of institutionalised punishment. Nor is it my aim to simply cover the history of the discipline and outline and retell the stories of the core contributions. Instead, in this text I am seeking to try to navigate between these aims, and produce a comprehensive, single guide to the topic that gives an idea of what the method entails, how it might and can be done, how it has been used. However, my main aim is that I hope this book will equip readers with a desire to go out and do some ethnographic research. I hope that it will get people as excited about criminological ethnography as I am and demystify the approach. I hear a lot of confusion about the ethnographic approach, especially from those who have not previously used it, and I really hope that this book will help reduce this and, in the process, make ethnography more accessible to emerging researchers, at whatever stage of their studies or career they are.

As a practised ethnographer who has used the approach in a range of settings and contexts, I know well that while it is certainly not easy, criminological ethnography isn't that hard either. It can be undertaken in a range of places, and it can be fruitful in them all. From the street, to the shop, the pub, the custody suite, even the prison, there are plenty of settings where an ethnographic sentiment can shed light on human interactions and help us make sense of the world.

Moreover, while there are many ways to measure and consider crime, crime is a human phenomenon, and while crime can be variously researched, a significant and important part of the crime story should be that human story of crime. Qualitative research, and particularly ethnography, has long been well placed to explore the human stories behind real life crime events and their control, both the mundane and the occasionally spectacular. Of course, this brings methodological, practical and ethical challenges. Undertaking ethnography on crime and control in criminological studies, using participant observation, semi-structured interviewing and analysis of personal documents, has now been commonplace for more than a century. These research techniques can be employed to develop and test theoretical explanations and to examine the process of policy implementation and, importantly, to challenge the often common sense notions of criminality, comparing ideas about law-breaking and violence with the realities and frequently highlighting how reality can be counter to the intuitive position that many people may hold. Ethnography therefore undoubtedly has much to offer criminology.

David Downes has famously claimed that criminology is a rendezvous discipline (Young, 2003: 97), that it is a meeting place for ideas from a range of disciplines and draws on an eclectic range of influences rather than standing as a distinct discipline in its own right. In a similar manner, ethnography as a research approach is something of a rendezvous approach, as strictly speaking and in praxis, ethnography is a collection of qualitative methods. That said, before I attempt to introduce criminological ethnography, I shall attempt to give a brief and simple overview of research in criminology

CRIMINOLOGICAL RESEARCH – THE BASICS THAT YOU NEED TO KNOW

I perhaps ought to start out by simply saying that research, as most will accept, is a systematic investigation of sources and materials in order to establish facts and reach conclusions. Most texts on research methods will start from the point of describing variously the features of research as being a structured, systematic, controlled, empirical and critical investigation of hypothetical positions, questions or propositions about presumed relations and hence, for the most part there is acceptance that:

- research is a *process*
- it must be planned and intended: it does not happen by accident but by design
- facts and data are not necessarily the same as knowledge

- describing a phenomenon is not the same as explaining it
- research must be robust and rigorous
- it must be capable of withstanding external criticism and challenge from individuals who may not agree with the methods employed or findings produced
- for that reason, ethically it should be as transparent as possible to allow for critique.

As I note above, research is a process, and the nature of that process is that it will always have in common three stages in the process:

- the question
- data collection/gathering
- the answer.

On this basis, the generation of the question in research is sequential, and influences the later stages.

That said, if research requires a 'question' as simply put, it also needs to recognise that there are different ways of acquiring knowledge.

We discuss epistemology and ontology specific to ethnography below, but for now I will simply clarify those terms.

> **Ontology** is perhaps understood as the term we give to the philosophical study of being. More broadly, it involves the concepts that directly relate to being, becoming, existence and reality, as well as the basic categories of being and their relations. Traditionally listed as a part of the major branch of philosophy known as metaphysics, ontology often deals with questions concerning what entities exist or may be said to exist.

> **Epistemology** is the science of knowledge, and essentially a debate between empiricism and rationalism, in which the former claims knowledge can only be gained through experience whereas the latter believes that knowledge can be acquired through reason alone.

Social science researchers use the terms ontology and epistemology to describe these two things because, essentially, they describe the parameters of a researcher's view as to the nature of the social world, and the assumptions made about how and what we study.

In criminological research (as a field of study) there are essentially different ways or methods for acquiring knowledge, and these will be influenced by views on ontology and epistemology.

Debates about the acquisition of knowledge therefore are epistemological. In the social sciences there are generally two main systems or paradigms that relate to knowledge acquisition, these are the *positivist paradigm* and the *interpretivist paradigm*.

THE POSITIVIST PARADIGM

Sometimes called the scientific method, the basis of the positivist method is an ontological view that the world is a real, tangible place. Research based on this assumption relies on facts observed in nature as the only true elements. The positivist method stresses the objectivity of the observation, and only that which is observable, or which can be perceived by our senses, can constitute knowledge. Interpretation in the search for a relationship between facts is considered a distortion.

The positivist paradigm stresses two main components:

- experience
- reasoning (rationality).

As members of society and as individuals we learn from experience. Personal experience is obviously the most immediate form. Personal knowledge may be disseminated to others, and this is termed authoritative knowledge. Authoritative knowledge commonly refers to the wisdom of prominent people who are perceived to have a better understanding than that of ordinary people. However, such experiential authoritative knowledge may be random and uncontrolled, so for example claims to 'common sense' can be self-evident, but there are numerous examples of phenomena that contravene common sense.

The reasoning (rational) aspect of the positivistic paradigm is based on the idea of human reason. Human beings can think logically, to reason and to discover rules and laws using pure, abstract intelligence. Humans can reach conclusions using logical argument. Rationalists aver that the basis of all knowledge is proper reasoning, which allows us to know what must be true by principle. As an example, in subjects such as mathematics, principles and rules are generated without reliance on any form of reality, but on the basis of axioms. Observation of reality and collection of facts are not necessary.

Reasoning is usually subdivided into three different types, and these are important because, as you will see, most of those who describe 'ethnography' talk of its inductive base.

Deductive: e.g. all cats are animals, Kitty is a cat, therefore, Kitty is an animal (deduction).

Inductive: all the cats I have seen have fur, therefore Kitty the cat will have fur (induction).

These positions can be combined in what is essentially a **hypothetico-deductive** form of reasoning. which can be regarded as a process of developing hypothesis (that is testable ideas) by inductive reasoning from observation and mapping their implications by deductive reasoning, which is the basis for most modern scientific research. But essentially what is important for now is understanding that the positivist paradigm believes in an ordered universe which is predictable and where the same actions will reproduce the same reactions; that reality is external and universally recognised (i.e. there is an external truth); that human senses (including human memory) are reliable and that reason and logic are important research tools; that phenomena should be explained in the simplest manner, and that there is a valid relationship between individual phenomena and the rest of the wider world.

THE INTERPRETIVIST PARADIGM

Interpretivists have a different ontological and epistemological standpoint from that of positivists. They suggest that the social world that we live in and that we experience is a social creation; a construction of the individual and the collective mind (idealism). This argument does not suggest that the world is not real (although some such social constructionism can be extended to deny realities) but rather that we experience the world through our personnel perceptions which are influenced by our own preconceptions, beliefs, experiences and so forth.

Numerous eminent philosophers (for example Kant, Kuhn and Foucault) supported such a concept of the world being open to interpretation. Furthermore, reality is not some objective truth waiting to be uncovered through positivist scientific inquiry, but rather, there can be multiple realities that compete for truth and legitimacy. Social constructionism often understands the fundamental role of language and communication in constructing reality and hence, many social constructionists abide by the belief that language does not mirror reality; rather, it creates it. As such there is no 'objective reality' because we construct reality in social context. What counts as real are those things we are conscious of. Moreover, knowledge must be gained via interpretation and questioning the meaning that people attach to their experiences.

The reason these paradigms matter in criminology is that historically they inform two diametrically opposite methodologies in social science: positivism tends to be associated with quantitative methods and hypothesis testing, while the interpretivist paradigm is associated with qualitative data collection methods.

QUANTITATIVE AND QUALITATIVE APPROACHES TO DATA COLLECTION

Quantitative data is numerical; however, because the world does not take a numerical form, a process of measurement is needed to turn the world into numbers. From the earliest days, some criminologists sought to do this by measurement and mimicking approaches that would more commonly be encountered in the natural sciences such as biology, chemistry and physics.

Quantitative research is used to quantify the problem by way of generating numerical data or data that can be transformed into usable statistics. It is used to quantify attitudes, opinions, behaviours and other defined variables, and to generalise results from a larger sample population. Quantitative research uses measurable data to formulate facts and uncover patterns. Quantitative data collection methods are much more structured than qualitative methods and include the administration and evaluation of various forms of surveys – online surveys, paper surveys and longitudinal cohort studies – and, in keeping with positivist ideas, scientific experiments that aim to reduce bias when testing a new treatment, such as randomised control trials. Measurement and, by implication, quantitative and positivistic approaches to data collection necessarily impose a structure on the world. In opposition, qualitative approaches to data collection seek to allow subjects to develop their own meanings and structures.

Qualitative research instead generate non-numerical data. Qualitative research is primarily exploratory research. It is used to gain an understanding of underlying reasons, opinions and motivations. It provides insights into the problem or helps to develop ideas or hypotheses for potential quantitative research. Qualitative research is also used to uncover trends in thought and opinions, and dive deeper into the problem. Qualitative data collection methods vary using unstructured or semi-structured techniques. Some common methods include focus groups (group discussions), individual interviews and participation/observations, and hence ethnography, phenomenology and field research based on interviewing tends to be qualitative (so long as it aspires to elicit more than simple numerical and statistical data).

WHAT MAKES RESEARCH GOOD QUALITY?

A final point that I noted above is that research (whether qualitative or quantitative) generally tends to follow rules (although these rules are sometimes broken) that impose structure and guidance and give research its systematic and structured nature and against which its quality is often assessed or adjudged. These are:

1.   Reliability (also sometimes known as reproducibility or repeatability)

Reliability is regarded as an important characteristic for assessing the quality of research and holds that if high-quality research is duplicated by other researchers, the same results would be encountered. In hard and natural sciences, such as physics, researchers would expect to yield exactly the same results from the same experiments. (The controversy of Fleischmann and Pons Californian

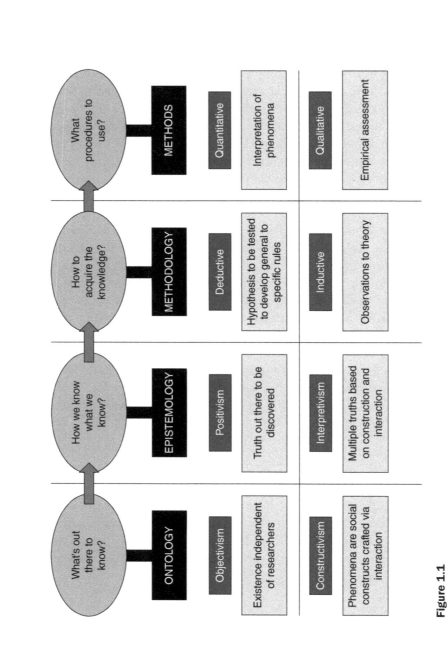

Figure 1.1

'Cold Fusion' experiments, or French immunologist Jacques Benveniste are evidence that this does not always happen, even in the STEM subjects.) However, in social sciences, as the subject matter is people not weights, measurements or chemical processes, we expect individuals to act differently. For this reason, social science researchers do not expect *exactly* the same results with repeated experiments, and yet, a high degree of consistency and similarity for similar studies are evidently useful indicative evidence of their quality, and hence reliability is not researcher specific.

2.   Validity

Validity is seemingly a simple concept to explain, as essentially the term means: 'Are you researching the thing that you think you are? Are the data that you are getting relevant?' For example, if you discover that there are inequalities in crime levels between different socio-economic groups, on average that more young unemployed men are incarcerated than middle-aged employed men, what does that tell you and what are you researching? There may be are a range of important factors:

- social class
- income
- employment
- age
- geography
- criminal justice processes
- social justice.

And many factors more beside. Research validity in surveys relates to the extent to which the survey measures the right elements that need to be measured. In simple terms, validity refers to how well an instrument measures what it is intended to measure. So for example, specifically with a mind to criminological ethnography, the human processes of crime and crime control tend to be the object of study. It is valid to use ethnography to discover the inner life world of the policing occupation or the everyday practices of young criminals on an estate in central England.

3.   Generalisability

Generalisability is applied by researchers in an academic setting, to discuss the extension of research findings and conclusions, and how much the findings from a study conducted on a sample population are applicable or relevant to the wider population at large. This is based on the fact that in the social sciences, much research is based on sampling and hence an entire population is not studied, only a part of it. Generalisation asks whether the findings of a research project on a sample population are true for the entire population, because small scale research may not be generalisable. As you will see, this is one of the traditional criticisms made of ethnography and used to suggest that it cannot be used to examine wider social processes and trends.

4. Credibility

The criterion of credibility concerns the need for researchers to provide detailed information on the way in which research was undertaken and a project of study carried out. In effect, it concerns the transparency of a research project so that those who later seek to evaluate it, or to replicate it, can be clear on the parameters of the study and what was done. Of course, this must be balanced with a mind to research ethics, but in essence the principle is that good research embraces a degree of openness. It is an assessment of whether or not the research findings represent a 'credible' conceptual interpretation of the data drawn from the participants' original data.

TASK

Criminologists will no doubt be aware that virtually everyone has common sense knowledge about crime, and accordingly many ideas about the causes of crime and the best ways to tackle it. However, what characterises criminologists, for Garland, is that they subject these ideas to rigorous enquiry using either quantitative or qualitative research conducted by themselves or other researchers.

With these points in mind consider the following questions:

- What should be the point of criminology today?
- Should criminology be tied to a governmental project?
- Is good research only dependant on reliability, validity, generalisability and credibility, or are there other moral and ethical principles at play?
- Is all good criminology empirical?

THE USE OF THEORY IN RESEARCH

Theory is important in social research. Social research uses theory in something of a symbiotic manner: good research is often used to generate theory, theory is then also used to inform and guide research, where research can test the theory. Additionally, when considering social research, we need to be aware of the way research is both influenced by external factors and by the perspectives we use to understand it.

Simply put, when we investigate the social world in subjects such as criminology, its components combine and recombine into new patterns as they are viewed through different theoretical perspectives. Indeed, theory can be thought of as the different lenses that might be put into a pair of glasses, each lens will make people view the world in a slightly different way. Different theories, like different lenses, bring different parts of the world into view or can lead to the image being blurred, or clear, patterns or outlines that were indistinct become clearer, and some make the vision blurrier or sharper.

The role of theory is to make things that are initially hidden visible, to define some patterns and give some meaning to the sorts of observations that social science researchers continually make when investigating society. In criminology there are a range of criminological theories (sometimes termed perspectives), some (although by no means all) built upon empirical research. In criminology, many theories have emerged over the years, and they continue to be explored, individually and in combination, as criminologists seek the best solutions in ultimately reducing types and levels of crime. To this end, criminological research both produces theories and employs them as a foundational basis for examining contemporary and historical issues. It is important to remember that criminological research does not take place in a void: human beings are at the heart of the issues and processes, not only the offender, the victim and the capable guardian, but also the prisoner's young daughter, the victim's grieving mother, the witness who was traumatised, the producer who took up the story and the politician who used it in their speech. Just as research is linked to perception-based arguments and perspectives, so is the criminal justice process. There are now few social scientists who hold the traditional positivist orthodoxy that research is value neutral. Yet even if research is considered to be value neutral, an unescapable aspect of criminology is that issues of crime and control are never value neutral. The research that is undertaken by criminologists can have an influence (intentional and not) both for the good and for the bad of society, and that arguably makes criminology quite distinct as a subject area.

CRIMINOLOGICAL ETHNOGRAPHY AS QUALITATIVE RESEARCH

Historically in the social sciences, ethnographers studied single groups of people. As a research method, ethnography was arguably somewhat imported from anthropology and incorporated into a burgeoning social science as part of the early work among the Chicago School of sociologists (I will document more of the roots of the discipline in the coming pages). Ethnography was therefore one of the qualitative approaches championed in the US as part of the reformation of the social sciences in the early 1920s. Ethnography prior to that was one branch of anthropology (given the anthropological roots of the term, it is worth noting that anthropologists use the term ethnology for another branch which is, in contrast to ethnography, the comparison and analysis of the characteristics of different peoples and the relationship between them, although this term has not been used in criminology[2]), which all the same normally employs the techniques of participant observation and interviewing.

Ethnography today uses various methods of empirical investigation and critical analysis to develop a body of knowledge about social order, processes, social disorder and social change. Therefore, as a social research methodology it is undoubtedly attuned much more broadly to the social world than the issue of crime alone. Many ethnographies do not concern crime at all, and by no means is all ethnography criminological.

SO, WHAT IS CRIMINOLOGICAL ETHNOGRAPHY?

The answer is that what constitutes criminological ethnography is not clearly defined. Indeed, the answer to 'what is ethnography?' is also hard to pin down, because as numerous commentators observe, what constitutes ethnography is far from universally agreed upon. If a lack of agreement surrounds ethnography, then greater conceptual clarity will arguably never be likely to come from combining ethnography and criminology.

I am acutely aware of this problem from the outset. I share a concern that there is a flaw with contemporary social science, perhaps resulting from the common inclination of practising social scientists towards self-identifying into siloes and retreating into ever more specialist niche subject study rather than developing a rounded, broader intellectual subjectivity. It is also worth noting that traditionally and historically, there has been something of a qualitative and quantitative divide in the social sciences that has seen some researchers engage in a disparaging and dismissive critique of the alternative approach while arguing that their selected methodology is the superior and more robust means of conducting meaningful research in criminology and crime control.

Arguably, historically in the social sciences, quantitative research is archetypally regarded as the more 'scientific' means of undertaking empirical social science. The focus is on using specific definitions and carefully, meticulously determining what particular concepts and variables mean. Qualitative research

---

[2]Yet the overlap between these disciplines is an interesting one when we consider that at least in part, the aims of both ethnology and criminology could be regarded as common or shared, if we sceptically hold that both were designed to brand subdominant peoples as inferior and understand that inferiority.

methods, in contrast, are associated with more subjective emphasis on interpretation. Yet both are necessary. Undeniably quantitative methods and approaches provide a glimpse of the bigger picture and set the scene against which qualitative methods and approaches, such as ethnography, provide a depth of understanding of issues that is not possible using quantitative, statistically-based investigation alone. Hence from the outset I am keen not to rekindle the old qualitative–quantitative divisions long characterised by infighting. In that vein, I do not seek to use 'criminological ethnography' as an exclusive term, and I am not suggesting that it is a superior method or the only method that criminologists should be schooled in.

Perhaps the claim that criminological ethnography should be worthy of consideration in its own right will be controversial, but in the pages that come *we* intend to make this claim, and I intend to tread a path that is partly a call for action, partly a suggested map of how that action might be undertaken. A central desire was to redress a research imbalance in criminology that still tends to promote quantitative research as more useful, more rigorous and more salient to policy. On this point (and having noted a recent study which showed that less than 6 per cent of articles in the top five criminology journals are based on research that used qualitative methods), Steve Hall convincingly argues that such a situation is the result of the contemporary character of academe, and warns:

> Today's academics are under intense pressure to publish their research. Because researchers' own evaluations of the chances of getting their research published affect their choices of methods, the striking bias towards quantitative research continues to be reproduced. Criminology students who opt for qualitative research should be aware that they are not only entering a struggle to explain crime and evaluate systems of justice, but also a struggle for credibility within the discipline itself. (Hall, 2018: 385)

Yet I wrote this book, as an active ethnographic researcher, at least in part in agreement with Hall, and out of a desire to see that situation changed. Only someone who has not spent the time or expended the effort to undertake rigorous ethnography could doubt its credibility or value, and I want to see it demystified at least in part, so that it is used, and well used. It is neither a 'how to do it' handbook or a historical textbook guide, but is intended to sit somewhere between the two, and provide both a meaningful guide to terms and method while also giving a historical context to the rise of criminological ethnography.

Perhaps there is a further problem that arises at the outset with the term 'criminological ethnography', which necessitates immediate attention, and that is the extent to which any guidance on how to carry out ethnography truly has a function or purpose. It would seem safe to assume that a number of social researchers would hold the view that good social research skills, and the capacity to do ethnographic and qualitative research well are more the product of nature than nurture. Put quite succinctly, when it comes to undertaking ethnographic research, as put in the words of one criminological colleague, herself an experienced ethnographer; 'you have either got it or you haven't'. In short, there is a view that the skills, techniques and abilities that are required of someone who is a successful ethnographer cannot be learned, and certainly not from a book.

Again, this is a worthy debate and one which cannot easily be resolved, and one which should be kept in mind as a recurrent theme that underscores the discussion in this book. Ethnography comes into being in the doing that is both the conducting of research, and then the process of producing that work in written form. Indeed, what I aim to do here is not provide a how to instructional manual, but rather to help the reader to 'understand' and have some knowledge of the issues connected to ethnographies of crime and deviance, the lineage and histories of these studies, the differential ways in which those who have trodden a path of utilising the method have variously encountered challenges, difficulties, dilemmas and opportunities. It provides an opportunity to raise broader questions, to deal with the debates about access, ethics and realities of fieldwork, of thinking about issues of presentation, representation, style and voice; to consider the way in which ethnography can inform, shape knowledge or, to use contemporary higher educational parlance, have 'impact'. Yet more than anything else, this book seeks to provide something more to the emerging momentum that has sought to promote a re-engagement with real world social research. Criminologists have variously called for a revitalisation of contemporary criminology, a re-awakened criminological imagination, and a return to criminology's creative and critical potential (Young, 2011). Without pressing this point or revisiting the history of criminology's endeavour, I would simply highlight the difference between the current momentum and appeal of ethnography and the situation just a few years ago.

Certainly there was a period in Britain and the USA between the late 1960s and 1980s when many ethnographies were published in criminology, socio-legal studies and the sociology of deviance about different criminal subcultures and the criminal justice process, but between the 1980s and the present day, for the most part, there is a common disciplinary agreement that the most significant and respected criminology journals mostly publish quantitative studies.

For the most part, there is a neglect of ethnography and, perhaps more importantly, a lack of interest among mainstream criminologists in the methodological issues that arise when employing this research method and in qualitative research more generally. Perhaps this alone forms the case for putting 'criminological ethnography' on the map and recognising it as a unique, valuable empirical and inquisitive endeavour. Yet I would argue that at this moment, the ethnographic tradition and its approach to research have never been as current and essential as they are now for criminology, including quantitative criminology. How many more criminologists might have been reluctant to talk of the crime drop in the 1990s and early 2000s so authoritatively if (like Treadwell, 2012) they had an ethnographic attachment that allowed them to see crime mutating and changing rather than falling?

Yet while criminological ethnography has been growing in popularity and showing its utility in understanding a range of crime and crime control phenomena, it is also true that in many ways it has never faced such a sustained period of threat as it does right now. While it is reassuring that several theoretical criminological perspectives (which I will visit in the coming pages) have come out as veracious defenders of ethnography, so it is also true that restrictions and even outright prohibitions currently exist that restrict the possibility for social researchers to utilise these long-established methods. In the pages to come and drawing on real world examples, I will illustrate the threats and opportunities as they are currently constituted, or at least my perspective and reading of them. Not all will necessarily agree with me, and as such *Criminological Ethnography* aims to be provocative, if I can generate a debate then all the better. Perhaps Robert Park's call for action needs an update: perhaps ethnographers need a new manifesto. A new call for action. I hope that this book goes some way to providing that, and most of all I hope that it is interesting, engaging and sparks debate about the method that will guide the criminology of the twenty-first century.

CHAPTER SUMMARY

This chapter has sought to introduce readers to the basics of social research and criminology, to move towards understanding the specific nature and character of 'criminological ethnography' as research sensibility. From reading it, you should have a better grasp of the fundamental concepts that all social research broadly rests upon and understand the traditional and historic differences between different ways that research specific to criminology has been understood.

FURTHER READING

Criminological ethnography as a term ties the ethnographic approach to the subject of criminology and so texts that introduce the basics of criminology and its theories are useful, such as Treadwell (2013) *Criminology: The Essentials*.

There is an array of edited collections containing chapters written by criminologists that explore the significant role of research in expanding and refining understandings of crime and justice, but as a solid introduction and foundation to the topic, students might benefit from accessing and reading good texts on the essential scope of criminology and qualitative research, and I would recommend: Wincup (2017) *Criminological Research: Understanding Qualitative Methods*.

2
CLASSIC CRIMINOLOGICAL ETHNOGRAPHY

LEARNING OBJECTIVES

This chapter looks at the history and development of qualitative research in criminology, and criminological ethnography more specifically. It explains the roots of criminological ethnography as an iterative and inductive approach tied to qualitative criminology and charts the emergence of the terminology of criminological ethnography. By the end of this chapter you should have a better understanding of:

- early ethnography and the link between ethnography and social documentation and journalism
- Chicagoans' first and second wave interactionism
- the National Deviancy Symposium and the emergence of British social criminology and cultural studies
- the place of criminological ethnography today.

ETHNOGRAPHY, CRIME, DEVIANCE AND DISORDER: A SHORT HISTORY

This chapter serves as an introduction to ethnography more broadly, and its specific criminological sensibility. In that way it is in keeping with the general assertion that there is something specifically criminological about some forms of the ethnographic endeavour, and that these works, and their contribution, can be examined meaningfully as a collective. Ethnography has a long history and intellectual trajectory, and by no means is all that record linked to issues of crime and control. This chapter will seek to focus on both the conduct and conceptualisation of ethnography, although immediately such an aim requires a conceptual clarification. The term 'criminological ethnography' is not necessarily one that has a contemporary currency, though for those who occupy the criminological field it carries a common sense and familiar meaning that is far from perplexing or inexplicable. For decades now, the ethnographic tradition has formed part of the bedrock of social scientific research techniques on which empirical social study and policy draw. Yet the field and studies that constitute that ethnographic tradition in the social sciences are diffuse, and in many ways escape neat categorisation or the long-established tendency to attempt to usher into neat, clearly demarked categorical configurations of discernible difference. Ethnography generally escapes neat categorisation, and while on one level it is self-evident and commonly understood by those familiar with the social sciences generally, the headline descriptors betray the complexity of the realities of the subject.

There is no single definition of 'ethnography', and nor should there be. Ethnographic research practice arguably is one of the most flexible and adaptable, and the fieldworker responds and adapts to field research situations. As ethnography, through participant observation, interviewing and other qualitative techniques, is a deliberate attempt to generate data and is thus eminently suited to the study of unpredictable situations and outcomes, it is, by its very nature, fluid and adaptable.

Yet while ethnography has long been part of the wider project of constructing sociological accounts of deviant life and documenting the rich variety of human interaction that is associated with crime and law-breaking, the very word often does not feature prominently within the internal discipline of sociology in these same oft cited seminal works. Ned Polsky's often highly praised *Hustlers, Beats and Others* (1967), a seminal study of deviance and the value of the 'unconvicted felon', which unashamedly promotes empirical qualitative engagement (and is often used as a go-to by ethnographers) yet does not employ the term 'ethnography' nor cite it in the book's index. That is similarly the case for William J. Chambliss seminal study of organised crime in the United States of America, *On the Take* (1978). Although Jason Ditton incorporates the term in his seminal study *Part-Time Crime* (1977), he first talks of 'a period of relatively unstructured participant observation research wherein I hoped that those studied would suggest the direction and substantive content of analysis' (Ditton, 1977: 4). In many ways, Ditton evokes the very often prominent image of what Westmarland calls:

> the classic, or some might argue over-romanticised, view of this sort of approach is the young single graduate student, going to live in an exotic, unheard-of, off-the-beaten-track place. They learn the language, become immersed in the lives of people, become a trusted friend. The aim of this approach is to live or walk in someone else's shoes, to see the world from their point of view or, as some have described it, understand 'their' world-view. (Westmarland, 2011: 118)

Of course, there is a range of ethnographies both historical and contemporary that accord with this characterisation. Recent ethnographic works in a criminological vein, for example Randol Contreras's ethnography on Dominican men who violently rob drug dealers (2013) or Sandra Bucerius's five-year study of a group of 55 second-generation Muslim immigrant drug dealers in Frankfurt, Germany (2014), have inspired wider academic debates about the extent to which the ethnographer can claim 'outsider' status and difference from those studied, which is, of course, always a matter of variation. What is more certain is that ethnography as a term is somewhat imprecise.

The texts above (and a wider range of criminological, ethnographic studies) have clearly been part of the driver of various and increasingly prominent public debates about the approach, and accompany the rejuvenated recent interest in it as a research technique – partly prompted by the growing popularity of emergent criminological perspectives that are 'cultural' (Ferrell et al., 2015), 'narrative' (Presser and Sandberg, 2015) or 'ultra-realist' (Hall and Winlow, 2015). As this book will demonstrate, the ethnographic tradition within criminology has a long and venerable history, and it underpins many of the theoretical perspectives and empirical studies in criminology that are now regarded as 'seminal'. Yet despite the very firm foundations, there is a continuing debate about what ethnography is. Broadly speaking, ethnography involves the study of people in their natural setting, typically resulting in the researcher being present for extended periods of time in order to collect data systematically about daily activities, and the meanings that are attached. As Fassin has suggested:

> For most people, the term evokes far-away societies and probably traditional cultures … [Yet ethnography is] about entering and communicating the experiences of men and women in a given context: Their way of apprehending the world, of considering their place in society and their relations with others, of justifying their beliefs and actions. It is an attempt to go through the looking glass, so to speak, and explore another universe, often initially foreign but progressively becoming more familiar. In other words, it is not about producing otherness … but on the contrary, it is about bringing closeness, discovering that those who seemed so different, irrational or incomprehensible resemble us more than we thought, act more coherently than we conceive, and, in any case, think and behave in a manner that can be rendered intelligible to everyone. (Fassin, 2013: x)

When it comes to crime this issue of proximity that Fassin raises is an interesting one, because while for some individuals, crime will feel close and constitute a pressing issue, for others it may largely be quite abstract and rarely intrude on their lives. However, for me, ethnography is largely a sentiment and an approach that keeps the academic subject of criminology anchored to everyday lived realities of crime. What I ought to start by saying is that, although on occasion it is possible to fall into the trap of looking at ethnography as a research method, for me, it is far more. It is crafting a willingness to be in the world and to look at the world critically. Ethnography is not, as I note above, a research method *per se* (it is not a strictly defined data collection technique), nor as such a methodology with a philosophical framework. In the classic application it is tied strongly to interpretivist and naturalist ideas, and historically at least it was often iterative and inductive rather than deductive (though this is no longer always the case).

By **iterative** and **inductive** I mean that it is a repeated process, where an inductive approach is used. An inductive approach (which I examine in the context of research in more detail below) is one where the researcher begins with as few preconceptions about what he or she is studying as possible; rather they enter into the study with an open mind and no preconceptions and see what is happening. Here theories are devised to explain what is encountered, rather than the other way around. Some people talk of this as starting out with a blank sheet. Ethnographers tend to believe that if they begin their work with theories to test they will end up only seeing things in an un-objective manner and cloud the findings of their research. Additionally, ethnographers are less likely to be looking for patterns and regularities and more likely to be interested in the complexity, nuance and contradictions of the settings that they participate in and observe. In contrast, in **deductive** (and often in quantitative) studies, the researcher comes up with a hypothesis to be tested or an idea based on what he or she thinks is already known and then the topic is explored, and data are collected, in order to test this hypothesis and prove if it is correct or not. A hypothesis (a suggestion that needs testing), however, is usually not used in ethnography. The traditions of ethnography, perfectly captured by Spradley (1980: 12), are to ask, 'What is going on here?'.

However, most commentators now recognise that it is somewhat naïve to think that an ethnographer can be entirely inductive; such neutrality is impossible to achieve. Everyone starts their research with some preconceived views and ideas, and every ethnographer is necessarily the person who ultimately determines the focus, what is put into and what is left out of the picture.

Often an ethnographer accepts that to an extent they hold some preconceptions, some goals and theories. They recognise that their work may have practical limitations, but still attempt to minimise the effect of their own impact on the setting, or they work with these preconceptions and turn them into advantages. An ethnographer's job is not just to watch and listen, but it is also to attempt to get to grips with the complex nature of the world around them, and not to close the mind to things that would otherwise surprise. In doing this the ethnographer as researcher will draw on the theories and concepts from their studies as they become useful. This involves a constant to and fro (an iteration), of participating, observing, writing, reflecting, reading, thinking, talking, listening, participating, in a circular and repetitive manner. Hence, ethnography is both iterative and inductive, it is more like an expedition than a well-planned scientific experiment, and like an expedition or voyage of discovery, it often comes with unexpected and unanticipated dilemmas, wrong turns, delays, frustrations and moments of excitement and discovery.

In undertaking such a voyage of discovery, the ethnographer draws on two forms of data collection technique: participant observation and in-depth interviewing. Again, this owes something of a lineage to anthropology and borrows heavily from that discipline's fieldwork traditions where ethnographers look to craft very detailed descriptions of what they witness and encounter. Because of that, ethnographic works often contain very vivid, evocative and detailed descriptions and long passages of verbatim quotes taken from research participants. For that reason, and from the proximity of the researcher, ethnography is regarded as being able to provide a depth of understanding of issues that is not possible using quantitative, statistically based investigations or even less immersive qualitative methods. It is also for that reason that the late Geoff Pearson suggested that:

> [E]thnography is often said to be a way of 'telling it like it is', looking at the social world of the subject as it is seen 'from the inside' … Some perceive, it is not, and never can be that … In my view, the ethnographic text cannot 'betray' the experience of the field since the vital opposition of authenticity and distance means that the experience of fieldwork is never quite as 'real' as it is sometimes supposed to be … What is required of a good ethnographer is neither full membership nor competence, but the ability to give voice to that experience, and to bridge the experiences of actors and audiences. (Pearson, 1993: xviii)

Elsewhere Alison Liebling, a professor of criminology and prominent prison scholar suggests:

> Ethnography is the most basic form of social research – and resembles the way in which people ordinarily make sense of their world … It can include observation, participation, interviewing and almost any other form of interaction between ourselves, the researchers and the social world. (Liebling, 2001: 475)

Indeed, there are countless definitions of ethnography offered by countless people who are attached to criminology, at least in part because criminology as a growth subject is now an area that produces quite a volume of social research that proclaims to be 'ethnography' (and perhaps arguably always has been one of the areas where ethnography is most frequently applied). Both Liebling and Pearson capture the essence of ethnography as a social research approach, grounded in interaction and engagement. Yet while this may capture some essence of the aims of the ethnographic approach, which seeks to bridge a gap between practice, experience and knowledge, Pearson notes that there is, and must be, something more to the approach and an ethnographic orientation than just bringing forth stories of tales from the field alone.

Once it was certainly the case that ethnography was considered something of a marginal method, and subject to an array of criticism. Famously Alexander Liazos described the sociology of deviance as the study of 'Nuts, sluts and perverts' (Liazos, 1972) and the ethnographer Dick Hobbs notes, 'Ethnography is an academic vice, and academic life has its hierarchies' and recalls how in the 1980s 'one colleague' used the description, 'petty, trivial, irrelevant ethnography' (Hobbs, 1993: 46–54). However, since the mid-1990s the value of ethnographic and qualitative research approaches has come to be increasingly recognised and valued by government officials and agencies, although it is not always tempered by a recognition of the complexity of transforming observation into social scientific data. For example, in the United Kingdom, the UK government has offered a definition of ethnography via the online Service Design Manual (which assists those in governmental roles to commission and design appropriate research). That definition suggests:

> Ethnographic research usually involves observing target users in their natural, real-world setting, rather than in the artificial environment of a lab or focus group. The aim is to gather insight into how people live; what they do; how they use things; or what they need in their everyday or professional lives. (Gov.UK, 2016)

Interestingly, the same source goes on to suggest:

> The term 'ethnographic' can be misused, it's currently a bit of a 'buzzword' with some agencies who may not fully understand the approach. (Gov.UK, 2016)

Indeed, it is not only the UK government who will attest to the somewhat complex nature of ethnography and the fact that it does not necessarily lend itself to ready definitions, hence ethnography is often poorly defined and understood.

There is, for example, an increasing (and to my mind very frustrating) tendency in the social sciences to equate ethnography will qualitative research (and interviews) generally and then conflate the terms so as to use them as if they were synonymous with one another. Yet for me, undertaking several interviews in a setting that is not the university office is stretching the term ethnography. While there is a complex debate to be had about how long is required observing and participating for research to be able to claim ethnographic status, there is arguably a value in recognising that ethnography describes a different form of immersion in a setting than qualitative research alone. In essence, then, some form of 'fieldwork' and 'being there' must be at the centre of ethnographic sensibility.

For many the halcyon period of ethnography accords with the rise and incorporation of the method in Chicagoan sociology, a point to which we will return shortly (and that Chicagoan sensibility is captured well in the quote at the start of this chapter). Ethnography as a social research strategy has proved to be popular in different contexts at different times. Arguably an ethnographic sentiment was apparent during what many call a second Chicago School of sociology between the mid-1940s to the 1960s, which again prioritised qualitative social research, and saw the likes of Howard Becker, Erving Goffman and others create a large, enduring body of academic work that renewed a commitment to participant observation as a method and symbolic interaction as a guiding theory. Similarly, much of the English cultural studies tradition emerged out of the fusion of disciplines at and around the University of Birmingham and the Centre for Contemporary Cultural Studies (BCCCS), which rose to prominence after it was founded in 1964 by Richard Hoggart. In the 1960s Howard Becker's *Outsiders* (1963) proved so influential on the early National Deviancy Symposium (or National Deviancy Conference) that a group of British criminologists broke away from the National Conference of Teaching and Research on Criminology organised by Professor Sir Leon Radzinowicz at the University of Cambridge. These academics expressed dissatisfaction with orthodox British criminology of the legal and medico-psychological professions, social democratic politics, and the dominance of what they termed 'positivist criminology' and its close links with the state, and instead became the founders of a much more critical criminology rooted in sociological concerns.

As society shifts and changes, what is considered worthy of study was to become increasingly diverse, a process that continues to be refined today as we consider the nature, scope and value of, for example, the cyber and virtual world as a place worthy of ethnographic study and a place where meaning and culture are crafted. Just as the Chicago School and BCCCS adapted to and tracked a world in motion and flux, so too today ethnographers find themselves facing critical discourse on shifting and emerging practices. Reflexive, critical and feminist ethnography and auto-ethnographic accounts, as well as a reconfiguration of what constitutes the 'field' (as new sites, including the virtual, mobile, multi-sited and global), come to the fore. Suffice to say, ethnography has not remained static, but rather has shifted and changed in light of new and emergent debates and critical perspectives, new opportunities and new challenges.

While the need for rigour, critical thought and practical skill may be unchanging and unwavering aspects of the social sciences and the ethnographic approach (as is the tension to keep ethnographic works both theoretically informed yet accessible) the settings that the ethnography is used in can and do shift and alter. Many historical ethnographies contain language and description that can appear quaint, or even offensive, such as casual sexism, or unacceptable terminology around race. With the passage of time ethnographies become not a study of the here and now, but a historical document, at best a vivid, evocative picture of the world as it was. One historical epoch is not necessarily like another, and while undoubtedly there are always similarities and continuities between different eras, so too, ethnography as praxis is a technique that can be finely attuned to social change and society in a state of change or flux. Indeed, arguably ethnography has tended to be at its most ambitious and popular when it is used in society undergoing rapid periods of social transformation, such as pre-Second World War and post-war Chicago, and the cultural reformation around Britain in the 1960s and 1970s as affluence and optimism and the first sparks of consumer capitalism replaced post-war austerity.

I firmly believe that ethnography should be perceived as a research praxis. Hence, I intend to spend some time considering how epistemological and ontological frames at various phases influenced the dominant ideas that were implicit in various phases of ethnography's lineage, which perceive human beings as part object and part subject. These were and are based on often implicit assumptions about the extent to which humans are free agents, or they are determined by social forces and social structures. There has been a tendency in more recent ethnography to focus on individuals' and groups' perspectives, viewpoints, attitudes and feelings, or on their cultures and practices while perhaps forgetting to adequately consider the wider social structures and forces that both frame and inform human choices.

Here, I suggest that ethnography should always be informed by a theoretical perspective that understands social life as the outcome of the interaction of structure and agency through the practice of everyday life; that examines social life as it unfolds, including looking at how people feel, but crafting an understanding that is always attuned to a wider context of the socio-economic, political, cultural and technological forces. If it is anything, ethnography is a research praxis that comes into being in its doing, but that doing is always socially and situationally framed.

So ethnography then is not one particular method of data collection, but a style of research, a sensibility perhaps, as so brilliantly captured by Raymond Madden, it is about 'Being Ethnographic' (Madden, 2010). Ethnography is inexorably connected with its end objective, which is to understand humans and their social meaning in each setting, sphere or culture. Where Madden is right then is that ethnography is perhaps better considered an orientation towards research, so we might talk of an ethnographic imagination (Willis, 1990) or sensibility, or a criminological ethnographic sensibility. In perusing that end, as a praxis it is often associated with those studied, and often with researcher participation and immersion in the said field.

Ethnography is intended to explore cultural phenomena through close researcher proximity, and often involves data gathering where the researcher observes society from the point of view of attempting to appreciate, capture or understand the subject of the study. At a deeper level, ethnography historically and traditionally means to represent graphically and in writing, and historically this writing and producing is a core part of the end aim. Indeed, the very etymology of the word is derived from Greek *ethnos* (folk, people, nation) and *grapho* (I write). Indeed, while it may be possible to subsequently present ethnographic material in alternative forms, an ethnography is, and must be, the written product of the research process. Hence ethnography, what is written, and how it is written, is important.

As I will suggest in the coming pages, ethnography developed in the discipline of anthropology in the past century as a research practice involving participant observation in a locale. The written account that described and interpreted the place and people through a cultural 'lens' or 'frame' is the ethnography. Undertaking immersed fieldwork in the unfamiliar setting or the foreign field was an integral component of research orientation where the researcher became familiar with an unknown socio-cultural context to better understand and translate social ordering and meanings of the milieu. Yet so too, ethnography only comes into being when something of that process is produced in written form. As ethnographic techniques, and participant observation, were increasingly adopted by other disciplines in a wider range of settings in order to investigate a broad range of questions, the degree to which the researcher became 'immersed' became a subject of reflection and debate.

Yet as ethnographic methods came to be more commonly accepted in a range of social science disciplines (such as sociology, pedagogy, philosophy, psychology, geography, socio-legal studies and economics) so too the debates, contestations and controversies within the broader ethnographic endeavours were replicated and played out in distinct and often quite disconnected disciplinary fields. The imprecise and various applications of ethnography across a range of subjects in the social sciences and humanities that often are concerned with crime now means that when the term ethnography is connected with criminology it arguably becomes even less conceptually precise.

Of course, that at least occurs in part because criminology (like ethnography) is something of a meeting point in the social sciences. Yet by using the term 'criminological ethnography', it is possible to straddle academic disciplinary boundaries and truly practise inter-disciplinary scholarship that is more intellectually coherent and better informed. While I recognise that I potentially face the allegation that in attempting to fuse the often diffuse, misunderstood and contested strategy of ethnography to the equally nebulous and amorphous vehicle of criminology, I have not suggested a clearer discipline. I hope that by the end of the book I will have refuted and disproven any such accusation.

Having spent some time clarifying what is meant by ethnography, we are now better placed to consider what constitutes its specific criminological variant. For some, criminology is the 'scientific' study of the nature, extent, management, causes, control, consequences and prevention of criminal behaviour, both on the individual and social levels. Yet there is often some disagreement about what constitutes the proper parameters of criminology (and what focus and parameters of social study the discipline should encompass; see, for example, recent criticisms from criminological perspectives such as Zemiology and ultra-realism).

While terms such as 'scientific' regarding criminology are not universally accepted, some scholars, such as David Garland, have traditionally suggested that the separation between criminology and the wider sociology of deviance and control is at least in part linked to that disciplinary distinction (Treadwell, 2013). What is less disputed is that academic criminology undoubtedly is an inter-disciplinary endeavour that draws upon an eclectic range of other disciplines in the social sciences. Most notably, this broad church often prominently includes sociology, psychology, psychiatry, political science, economics (as well as law and socio-legal studies, which feature prominently) but which really came to fruition in the post-war period. In Britain at least, 'criminology' had, until the arrival of the European émigrés, been a minority interest of the medical profession, often tied to the desire to treat juvenile offenders.

While the first lectures in criminology were given in the medical school at the University of Birmingham before the Second World War, 'criminology' was having little relevance to policy or praxis. That was to change particularly via the work of the Institute of Criminology established in Cambridge in 1959, where Leon Radzinowicz became the first professor of criminology in Britain.

This history at least explains why in the UK, the roots of criminology are heavily connected to a scientific status with origins in both a legalistic, positivistic (although Radzinowicz latterly described himself as moving away from positivism – he was formerly a pupil of the great Italian positivist Enrico Ferri) empiricism. Radzinowicz understood and promoted a criminology tied to a reliance on those in government departments for both funding and much of the access to the field. This is supplemented by a necessary part of the subject that is in a legal sense a relatively doctrinal, philosophical (or jurisprudential) subject where, for example, consideration of legal mechanisms at least in part provided much of the steer from Jeremy Bentham onward.

In the post-Second World War period in the UK the governmental and disciplinary foundations of criminology were strongly connected with European legal scholars such as Radzinowicz, Manheim and Grunhut. Hobbs notes that 'mid-nineteenth-century London, both as the centre of the world's most powerful military and trading empires and as a byword for urban squalor and social decay' (Hobbs, 2001: 204) gave birth to a range of social commentators whose work could rightfully be acknowledged by criminology, but often isn't. Similarly, Wilson has noted that Charles Dickens, in his 1842 visit to the Eastern Penitentiary in Philadelphia in America, was demonstrating skill and mastery as a writer to document the inhumane and barbaric application of involuntary solitary confinement and in doing so was 'closer to ethnography than many criminologists would now recognise, with his use of interview and observation and his desire to immerse himself in the world that he is seeking to describe' (Wilson, 2009: 228). As Hobbs argues, figures such as Henry Mayhew predate discussion of an ethnographic method, but ultimately use similar naturalistic, engaged and observational approaches (Hobbs, 2001). Arguably those figures also have a long legacy, for it is almost impossible to think of Victorian crime in England without the Dickens characters Bill Sykes and Fagan quickly coming to mind.

As Edwin Sutherland, in his classic work *Principles of Criminology* suggested, criminology at a most simple level can be understood as: 'the body of knowledge regarding crime as a social phenomenon. It includes within its scope the processes of making laws, of breaking laws, and of reacting toward the breaking of laws' (Sutherland, 1939: 1). Hence, it is arguable that if criminology involves law making, breaking, enforcement and social reaction, then any ethnography that considers these, might be considered criminological. However, the issue here is that for the most part almost every ethnography, given its focus on the everyday and ground level experiences of life, will have to take as part of its focus the laws, rules and customs that are apparent in the social system under study, which does not mean that all ethnography is criminological.

CASE STUDY

JASON DITTON: *PART-TIME CRIME*

Jason Ditton, who died in 2015, was a pioneer of criminology. He studied sociology at Durham University and founded the first Criminology Research Unit in 1988 at Glasgow University and in 1994 created the first Scottish Centre for Criminology in Park Circus in Glasgow before becoming a professor of criminology at Sheffield University.

Ditton's PhD thesis formed the basis of his first book, *Part-Time Crime: An Ethnography of Fiddling and Pilferage* (1977), a seminal study of what is now known as the informal economy (earlier known as the black or hidden economy). The subtitle of that book, *An Ethnography of Fiddling and Pilferage*, was perhaps one of the most notable specific uses of the term ethnography in criminology, and arguably remains so, and yet Ditton was arguably a remarkably productive, innovative and influential qualitative researcher whose work noted crime trends before many others were considering them; with topics as diverse as heroin addiction in Glasgow; probation in Scotland; evaluating Scottish syringe exchanges; cocaine use in Scotland; illicit drug use in HMP Barlinnie; crime and fear of crime; drug use by ethnic minorities in Scotland; ecstasy use in Scotland; CCTV and crime; Scottish ecstasy users on

(Continued)

(Continued)

holiday abroad; and the rise of heroin addiction in Glasgow. In all this work, he astutely combined his main academic interests in the sociology of deviance, criminology, ethnography and social science research methods more generally.

For his PhD Ditton undertook a lengthy period of participation observation and subsequent semi-structured interviewing among the bread salesmen in an English factory bakery he calls the 'Wellbread' bakery, and from that work showed that the salesmen regularly stole small sums of money from their customers. Paradoxically, although this is clearly theft, Ditton suggested that the salesmen (or roundsmen) were taught to steal by the bakery management, and muses on the way that criminal conduct was not simply the preserve of outsiders, but rather could be part of the fabric of everyday business. In his introduction Ditton describes how he generated 4,560 hours of participant observation, and how the research 'was not set up to answer any empirical questions' (1977: 11). *Part-Time Crime* remains a fantastic overview of how traditional ethnographic work was undertaken in criminology and is much more than a moral account of the career development of the fiddling roundsmen.

See Ditton, J. (1977) *Part-Time Crime: An Ethnography of Fiddling and Pilferage.* London: Macmillan.

Much debate has surrounded what constitutes crime and criminals. Some have argued that the definition of crime is fully a legal matter; that is, if something is prohibited by law it is then and only then a crime, and such crime as legally defined is the proper stuff of criminology. Others answer that because the laws are not really concerned with behaviour itself, such strict legal definitions do not provide a clear-cut focus for behavioural distinctions. For example, the act of taking a life, or homicide, encompasses far more, and much more broadly allows for discussion than the narrow legal category of murder. Hence a social definition more attuned to harm or deviance in its multiplicity of forms might be a better conceptual framework for criminology.

In many ways, it is perhaps unsurprising that traditional ethnographies involving 'crime' tend to be associated with an acceptance of the problematic nature of narrowly defining what is constituted as crime. As ethnography generally evolved over time it has been buffeted and shaped by wider epistemological and ontological shifts in the social sciences more broadly, and much of the qualitative work that criminologists now regard as seminal, including ethnographic works, did not necessarily use the term or the reference of crime *per se*. Rather, they tended to be easier to categorise in respect of the dominant theoretical ideas and perspectives which inform them. For example, Adler and Adler suggest that ethnography (including works on crime and deviance) has moved from the 'Impressionism' of the early Chicagoan phase of the 1920s, through a renaissance phase during the post-war period, to an abstract expressionism of the 1960s, surviving a 'Dark Age' lasting from the 1970s until the mid-1990s and finally being framed by a new 'Enlightenment' phase commencing in the twilight of the 1990s with the emergence of cultural criminology (Adler and Adler, 1998: xii–xvi). As a broad characterisation, that model may work, although it is perhaps better attuned to the contours of the United States of America than that of Europe.

Additionally, to return briefly to the ethnographic tradition and its connection with criminology, there is a clear historical separation that divides qualitative and quantitative criminological research in terms of its ontological and epistemological orientations. Historically the split between quantitative and qualitative social science is both ontological and epistemic, with the former concerned more directly with the testing of hypotheses, the principle of value neutrality, and claims to scientific status than the latter.

Yet because of the dominance of quantitative traditions and because of criminology long having a connection to medico-psychological research, the frame of the reference points for scientific qualitative research have affected the conditions under which qualitative researchers operate. For example, Yvonne Jewkes has recently suggested that 'the academic environment arguably trains researchers to be rational and objective, to "extract out" emotion and not disclose feelings of anxiety, confusion, vulnerability, or anything of their selves' (Jewkes, 2011: 64). It is only relatively recently that academics have had the confidence to propose that such emotion is the stuff of criminology. In particular, the inspiration and steer of cultural criminology (Ferrell et al., 2015) has been important here, along with new ideas from narrative criminology with its appeal to understand the stories of crime (Presser and Sandberg, 2015).

For many criminologists, qualitative research remains inferior to quantitative methods, as the former provide only anecdotal, non-scientific examples of marginally interesting and valuable insights. For them, ethnographic research is the realm of pseudo-science, journalism or narcissistic self-indulgence. Ethnographic research accordingly can provide little or no value for addressing how crime and societal responses to crime transpire and play out and tells us nothing useful that might solve the problems of crime and its control. One only has to look, for example, at the wholesale dominance of quantitative works at the American Society of Criminology to see that the frame is still largely set around the dominance of statistical quantitative research in criminology generally (Hall, 2018).

Yet ethnographic research, while often viewed (especially by those unversed or unfamiliar with it) as simpler and easier than quantitative research because the actions of researchers resemble what people do in daily life, is in fact very often far more time consuming, difficult, complex and emotionally charged.

Ethnographic fieldwork especially requires a greater emphasis on researchers themselves clarifying and defining what things mean and relies on the intellectual abilities of researchers to interpret and theorise. Furthermore, as experienced ethnographers will know, the field can be a lonely place. While there are certainly general guidelines and textbooks (often based on the successful experiences of previous qualitative researchers) that can provide template guidance on how to resolve some of the ethical quandaries that can arise in a project, I hope that this book will serve for criminologists, and those interested in ethnographies of crime, as a go-to introduction.

To this end, it is not written as a research methods textbook or how-to guide, but neither is it simply a history or overview of how ethnography has been used in criminology and the sociology of deviance. Rather it seeks to be something of both, giving a comprehensive overview of the real task of undertaking criminological ethnography, be it data collection, analysis, practising reflexivity and managing a project, while showing how this has been undertaken previously in criminology. More than anything else, I want to demystify ethnography and show that it is something that can be done.

For one, I am unequivocal in my view that those seeking to undertake ethnographic research should seek to know ethnographic texts well. A lamentable feature of some methods-based textbooks is the tendency to point those looking to understand ethnographic research too readily towards the literature on research methods, at the expense of research monographs. Yet substantive methodological insights can be gained from reviewing the various ways in which researchers reflect on their own methods and the manner in which they sought to conduct ethnographic research in a variety of criminal justice agency settings: for example, with the police (Westmarland, 2001; Fassin, 2013; Stuart, 2016), in courts (McBarnet, 1981; Scheffer, 2010; Gonzalez Van Cleve, 2016), in prisons (Crewe, 2009; Ugelvik, 2014; Fassin, 2016; Sloan, 2016), in criminal gangs (Venkatesh, 2009; Densley, 2013; Ward, 2013; Goffman, 2014; Fraser, 2015) or with serious offenders and criminals generally (for example, Nordstrom, 2007; Hall et al., 2008; Bergmann, 2010; Contreras, 2013; Hobbs, 2013; Ellis, 2016). When reading criminology and sociology, it is ethnographic studies that capture the imagination most and appear to reveal the greatest depth of understanding, texture and nuance of the relationship between macro socio-economic structures and their manifestation in the micro-context of everyday life, and it is very common to see ethnographers cite successful fieldworkers whose studies they have used as inspiration. A number of texts reveal a continued appetite for criminological ethnography and good qualitative research, not only monographs but also edited collections such as Bartels and Richards, *Qualitative Criminology* (2011), Rice and Maltz (eds), *Doing Ethnography in Criminology* (2018), Drake et al. (eds), *The Palgrave Handbook of Prison Ethnography*, Presser and Sandberg (eds), *Narrative Criminology* (2015),

Lumsden and Winter (eds), *Reflexivity in Criminological Research* (2014), but this book is my attempt to draw the strands together and provide a text that those new to criminology can dip into as a starting point to gain a better understanding of where ethnography is used in criminology.

Of course, there are things I cannot give readers in this book. Any successful aspirant ethnographer (and I hope at least some readers of this text will be in that category) probably needs tenacity, good people skills, fortitude, personal strength, humour and determination. They need to be a person of sound judgement and sound mind, and clearly you are at least some of the way there, you have shown those qualities by reading this book. On a serious note, as an experienced field ethnographer I know the sheer range of qualities necessary to successfully see an ethnographic criminological project successfully to fruition, and that goes some way to explaining why I think ethnographers often make the best criminologists. I hope that the book provides an inspiration for readers, and then, that some might practise 'being ethnographic' everywhere they can. Practise the basic ethnographic methods of watching and listening, thinking and writing. If this book helps readers in that end, it will have served its purpose well, but in many ways it plans to be the starting point on a journey, and the real depth of knowledge on ethnography comes not from reading textbooks but from reading and engaging with ethnographic works, contemporary and historical, and I hope that this book will assist interested readers in the task of tracking down some excellent works, and being better prepared to approach these with a critical mind.

CHAPTER SUMMARY

This chapter has started to weave together threads on the themes of ethnography with the subject of academic criminology, and to show how academic criminology is regarded by some of its academic practitioners. However, what appears here is a relatively short overview of some academic criminologists and their views on ethnography; to gain a better insight it is necessary to read a range of criminologists who have provided a broad introduction to the history and perspectives of conducting research and analysis that informs public understanding of crime, criminal justice, control and associated policy formation.

FURTHER READING

It is arguable that a better understanding of social research methods generally will assist readers in coming to terms with the position that criminological ethnography today occupies. The best overview of the place of ethnography in studying crime and deviance remains Dick Hobbs' chapter in Atkinson et al. (2001) *Handbook of Ethnography*, although it omits many of the excellent criminological ethnographies that have emerged in the last 18 years. Edited collections such as Bartels and Richards, *Qualitative Criminology: Stories from the Field* (2011), Rice and Maltz (eds), *Doing Ethnography in Criminology* (2018), Drake et al. (eds), *The Palgrave Handbook of Prison Ethnography* (2015), Presser and Sandberg (eds), *Narrative Criminology* (2015), and Lumsden and Winter's book, *Reflexivity in Criminological Research* (2015) also give a useful backdrop, but in many ways there is no substitute for reading original criminological ethnographies, as even extremely dated texts continue to be an indispensable guide to the social conventions and mores of the time and context that they were produced in. What is more, gaining familiarity with classic texts is part of the passage of becoming a skilled and knowledgeable ethnographer.

3

CORE ETHNOGRAPHIC PRINCIPLES AND APPROACHES

LEARNING OBJECTIVES

This chapter provides a brief introduction to the ethnographic approaches and perspectives that are used in contemporary criminological research. It offers some further clarification of the principal methods and research approaches used in contemporary criminological ethnography. Specifically, here I want to begin to outline the research techniques and varying theoretical perspectives specific to criminology that inform and underpin real world criminological ethnography. By the end of this chapter you should have a better understanding of:

- participant observation, interviewing and fieldwork as specific to criminology
- overt and covert research and the core criminological perspectives that embrace the ethnographic enterprise
- emic and etic approaches and thick description
- the place of criminological ethnography today in critical, cultural, feminist and ultra-realist criminology.

THE ETHNOGRAPHIC APPROACH IN CRIMINOLOGY

In being allowed into this very exclusive world, I went halves on a bag of cocaine with Linden ... After Linden procured the cellophane bag, we went off for a game of pool ... Tony went over to an empty table, took a small cellophane bag from his pocket and emptied the contents of the bag onto the table: an entire gram. After lining up the entire contents with a beer mat, Tony took it up both nostrils. (McAuley, 2007: 51)

A dank little kitchen holds the shadow of a man crouched down on its bare black floor. Rays of light pass through holes in a dirty old towel strung up over the window, they ripple over him as his eyes scan his folded forearm with precision, purpose and poise. A syringe nestled behind his ear is plucked from its resting place and as it punctures his skin the noir serenity of the scene ends. Repeatedly the plunger is pulled back and forth; the needle goes in and out many times but all seemingly to no avail. I know what he wants; I know what he needs – yet that tiny inverted mushroom cloud is just not forthcoming. The blood trickling down his arm is sucked off with loud kissing sounds that echo round the whole flat. (Wakeman, 2014: 717)

How do the above extracts make you feel when you read them? What is going on in them? What are the people doing? What are they describing? Why do the authors use the terms that they do? How does reading them make you feel? In both descriptions the people being described are taking illicit drugs, and while they are doing it they are being observed or watched by ethnographers. But why are they taking drugs? Is it addiction, hedonism, poverty, boredom, routine, impression management, cultivation of peer status? What is happening and how do we know it to be the case? While these questions might seem overly philosophical, they are in many ways at the crux of ethnography.

As I have suggested, criminological ethnography is at heart not merely a technique for doing research, but a sensibility, a way of being, a style of thinking and doing, yet while we might make such claims in ethnography generally, there is a widespread disagreement about what the purpose of ethnography can or should be. At the forefront, most ethnography, like the passages above, will at some juncture involve the use of what is termed 'thick description' and will produce findings from the field, observations, reflections, stories, narratives, interpretations, explanations that bring to life the subject. Yet there are competing views about what constitutes ethnography, and more debates still about what is required for good and ethical ethnography. Yet most criminological ethnographers would agree that what also undoubtedly separates and unites qualitative research generally, with its interviews, surveys and questioners, from ethnographic methodology and its fieldwork is that while qualitative researchers examine what people say, ethnographers more routinely examine both what people say and what they actually do. There is huge gap between described relationships and behaviours and the realities as they are encountered and witnessed. The fact that ethnographers can differentiate between deeds and words makes ethnography more informative and, I would suggest, more penetrating and insightful.

The two passages above are based on ethnographic observations. They tell us something, in each case, about the culture and way in which people consume illicit drugs. Of course, we could find out about drug use from surveys or interviews, but ethnography, and participant observation, can arguably give us something more. There is an evocative richness that is different and distinct, which comes from good, well-written ethnography which gives us more. Ethnography as a research sensibility gives priority to the experience of witnessing and seeing, of observing, believing that that observation, underpinned by an array of complementary strategies, can tell us something of the world. Ethnographic research is a distinctive method that involves the immersion of a researcher in different social worlds, and managing the tensions between their insider and outsider perspective. Even a small amount of the thick description of ethnography can shed light on the world, especially where crime is concerned, but how it does this is the subject of a great degree of contestation and disagreement.

As should now be apparent, the principal methods that underpin criminological ethnography are **participant observation**[1] and **interviewing**. In ethnography, data are collected by the researcher in the environment in which participants experience their everyday lives in a process which is often termed **fieldwork**. Participant observation as a strategy used in ethnographic fieldwork involves sustained immersion in the research setting to allow the researcher to witness and, in some cases (depending on the subject and degree of immersion), experience first hand the behaviours, customs, norms and practices that occur in the setting for the subjects of the study, and provides the researcher with the opportunity to watch, listen, record and think.

Typically, ethnographic fieldwork is a lengthy and extended process that occurs repeatedly over a period of some time, with the researcher looking to achieve a high degree of immersion into the field. Firstly, the fieldworker negotiates some form of access, enters the field, encounters initial participants, revisits the field on numerous occasions, meets more participants, and comes to a point where a conclusion is reached. The researcher then leaves the field, and writes up the full account, producing the physical document and end product, a written 'ethnography'. Such a model, however, is perhaps a little too linear and uncomplicated to capture the often messy realities of how an ethnographic research project really unfolds.

What is more certain is that to see this process through effectively, the ethnographic researcher must develop and employ their skills: interviewing, listening, and watching. As the fieldwork process becomes more established, ethnographic researchers' will move from initial contacts to managing and maintaining unfolding relationships, communicating and understanding ideas and adapting a role and identity that is suitable to the research setting.

Immediately, this shows that ethnography is not dissimilar in some ways to many qualitative research methods more generally. Criminological ethnographers often apply a range of research skills and techniques to gather data.

---

[1]Some commentators use the term non-participant observation to differentiate between observation from a distance without interaction, and observation where the observer participates (e.g. see Gobo and Mollie, 2017), but here, for the sake of clarity and expediency, I have dispensed with a discussion of that distinction precisely because the majority of criminological ethnographers adopt a position that sits between being insider and outsider.

Hence, what is termed participant observation is in reality a somewhat complex catch-all term that is often employed to describe fieldwork and vice versa. So while participant observation may sit at the fore, the techniques ethnographers draw on are multifaceted and varied, ranging from interviewing and documentary analysis to more complex multiple techniques. Historically, it was often the term participant observation that was preferred by social scientists to that of ethnography, and it is only more recently that the term 'criminological ethnography' has come to be used. The first use of the term is in a piece about Jason Ditton published in volume 49 of *New Society* published in 1979. Daniel Murphy then used the term in 1986 describing his monograph *Customers and Thieves* as a 'criminological ethnography' of shoplifting (Murphy, 1986).

While participant observation and fieldwork remain the ethnographer's main research tools, and the activities that they spend much of their time doing, the broader processes that surrounds this is much wider, and in reality much more complex. I could spend a great deal of time considering the origins of ethnography, and the contested terrain of the various terminology that accompanies it. I have tried to draw clear lines, so I suggest that we try at least to understand the difference between:

- ethnography – as the research methodology (thought I prefer sensibility)
- participant observation and interviewing – research methods
- fieldwork – the period of primary data collection.

Additionally, while I intend to give a brief overview of the basic terminology employed in criminological ethnography, some of the central ideas and debates that surround ethnographic methodology necessarily must curtail some of the detail. That may be no bad thing. The tendency towards more obscurantism and lamentably abstruse style is undoubtedly encountered in some academic writing on research methods, and specifically in ethnography. I am convinced that this only serves to make the subject more daunting rather than less for many practitioners. Having stated that my desire is both to get people to 'do' criminological ethnography and encourage others to attempt to use it as a research method putting some of its ideas into praxis (to look at crime and its control), I do not now want to undermine my initial intentions and put people off by making the subject more complex than is necessary. However, it is necessary for criminological ethnographers to be equipped with some understanding about the overarching and underpinning ideas and theoretical perspectives that frame discourse on criminological ethnography, and to that end, I am going to attempt to provide just that here in this section. However, this can be no substitute for a fuller appreciation of the terms and debates, and I recognise that there is an array of good books on both ethnography and criminological research, and I would encourage readers to examine these texts to gain the fullest appreciation that they can of the method, its application and the potential issues that arise when putting ethnography into practice.

There are excellent texts that break down the core craft of ethnography and explain core terms accessibly and succinctly. To my mind, among the best of these are texts such as Karen O'Reilly's *Key Concepts in Ethnography* (2009), which is a great general guide to the subject. While there are a number of good generalist ethnographic methodology guides (long established favourites to new texts published), and these continue to be published and updated frequency, there can be a real benefit to reading around the subject and engaging with monographs and studies based on ethnographic fieldwork, both classic and contemporary.

TAKING IT FURTHER

GUIDANCE ON ETHNOGRAPHY

As I have suggested, my aim in this text is not to provide a text book *per se*, but a book that helps the reader understand the general principles of criminological ethnography, alongside some classic works. Good guides on how to use ethnography include:

Atkinson, P. (2015) *For Ethnography*. London: Sage.

Gobo, G. and Mollie, A. (2017) *Doing Ethnography* (2nd edn). London: Sage.

Hammersley, M. and Atkinson, P. (2007) *Ethnography: Principles in Practice* (3rd edn). London: Tavistock.

O'Reilly, K. (2009) *Key Concepts in Ethnography*. London: Sage.

Van Maanen, J. (2011) *Tales of the Field: On Writing Ethnography* (2nd edn). Chicago: Chicago University Press.

There is no single text that sets out all that can be known about ethnography, so reading around several different texts will expose you to different authors and their different ideas and perspectives. However, while there is a tendency to direct those looking to understand ethnography towards the methodological texts, I would respectfully suggest that there is much more value (and entertainment) to be had in reading the actual ethnographies, and here in criminology there are numerous excellent works. There are also several journals that serve to bridge subject boundaries, perhaps most notably the Sage journal *Ethnography*, a peer-reviewed, international and inter-disciplinary journal for ethnographic study.

Yet as Hammersley and Atkinson note, what constitutes ethnography is 'necessarily unclear' (2007: 2) and greater conceptual clarity is not guaranteed as the product of extensive engagement with the now vast literature on the topic of ethnographic methodology, as various authors employ terminology differently (and sometimes interchangeably), hold differing viewpoints and opinions, and ascribe to different theoretical positions. Any author's or expert's understanding and view on what are termed ontology and epistemology (see below) will necessarily dictate some of how they see ethnography. However, as a brief introduction, I have attempted to find a way to present these often-complicated framing ideas as simply and accessibly as I can.

ONTOLOGY AND EPISTEMOLOGY

Reading many of the textbooks on ethnography, those new to the subject might experience something of a sense of discombobulation, not least because some of these texts serve to make the topic seem more complicated than clear. Additionally, the terminology that is used can also confuse because different authors will variously employ different terms to describe the same thing. What most do share is an acceptance of a general history of ethnography, which regards qualitative traditions in the social science as emerging in opposition to positivism, then ethnography specifically moving through several phases or epochs. I have already partly covered this consensus history, as relevant to criminology, but here, for the sake of expediency I want to drag out and present some key terms.

Historically, perhaps the most fundamental divisions in ethnography arose because of competing views on the ontological and epistemological framework that researchers subscribe to. The words ontology and epistemology are often stumbling blocks, and hence, it is valuable to strip them down and present them as simply as possible.

Epistemology essentially concerns what constitutes valid knowledge and how it can be obtained. Ontology in contrast refers to what constitutes reality and how can we understand existence. Added to that are theoretical perspectives (by which we normally mean what approach is it that can be utilised to gain knowledge, for example, positivism and symbolic interactionism are theoretical perspectives in criminology that you are likely to be familiar with). Those terms are separate from methodology (essentially the system of methods used in an area of study or activity) and methods (the specific tools and techniques, interviewing, observation) from the sources (the providers of data). Necessarily, these elements are interconnected. Strictly speaking then, criminological ethnography falls between methodology and method, closer to the former, although as I have argued, it might not be considered a methodology in the purist sense.

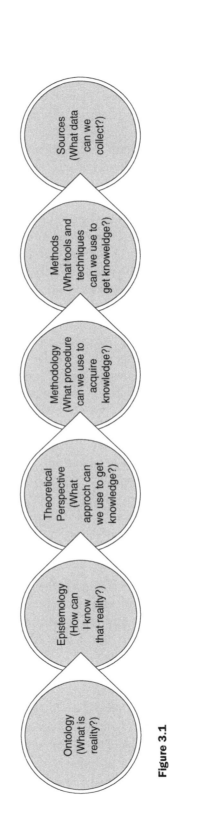

Figure 3.1

The terms ontology and epistemology are important ones that scholars of social science are advised to become familiar with, and while complex sounding, are basically descriptors that help in discussion of the set of ideas that conceptualises what exists in the world at the most basic level, and how we can know about it. That is perhaps the simplest way to explain what these quite complex sounding terms are. It is also against this framework that some quite complex methodological debates about the aims, function, utility and value of ethnographic research have played out.

Social scientists have quite different, sometimes opposing and contradictory views, depending on the ontological and epistemological beliefs that they have. The researcher's understanding of ontology and epistemology will influence not only the final analysis and theorisation of their work, but also the way that research (including ethnographic research) is carried out.

In qualitative research such as traditional criminological ethnography, this usually boils down to whether the researcher subscribed to an interpretivist framework or a realist framework. As a qualitative research methodology, ethnography is normally associated with inductive reasoning (that is, theory is built from the bottom up and emerges from the data, unlike deductive knowledge where a theory or hypothesis is formulated (or derived from existing data), then data are collected in order to test that hypothesis). Hence quantitative approaches and positivism tend to be deductive. While early ethnography made claims to be inductive, from the 1970s it faced a number of challenges, and the founding principles of early naturalist ethnography or 'telling it as it is' and documenting reality with complete objectivity and without researcher bias was naïve in the extreme. As these challenges came about, some, such as Barney Glasser and Anselm Strauss, suggested more systematic ways of defending the reliability of data collected qualitatively using grounded theory, an inductive data analysis approach informed by interpretivist and social constructionist ideas.

Yet a problem here is that realism and interpretivism are often opposing standpoints. Realists believe that things exist in the social world that are independent of thoughts and perceptions. As Hammersley and Atkinson (2007) note, early ethnography could be regarded as a break with positivism. In part as a challenge to the naïve naturalism of early ethnographers, interpretivism arose as a challenge. Interpretivist ideas emerged as an epistemological challenge to positivism and positivist assumptions that the natural sciences provide a fitting template for the scientific study of social life, and instead placed emphasis on the role of human beings' understanding, and the meaning that human beings give to their actions. Therefore, interpretivism is variously connected to symbolic interactionism, social constructionism, phenomenology, hermeneutics; but further complexity is added here because, as O'Reilly suggests:

There is no direct line between these ideas and ethnographic methods; researchers use the terms interpretivism, phenomenology, and hermeneutics in different ways with different implications for method ... contrary to what is often supposed, there is no link between interpretivism and qualitative methods. (O'Reilly, 2009: 122)

This confusion occurs at least in part because interpretivism and qualitative methods more generally grew prominent in the same epoch that witnessed the growth and ascendency of the American sociology of social constructionism and symbolic interactionism. In the 1960s and 1970s ethnography and the social sciences generally were to come under sustained critique as part of the postmodernist critique of social sciences. Postmodernism is a complex term, associated with different things in different subject groupings, but in the social sciences it might broadly be considered a challenge to and a contestation of grand theory. What often unites postmodernists in the social sciences is the notion that no single account of any reality has any more accuracy, veracity or claim to truth than any other, and hence we should accept the multiplicity of meaning and we can be generally pessimistic about the possibility of obtaining objective knowledge that might lead to social improvement or betterment. Postmodernism was, of course, as much an era or epoch as it was a broad movement straddling disciplines such as philosophy, the arts, architecture, literary criticism and the social sciences, and was typically characterised by a general attitude of cynicism or distrust towards grand narratives, ideologies and various tenets of enlightenment rationality, including the existence of objective reality and absolute truth, as well as notions of rationality, human nature and progress.

For ethnography the challenge of postmodernism was to substantiate any truth claims or expert status that the researcher might claim, in short, there could be no position of privilege afforded to ethnography as the accounts generated by researchers could claim to be no more reliable or representative than any other.

Some ethnographers took on board the challenges of postmodernism, and attempted to craft work that reflected the ambiguous, messy, multifaceted world of the postmodernists. For example Carol Rambo (formerly Carol Rambo Ronai) produced a distressing ethnographic article 'Multiple reflections of child sex abuse' in which she experiments with various styles of representation to reflect on being sexually abused at the hands of her father, and also seeks to produce what she calls a layered account, which aimed to break out of conventional writing formats by integrating abstract theoretical thinking, introspection, emotional experience, fantasies, dreams and statistics (Ronai, 1995). However, over time, there has been a return by ethnographers to realism as a means of escaping the defeatism of postmodernism and a greater appreciation and defence of ethnography as a useful method (Brewer, 2000; Hammersley and Atkinson, 2007). For Hammersley and Atkinson, the separation between naïve naturalist ethnography and its more contemporary works is the absence of reflexivity in the former, and they suggest that the presence of that reflexivity in ethnography is at least one way of meeting the challenges of postmodernism (Hammersley and Atkinson, 2007). O'Reilly argues that what is now required is what she calls 'reflexive-realist' ethnography, which is underpinned by a faith in the power of knowledge, accompanied by acknowledgement of the limitations of ourselves as data collection instruments' where 'the fact that we cannot achieve absolute truth need not lead us to abandon all attempts (O'Reilly, 2009: 185).

CRIMINOLOGICAL ETHNOGRAPHY TODAY

We have got to a point where we have competing epistemological standpoints, but we also have a deeper ontological question. Is the human world comprised of structures, forces and processes external to the individual and their culture or simply a set of cultural meanings and practices? While such arguments can at first seem complex and difficult to get to grips with, they are crucial divides between different researchers in terms of the nature of what they say involving crucial questions about the ability of ethnography to reveal truth or fact (or whether such truth or fact objectively exists to be discovered or is crafted in human interactions). The divide between these epistemological standpoints boils down to opposing positions regarding whether the researcher can or should employ moral and epistemological certainty to make clear judgements about what they experience, or whether they should be completely flexible, celebrate pluralism and epistemological uncertainty, and make no clear judgements at all and leave interpretation to the reader.

In ethnography (as in the social sciences generally), researchers face often quite complex debates about whose point of view is being presented, and how we differentiate between the views of insiders, participants or subjects and researchers. In ethnography (with its lineage from anthropology) we sometimes employ the terms emic and etic, which refer to two kinds of field research approach and the viewpoints obtained when using them. The term **emic** is used to detail and describe that which emerges from within the studied social group (from the perspective of the subject). In contrast, **etic** is that which emerges or is obtained from outside (from the perspective of the observer or the ethnographer). However, for most ethnographers today, the text they produce will seek to blend these two together and produce an account which is emic and etic, because most will believe that views are formed in a process of interaction where individuals who interact will shape one another's viewpoints, behaviour and interactions.

A further problem ethnography has with its claim to specialist scientific status relates to the generalisability of knowledge, analysis and theory. Generalisation is concerned with the application of research results to cases or situations beyond those examined in the study. Put simply, generalisability asks: can the results of the research be applied more generally and more widely than the study itself or are they only relevant to the specific context of this particular study and this particular instance? Can the researcher's account of what goes on in the chosen research setting be transferred into other research settings that might be different? Would the research findings be the same in other places or is it specific to the community or institution being studied? Will what the researchers found in their respective research settings also exist in the same or similar forms in similar research settings in similar structural locations elsewhere?

Traditionally, what has been termed the naturalist/realist and interpretivist divide emerged at least in part because there were concerns about how and to what extent ethnography could prove its value and merit as a social science research method and to what extent it was scientific in the traditional understanding of the term. More recently, criminological ethnography, driven on by a renewed sense of realist vigour, seems to have reached a point where there is now a much greater consensus among practitioners about what it involves, and hence naturalism has largely been jettisoned by both a widespread belief in social constructionism and symbolic interactionism. Most ethnographers subscribe to the view that they are not seeking out a single unified truth or a social rule in the way that early positivistic social sciences did, seeking to find general principles that explained the human world and human phenomena in a manner that the scientist might.

Ethnography is the writing of the people, the writing of society, the writing of culture. Ethnographies have long been what social researchers write and read, but recently we have also been using the term as a shorthand for fieldwork, saying we are 'doing ethnography' when we mean ethnographic research. By ethnographic research, anthropologists mean the ever-evolving Malinowskian programme of an ethnographer in the field conducting participant observation paired with a range of other methods, living within a community, and getting deeply into the rhythms, logics and complications of life as lived by a people in a place, or perhaps by people in an institutional setting. Ethnographic research, then, is more than a method. It is not simply to watch people or interview someone or assemble a focus group or 'shadow' someone; it is a much more all-encompassing and demanding way of knowing. But knowing about what? In short, some things are universal to all ethnographers, such as the idea that useful knowledge can come from observing human behaviour, and so some core features that are largely universally held apply, and we would suggest that these are the core features of criminological ethnography.

CRIMINOLOGICAL ETHNOGRAPHY – CORE FEATURES

- Criminological ethnography is not simply the study of people, but the study of both people and their socio-cultural contexts, processes and meanings within cultural systems that involve crime, social control, forms of harm and deviance.
- Good criminological ethnography is the study of these issues from both emic and etic perspectives, which is theoretically informed.
- Ethnography is a process of discovery, making inferences and continuing inquiries to achieve validity. It is (for the most part) an iterative process of episodic learning that is built on the methods of participant observation and interviewing, and a phase of fieldwork where the researcher is immersed in a setting.
- Criminological ethnography is an open-ended process, and while it is not a rigid investigator led process, the researcher has an impact, hence a high degree of self-reflection about the researcher's role in the process (reflexivity) is normal in good ethnography.
- Ethnography is a highly flexible and creative process, and can involve a multiplicity of techniques, but it is also an ethically complex and potentially risky research approach that can present complex dilemmas, some of which are unexpected, but which will often require negotiating.
- Criminological ethnography involves the regular and continuous recording of fieldnotes and thick description and comes into being (for the most part) in the process of writing and describing as a written product.
- Ethnography presents the world of its host population in human contexts of thickly described written form (thick description). While there may be other components to a criminological ethnography, reflecting the brevity of techniques available to criminological researchers, an ethnography, in some way, exists in written form and becomes a historical document that may give insight into the socio-economic, political, cultural and technological context of the study and its participants.

Most criminological ethnographies are products of a relatively unique time and place, in part because as a research method, ethnography does tend to be extremely time consuming and micro focused (looking at specific, small cohorts, groups or geographical locations) and traditionally, similar ethnographic explorations of research settings rarely materialise in actuality, and so cross comparison is unlikely. For that reason, ethnography has long faced criticism that it is macro focused and only useful in very specific contexts only as an illustration of what is happening and occurring in one specific place, at one particular time.

What counts as ethnography, and what constitutes good ethnographic methodology, are both long contested in academic literature. In his reflections on ethnography with heroin users, Agar describes how in his early career he was influenced by anthropological traditions and framing where, he suggests:

> In my day we followed the unwritten rules of the old model. Junkies were the 'they,' the so-called other. We looked at them as an urban tribe or band, a self-contained community wandering the streets of the city. We built a crisp, clean picture of how junkies are, what they know. And junkies were just out there, in the streets, doing what they do to hustle and cop heroin and inject it. In retrospect this was delusional. It wasn't wrong, but it was incomplete … The nature of US drug policy, and the institutions that junkies had to deal with, seldom entered the picture. (Agar, 2008: 5)

The point Agar makes is that, in contrast to subsequent ethnographic works, early ethnographic fieldworkers often became somewhat fixated on the micro rather than macro processes. The small rather than the big picture.

There are numerous texts written on ethnography and the underpinning ideas about how it makes its claims of validity. Much like Agar, the majority of contemporary criminological ethnographers would accept that most of today's small groups are not isolated from the broader economic, political and social worlds, just as the researcher is not value neutral in entering the field, and hence the researcher is likely to have developed a research question with an initial understanding of the broad social context in which they will place themselves (Agar, 2008). Moreover, most criminologists now recognise that their research is unlikely to ever be 'passive or neutral', to use Paul Rock's (2001: 30) words.

After Becker, many sociologists have convincingly argued that claims to the primacy of technically correct and value free research are in and of themselves deeply politically laden. While some practitioners of ethnography might claim to allow participants to speak for themselves, participants' voices are always then analysed, contextualised and theorised by the academic researcher. In these circumstances, how have those who participated in the research been given a 'voice'? As Lather (2001: 482) has suggested, it is the 'romance of empowerment that drives much current ethnography' rather than the reality of it and while many ethnographers claim to empower participants and give them a voice, that claim should perhaps not imply being taken at face value.

OVERT AND COVERT ETHNOGRAPHY

So as I have established, ethnographic researchers control many decisions about specific methods they will employ while located in the field, what they will highlight and what they regard as meaningful. For example, will they be **overt** or **covert** (by which we mean will they inform participants of what they are doing)? These two terms, overt and covert, of course are better regarded as

occupying different polar extremes, and the messy reality is that all ethnographic research runs on a continuum between these extreme positions. Even
overt researchers rarely reveal everything to participants. It is also very difficult
for researchers to observe the everyday lives of criminal individuals, in what are
sometimes dangerous places, as there are problems of infiltration and gaining
the trust of what may be unpredictable and dangerous people. If the researcher
is able to gain such access, they then face the tasks of remaining impartial in
their observations, continuing to observe without becoming involved in criminal activity themselves, and even trying to prevent crimes being committed. I
will talk at length about some of the risks, problems and dangers of criminological ethnography, and while I do not wish to overstate the risks of fieldwork,
so too I am not inclined to suggest that all the risks are simply imagined.

Traditionally, overt research is regarded as less problematic and ethically
dubious, as it can gain the full informed consent of notable participants
(although as I will later suggest, such a characterisation is simplistic). In contrast, covert (or undercover) research is an emotive and controversial field
often equated with deception and transgression (Calvey, 2017). Yet covert
research has obvious advantages, such as the increased authenticity of the practices that can be observed. However, a major disadvantage is that covert
research must be justified to satisfy ethics committees or institutional review
boards because it can be regarded as involving a form of deception and is
against the principle of securing the informed consent of research participants.
If overt research is chosen, and research subjects give their consent to being
researched, participants can act naturally. However, it often takes a long time
to build trust, there is no guarantee that participants will act consistently and
it can never be established whether they are actually being authentic. Moreover,
where crime is concerned, as many practices are illegal and hidden, and those
involved may not benefit (indeed, in many cases quite the reverse) covert strategies can be necessary. Moreover, covert research has a long, successful and
venerable tradition in the social sciences, and particularly studying illicit and
criminal contexts (Calvey, 2008; see also Winlow, 2001). Of course, additionally, in a covert ethnography it can be difficult to verify and confirm the presence of the researcher, making for concerns about accuracy and veracity.

FIELDWORK

Agar (2008) suggests that the very name for 'doing ethnography' is **fieldwork**,
and as I claim at the outset of this chapter, the real stuff of ethnography in
terms of the material it can generate comes from the field. Once access is negotiated (and now that often also means formally cleared by institutional reviews
or ethics committees) the ethnographic researcher can then begin the process

of fieldwork, meeting with participants in settings during periods when its participants are going about their everyday social or occupational lives. However, this frequently means that rather than being a finite process, access is negotiated and re-negotiated continually during the in situ phase of the participant observation. This is sometimes problematic. If the research is overt, and informed consent must be sought from all participants, informants and interviewees, usually in written form that explains the purpose and methods of the research in brief but clear detail, there are likely to be continual negotiations about access with differing explanations and guarantees. Furthermore, the more time spent in the field the more familiar the researcher becomes, and hence numerous methodology textbooks warn ethnographers to avoid over-rapport or 'going native' because should they do this they can end up exploiting participants and losing all sense of distance and objectivity. However, some question the purposefulness of such a term; it is debatable whether over-rapport is ever possible (given that the very stuff of ethnography is to gain insider understanding), or whether it is simply the objective of the skilled ethnographer and a grievance lodged by envious researchers who failed to develop a rapport (see O'Reilly, 2009). Furthermore, the very nature of objectivity in ethnography is highly contested by ethnographers themselves.

Fieldwork entails gathering data that is sufficiently full so as to produce a detailed description of everyday meanings and practices. As I have previously shown, over time, understandings of this within ethnography itself have shifted, but what is often regarded as the end goal of the participatory process is the production of clear, accurate and detailed fieldnotes, and this is regarded as an essential craft skill for an ethnographer. These can be written records, or in some cases audio recordings that are ready for transcription. Throughout the process of being in situ in the field, the researcher uses their experiences and observations to make sense. For some, this is also regarded as vital in the development of ideas, but a core component of much contemporary criminological ethnography is that of reflexivity, a term with rather different meanings in different contexts but which in general normally means 'reflecting', specifically as part of the social research, and hence reflexivity is the process by which the researcher reflects upon the data collection and interpretation process. Reflexivity in ethnographic research involves two things. First, it requires that researchers reflect upon the research process in order to assess the effect of their presence and their research techniques on the nature and extent of the data collected. Crudely put, researchers must consider to what extent respondents were telling them what they wanted to hear; whether the researcher(s) inhibited respondents; whether the format of the data collection restricted the kind of data being collected, and so on. Second, and perhaps more essentially, ethnographic reflexivity requires researchers critically to reflect upon the theoretical structures they have drawn out in their analysis.

Again, simply conveyed, researchers are expected to reconceptualise their evidence using other possible models, to think laterally. Ethnographers therefore should not just fit details into a preformed schema, but rather try to re-form the schema to see if the details have different meanings. Of course, all of this is perhaps a simplistic representation of the fluid and complex process of doing fieldwork, as often ethnographers will contextualise and enhanced field data by collecting documents, be it newspaper reports, news items from TV, radio or the internet, case notes, documents that are contemporary with the researcher's time in the field. In some instances, they will use photographs, recordings, letters and all manner of material that can then be drawn on in the process of research, reflection and writing.

WHAT IS FIELDWORK?

Although participation and observation over time can be said to be the core of ethnographic research, researchers often draw from a broad array of research strategies. These include interviews (ranging from formal to informal, structured to unstructured); the collection of life histories; focus groups; the review of documents, texts and records; and the development of relationships with 'key informants' within a community.

Criminological ethnographers use multiple strategies for recording their data, including audio recording, filming, photography and, especially, fieldnotes (essentially a term that describes copious and contemporaneous notes and reflections on what has occurred). Ethnographers combine data gathered via techniques such as these with direct observation, to create a representation of their subjects or participants. A convenient way to think of this range of ethnographic strategies is to recognise that participant observation (a term that historically was used interchangeably with the term ethnography) means that the criminological ethnographer might participate alongside an individual in their everyday routines, while, at other times, only watch and observe without participating.

The qualitative tradition in criminology developed in the United States. It owes a great deal to the work of the Chicago School. This school made important contributions to criminological theory, namely through developing 'social disorganisation' theory and their 'ecological model' of the development of cities and patterns of crime within them, with much of that work based on fieldwork study. While many aspects of their work, particularly the 'ecological model', have been discredited, they left behind a tradition of linking urban social problems to crime and provided the inspiration for the development of much subsequent qualitative criminology and an emphasis on fieldwork. They bequeathed a tradition of conducting criminological research that was distinctive in its prioritisation of ethnographic techniques to explore groups on the margins of urban industrial society in the United States in the 1920s and 1930s during an epoch of rapid change. Drawing their inspiration from developments within sociological theory, Chicago School researchers pursued innovative qualitative work making use of participant observation, life histories and documents. This work began to influence British criminologists in the 1960s and the qualitative tradition is now firmly established in criminology, with almost all mainstream criminologists of all theoretical persuasions involved in some form of applied research or fieldwork (although not all of it is ethnographic nor claims to be). Moreover, that fieldwork underpinned the very growth of new theoretical criminological perspectives, for example, Chicagoan symbolic interactionism inspired the development of the labelling perspective and the work of 'deviancy theorists' in the UK, and more recently 'cultural criminologists' in the US and UK. Such theoretical approaches have continued to support the use of qualitative methods and to emphasise the importance of gaining empirical insight in the real work, learning via fieldwork.

FIELDNOTES

Significant events can come and go very quickly in the field, therefore many ethnographers find it helpful to write **fieldnotes** or keep field diaries in stages of progressive complexity that allow for expanding reflection, starting with head notes for quickness and moving through scratch notes to later developing full notes for further reflection before the event becomes hazy in the memory and initial impressions are lost. Again, there are various ways that this is done, dependent on the setting.

Some researchers make audio recordings while in the field. Transcribing recorded data, if it is gathered, and the optimum time for doing that, are subject to some debate. Some ethnographers suggest that self-transcription is vital, while some will use others (such as research assistants) to do it for them. This creates debates about the purposefulness and utility of being close to data. It is unarguable that even for the most skilled and practised researchers, transcription is very time-consuming, and out of practical necessity many ethnographers will wait until the fieldwork is finished before commencing the process of transcribing. The drawback here is that such a delay can make it difficult to integrate transcribed data with insights that arise during the fieldwork process. Except in rare cases where a specific hypothesis is to be tested (which, as I have outlined, is not a universal accepted method of participant observation), ethnographic knowledge production, analysis and theory generation are normally inductive rather than deductive and hence premises, observations and data are viewed as supplying strong evidence for the truth of the conclusion. While the conclusion of a deductive argument is certain, the truth of the conclusion of an inductive argument is probable, based upon the evidence given.

THICK DESCRIPTION

Clifford Geertz stated in *The Interpretation of Cultures* (1973):

> From one point of view, that of the textbook, doing ethnography is establishing rapport, selecting informants, transcribing texts, taking genealogies, mapping fields, keeping a diary, and so on. But it is not these things, techniques, and received procedures that define the enterprise. What defines it is the kind of intellectual effort it is: an elaborate venture in, to borrow a notion from Gilbert Ryle, 'thick description'. (Geertz, 1973: 6)

Thick description was not Geetz's term originally, he took it and adapted it from philosopher Gilbert Ryle. Thick description then is really much of the stuff of good ethnography irrespective of the subject (you have already encountered some in the proceeding pages). It is text that is produced to evoke and provoke, it is words that serve to help the reader to arrive at what Hoey and Fricke term, 'a discourse of and about living in terms of meaning in a world subject to law' (Hoey and Fricke 2007: 596).

Ethnographers do this via a methodology that prioritises meanings and frameworks, and even terminology and argot that exist outside the discipline, generated not solely by scholars, but also by the community in which the ethnographer is situated and is conducting research. Often the hallmark of an ethnographic project is the genesis of more data than the researcher can be aware of at the time of collection or in the field, and only a small amount will be subsequently employed and used. However, in making several fieldnotes, gathering thick description and learning what is emic and etic, the ethnographer as researcher begins to arrive at some understanding.

Thick description is described by Lincoln and Guba (1985) as a way of achieving a type of external validity. By describing a phenomenon in enough detail, one can begin to evaluate the extent to which the conclusions drawn are transferable to other times, settings, situations and people. In the venture of criminological ethnography, it might be more immediate, for example, to describe the immediate outplay of a violent episode or situation that was encountered by the researcher in the field, and hence it may contain not only the events, but the words used, the feelings elicited. However, more sustained description of the mundane and everyday events is just as important in painting a true and accurate picture, as a traditional descriptor and criticism of ethnography is that it has tended to exaggerate focus on the exceptional at the cost of the more routine, mundane and common, and reading some of the best ethnographies, the tendency to show the reality of life with all its facets is a hallmark, and this arguably is the stuff of thick description.

FROM FIELDNOTES TO 'AN ETHNOGRAPHIC STUDY OF ...'

The final stage of ethnography, which often commences fully as the researcher leaves the field, is the analysis of the data, although again, to see criminological ethnography as neatly separated into easily demarked or neatly defined progressive sequential stages is problematic. Even though fieldwork is often primarily inclined towards data collection, it is often the case that the researcher conducts some initial analysis during fieldwork rather than leave it all to the end or a phase once they have removed themselves from fieldwork. Furthermore, ongoing and in situ analysis can help the researcher to come up with additional questions, and assist in developing understanding of significant events and cultural practices, which in turn then leads to the collection of more rich data and the construction of more sophisticated analysis and nuanced theory, as well as ensuring that they are acting reflexively.

At the heart of analysis of ethnographic data are techniques of coding, a term that is used to describe how the field data is categorised to facilitate analysis. This is often in actuality a two-step process, beginning with basic coding in order to distinguish overall themes, followed by a more in depth, interpretive code in which more specific trends and patterns can be distinguished.

Much of qualitative coding can be attributed to either grounded or *a priori* coding. Grounded coding refers to allowing notable themes and patterns to emerge from the documents themselves, where as *a priori* coding requires the researcher to apply pre-existing theoretical frameworks to analyse the materials or documents. Prior to constructing categories, a researcher must apply a first cycle coding method. There are a multitude of methods available here, and often the researcher picks one that is suited for the format and nature of their documents or materials. Not all methods can be applied to every type of document, but examples of first cycle coding methods include:

- **In vivo coding**: this method codes terms and phrases used by the participants themselves. The objective is to attempt to 'give the participants a voice' in research.
- **Process coding**: this method uses gerunds (that is ~ing words or verbs) only to describe and display actions throughout the document. It is useful for examining processes, emotional phases and 'rituals' that matter to participants.
- **Versus coding**: this method uses binary terms to describe groups and processes. The goal is to see which processes and organisations conflict with each other throughout the material.

- **Values coding**: these are codes that attempt to exhibit the inferred values, attitudes and beliefs of participants. In doing so, the researcher may discern patterns in outlooks, values and world views, i.e. attempting to map the group's or individual's 'world view' or outlook.

All coding involves the close examination of minute details of data. Some researchers will use data analysis software to assist them in the process of coding, but some argue that it encourages a lazy, mechanistic approach in which details vital to the eventual analysis and theory can be missed, therefore it is perhaps best used as an aid rather than a replacement. Again, it is important to stress here that qualitative research is inherently reflexive; as the researcher is involved in the process of data analysis, they are always encouraged to continue to be reflexive and hence, even while coding, it is vital that ethnographers continue to chronicle their own thought processes through reflective or methodological notes, as doing so may highlight their own subjective interpretations of data.

Finally, as part of ethnography is normally the creation of work in a written form, the fieldworker is regarded as entering a final phase termed 'writing up', a process that is usually marked by withdrawal from the field (again, this notion that ethnographers will fully leave the social world they write about may be problematic) and this stage again facilitates the further development of analysis and theory. As good ethnography should make a substantial contribution towards the understanding of the social life of those studied, should be reflexive and have an aesthetic impact on the reader, and should express a credible reality, the process of writing about the world witnessed is core: an ethnography is a written study. But what might at first seem straightforward (writing about what happened) is in reality another process that is often rife with problems. It is for that reason that we return to issues of writing later in the book.

THEORETICAL PERSPECTIVES UNDERPINNING CRIMINOLOGICAL ETHNOGRAPHY

While the above concerns ethnographic approaches to fieldwork rather generally, it is certainly arguable that criminological ethnography produces unique issues and problems that make orthodox ethnographic methods more difficult to utilise. Ethnography is used in a range of research settings and, for the most part, largely does not focus on issues of crime and crime control. The research settings and cultural groups investigated by anthropologists and sociologists are diverse and often relatively benign, whereas criminologists are more often compelled to address issues and practices that are moral, ethical and legal minefields.

Crime, as all criminologists know, has a significant impact, be it on the lives of perpetrators, victims, the communities in which they reside, or the authorities charged with regulating and controlling them. Hence, ideas such as value neutrality (if ever accepted at all in ethnography) become ever more stretched when issues of crime and its control come to the fore.

In some settings, it is very difficult, perhaps impossible, for the criminological researcher to suspend moral judgement and personal intervention. Whereas the traditional rule in sociology and anthropology is to show appreciation and understanding of human motivations and practices, criminology considers behaviours that can be immoral or illegal and hence potentially at the forefront of moral condemnation.

It is perhaps for that reason that various criminological ethnographers have encountered significant hostility from sociologists and some from within their own discipline, who accuse them of sensationalising, thrill-seeking, giving violent thugs and fascists too much publicity, or pathologising and labelling the poor by revealing too much of their harmful criminal activity. Other sociologists follow Gouldner's (1968) criticism that ethnographers are simply the 'zookeepers of deviance'.

Gouldner argued that in particular Becker's sociology of deviance tells us little about substantive structural issues such as political economy, power, poverty and the forces of exclusion, and this is a criticism that continues to this day, partly due to debates about culture and the significance of culture in terms of the history of ethnography. For example, criminologist Martin O'Brien has written about the efforts of cultural criminological ethnographers such as Jeff Ferrell and has been quite critical about the ethnographic work of cultural criminologists, ethnographers and their theoretical contribution to criminology (O'Brien, 2005).

Traditionally, criminological ethnographers enjoyed a measure of freedom, however, in recent years they have come to face increasingly restrictive and sometimes out and out prohibitive guidelines as they seek to negotiate ethical clearance from institutional review boards and research committees that specialise in research ethics. Moreover, as Fader argues, the accelerated culture of academia on both sides of the Atlantic has further created a pressure on ethnography and qualitative research methods that is multifaceted. But it is possible to keep ethnographic traditions alive, and to 'challenge the existing knowledge/power hierarchy that marginalises ethnographers and our products' (Fader, 2018: 144).

If I am to outline criminological ethnography, I must bear in mind that crucial imbalance of theoretical perspectives. While I, as an author, have ideas about which ethnographies are the 'classics' or seminal studies, such views are hardly universal and one of the joys of criminological ethnography is the plethora of exciting material concerning crime, control, harm and deviance. However, one argument I am keen to make is that the specific relevance of ethnography to criminology in its own right in many ways reflects the growth and popularity of criminology as a distinct academic subject area with its own theoretical positions and perspectives, and these, I would also suggest, are relevant and useful frames or lenses for the aspirant ethnographer, because ethnography is not, or should not be, simply description alone, but is inescapably bound to both the building of and testing of theory.

Just as crime is fluid and changing, so too are the methods used to study it, and while that is true for research methods generally, it is undoubtedly true when it comes to ethnography. Since the point at which my historical overview ends, in the 1980s, there have been a number of attempts to introduce new types of ethnographic research into the discipline in an attempt to overcome the short-comings of the 'classic' studies and move forward to show new understandings of crime and crime control. It is to these contemporary ethnographic approaches that I now turn to illustrate more emergent and current forms of 'criminological ethnography'. In making this case, I am suggesting that criminology as a subject is somewhat unique in so far as individuals who ascribe to criminological per-spectives will additionally identify as ethnographers, and this fusing of crimino-logical perspectives and ideas with research methods is unique.

THE CRITICAL CRIMINOLOGICAL ETHNOGRAPHY

The **critical** ethnographic approach openly encourages researchers to dig underneath everyday meanings and look for underlying significant meanings and events that reveal structures of power and control. For instance, researchers could look for the details in significant meanings and events that might indicate the motivations for and the responses to everyday instances of racism, sexism and other forms of domination. Critical researchers are encouraged to discover precisely how people are subjugated, in the sense of their rights, life chances and expressions of culture, by dominant social groups. Therefore, such critical research focuses on societies 'underdog' when seeking to expose power rela-tions, methods of subjugation and structural imbalances in social relations.

Both in criminology and in ethnography there is a strong critical research and activist tradition. Critical ethnographers generally gather and then politically and actively use ethnographic data, and analysis can inform policy and encour-age activism among the subjugated, with significant reform or social transfor-mation in mind. For example, Lisa McKenzie, an ethnographer of working-class life in deprived urban communities in England is also a self-declared political activist who seeks to promote emancipatory class politics. Some have suggested that the problems in this approach include the assumption of the subjugated as passive victims (Fleetwood, 2014) rather than already active resistors and the possibility that the rhetoric of 'empowerment' gives the subjugated false hope for the resolution of problems that require more fundamental political inter-vention in economy and society.

Yet it is undeniable that ethnographers working at the intersections of criminology today are using emic and etic perspectives to bring attention to harms that rightly require attention, and the tendency that Agar expressed above to look at participants in isolation as a group is now out-dated, as is the idea that the ethnographer will be value neutral and not take a political standpoint. For example, Gary Gray's insights on organisational safety culture stemming from his socio-legal ethnography of workplace safety fits the critical ethnography mantra well (Gray, 2009).

In his analysis of a medium-size unionised Canadian industrial factory that specialised in manufacturing automotive parts and involved workers in a variety of high-risk tasks, he was critical of the way in which the burden of responsibility for worker health and safety had been shifted onto individuals (Gray, 2009). Moreover, from new focuses on border security, to new forms of work-based harm, willing ethnographers who work in a critical manner have a range of emergent topics they could consider, from throw away fashion to green criminology, from local in Leicester to sweat shops in Bangladesh. 'Critical criminology' can be regarded as something of a lifeblood that flows through most criminological ethnographic perspectives.

CRITICAL CRIMINOLOGY ETHNOGRAPHIES – SUGGESTED READINGS

- Gray, G. (2002) 'A socio-legal ethnography of the right to refuse dangerous work', *Studies in Law, Politics & Society*, 24: 133–169.
- Gray, G. (2009) 'The responsibilization strategy of health and safety: neo-liberalism and the reconfiguration of individual responsibility for risk', *British Journal of Criminology*, 49 (3): 326–342.
- McKenzie, L. (2015) *Getting By: Estates, Class and Culture in Austerity Britain*. Bristol: Policy Press.
- Scheper-Hughes, N. (2004) 'Parts unknown: undercover ethnography of the organs-trafficking underworld', *Ethnography*, 5 (1): 29–73.
- Sollund, R. (2017) 'Doing green, critical criminology with an auto-ethnographic, feminist approach', *Critical Criminology*, 25 (2): 245–260.

POLICE ETHNOGRAPHY

While there has long been a stream of ethnographic work produced with ethnographers studying and observing policing, the mainstream policing literature perhaps positions this work at the periphery of the topic, and certainly, internally law enforcement agencies and particularly police themselves have tended to prioritise and prefer more quantitative, 'scientific' and statistical forms of research.

Early ethnographic works became visible and powerful icons of the policing literature, in both the US and the UK, telling much about the organisational culture and character of policing. In his overview of policing ethnography, Manning (2014: 532–535) suggests the nature of policing dictates the engagement of the researcher with the practice context as it is only in these circumstances they will have full access to the nuances and complexities that shape the ways officers make sense of, manage and perform their role within the occupational setting. Significant figures in the academic study of policing, such as Michael Banton, Jerome Skolnick, Egon Bittner, John Van Maanen and Maureen Cain, who employed broadly ethnographic strategies to examine policing, have begun to give way to broader examinations of the wider 'world of policing' (e.g. Fassin, 2013), which examine a wider number of contexts and draw on a now rich collection of ethnographic studies of policing in disadvantaged neighbourhoods that tend to straddle different continents, as police ethnography expands and considers contexts in both the Global North and the Global South.

Ethnographies of policing sometimes have considered police use of power and discretion and occupational culture, whereas other studies look at the more specific policing of some groups or issues. For example, in *Police, Drugs and Community*, Mike Collison concentrated on the policing of drugs. Collison's study presents the results of an ethnography, conducted in 1990 in an unnamed English town, of cops in the street, police who make 'shit bum arrests' of small dealers and hustlers (1995: 12). Ethnographers in police settings have referred to the difficulties that researchers face as they encounter corruption, malpractice and police deviance, but also have involved serving officers acting covertly as ethnographers. Perhaps one of the most famous examples of such research while still in uniform was Simon Holdaway's study: while working within a busy city police station, he was able to record the day-to-day frustrations, boredom and excitement of ordinary police officers. He provided a graphic and sometimes disturbing picture of law enforcement in action (Holdaway, 1983).

POLICE ETHNOGRAPHIES – SUGGESTED READINGS

- Fassin, D. (2013) *Enforcing Order: An Ethnography of Urban Policing.* Cambridge: Polity.
- Loftus, B (2012) *Police Culture in a Changing World.* Oxford: Clarendon.
- Stuart, F. (2016) *Down, Out and Under Arrest: Policing and Everyday Life in Skid Row.* Chicago: University of Chicago Press
- Westmarland, L. (2001) 'Blowing the whistle on police violence: gender, ethnography and ethics', *British Journal of Criminology*, 41 (3): 523–535.

PRISON ETHNOGRAPHY

Again, prison ethnography has long been at the heart of prison scholarship, and some have argued that early penal reformists such as John Howard, and authors such as Charles Dickens might have shown a tendency towards the ethnographic sensibility. However, modern prison ethnography really began with works such as Donald Clemmer's *The Prison Community* (1940) was written while its author was a staff member at the Southern Illinois Penitentiary. Based on his research in the Menard Branch of the Illinois State Penitentiary, Clemmer put forward and established the notion of 'prisonisation'. This concept can be understood as the impact of the prison experience on prisoners and is thus a descriptor of the process by which those who enter prison take on the 'folkways, mores, customs, and general culture of the penitentiary' (1940: 299). Clemmer documented the process by which the psyches and behaviours of convicts were moulded by the social and structural hallmarks of prison life. His research led him to suggest that 'prisonisation' largely confounds the social ideal underlying the penitentiary concept: it not only thwarted attempts to rehabilitate convicts but also inspired behaviour that was contrary to accepted standards of social conduct.

Perhaps better known is Gresham Sykes 1958 publication, *The Society of Captives: A Study of a Maximum-Security Prison*, based on research in the New Jersey state prison. A formative influence on the microsociology of prison life and penology, Sykes' work is now considered a classic and his internalist account of prison culture in a New Jersey maximum-security prison is still much read and cited by prison scholars today. Sykes described how inmates grouped together to counter the institutionalising effects of the carceral realm and the pains of imprisonment, how prison staff were only imperfectly able to control the prisoner population because of the defects of total power, and checks on custodial authority were the result of inmate resistance and the scrutiny of external society.

Erving Goffman, the Chicago School sociologist, published *Asylums* in 1961 (based on ethnography in mental health settings). Goffman coined the term 'total institution', which he defined as institutions that have an 'encompassing or total character, [as] symbolised by the barrier to social intercourse with the outside' … 'such as locked doors, high walls, barbed wire …The central feature of total institutions can be described as a breakdown of the barriers ordinarily separating three spheres of life [work, play and sleep]' (1961: 16–18). Goffman utilised a symbolic interactionist (or interpretivist) approach to consider the experience of confinement and suggested that through the inherently artificial and degrading environment of the total institution, inmates experience a 'mortification of the self'. The first sociological study of prison life in Britain was conducted by Terence and Pauline Morris in Pentonville prison (Morris and Morris, 1963). There were various additional forays into ethnography, including Stan Cohen and

Laurie Taylor's *Psychological Survival* based on their time teaching at Durham prison. Sparks, Bottoms and Hay's classic and seminal British work *Prisons and the Problem of Order* (1991) was based on ethnographic research in two maximum-security prisons (Albany and Long Lartin) in the late 1980s, and considered the factors which influenced the orderliness (or otherwise) of a prison regime. However, by the turn of the century Loïc Wacquant was lamenting 'The curious eclipse of prison ethnography in the age of mass incarceration' (2002) in a special issue of the journal *Ethnography* and asking why, given the backdrop of soaring rates of incarceration, ethnography of the carceral, particularly in the US, had been so infrequent. That ethnographic research appeared to be disappearing under the weight of more conventional and profitable 'correctional' research was a concern for him. Yet whether that trend was widespread, or more restricted to the US, is debatable. In the UK, for example, ethnographic work was being undertaken in prison settings, at least as much as in any criminal justice settings, although as I noted earlier, the 1980s and 1990s, according to Hobbs, were arguably not a good time for ethnographic criminological research generally). Recent times have seen the publication of *The Palgrave Handbook of Prison Ethnography* (Drake et al., 2015) and the use of ethnography is undergoing a resurgence in popularity in carceral settings beyond prisons.

PRISON ETHNOGRAPHIES – SUGGESTED READINGS

- Crewe, B. (2009) *The Prisoner Society: Power, Adaptation and Social Life in an English Prison*. Oxford: Clarendon.
- Fassin, D. (2016) *Prison Worlds: An Ethnography of the Carceral Condition*. Cambridge: Polity.
- Liebling, A. (1999) 'Doing research in prison: breaking the silence?', *Theoretical Criminology*, 3: 147–73.
- Sloan, J. (2016) *Masculinities and the Adult Male Prison Experience*. London: Palgrave Macmillan.
- Ugelvik, T. (2014) *Power and Resistance in Prison: Doing Time, Doing Freedom*. London: Palgrave Macmillan.
- Wilson, D. (2006) 'Some reflections on researching with young Black people and the youth justice system', *Youth Justice*, 6 (3): 181–193.

FEMINIST ETHNOGRAPHIES

Traditionally male ethnographers, and particularly those early on who were focused on gangs and youth subcultures, tended to situate females not as subjects but as peripheral and bit part players in the world, and there remains a tendency to regard crime (unless it is victimisation) as largely the exclusive preserve of men. However, female ethnographers such as Anne Campbell (1986) on female gang members, and Jody Miller (2001; 2008) have gone a long way towards rebalancing the one-time shocking neglect of women's experiences.

Yet in many ways to talk of feminist ethnography is difficult. Feminist ethnography does not have a single, coherent definition and is caught between struggles over the definition and goals of feminism. Yet speaking generally, the broad church approach is associated with critical ethnography, but researchers are encouraged to discover in fine detail how historical and structural subjugation specifically affects women's lives. Pat Carlen's (1976) study of a magistrate's court in Britain demonstrated how one could employ interactionist methods and concepts in researching the oppressive treatment of defendants at the 'micro' level, within a Marxist analysis of law as a 'macro' institution. She went on to pursue a feminist critique of the penal and welfare systems based on interviewing women about their experiences (for example, Carlen 1983) and while much of this work does not claim to be ethnography *per se*, she clearly held a very real ethnographic sensibility.

In many ways it could be suggested that there are several overlaps between feminist research agendas more generally, and ethnography specifically. All feminist research, including ethnography, tends to share in common that it selects as a focus an issue pertinent to women, a preference for qualitative research and a commitment to reflexivity as a means of highlighting issues of power and control and the subjective experiences of doing research. Some feminists, in particular Judith Stacey, highlight the concern that for all the merits and emancipatory potential of ethnographic methods as a means of building equal, reciprocal relationships with an emphasis on empathy and human concerns, there is paradoxically a dark side to such methods insofar as they heighten the potential for manipulation and betrayal and always result in a power imbalance between researcher and researched, where the former is given greater status and privilege than the latter (Stacey, 1988). This is the extreme end of concern though, as a number of feminist ethnographers argue that there is a natural or perhaps cultural affinity between feminism and ethnography just as there is between women and qualitative data, and an orientation to regarding people as humans rather than numbers. Some also suggest that women are notably adept at forging equal and appreciative relationships with participants and conducting all interactions in a warm and receptive rather than an interrogative manner. Like critical ethnographers, feminist ethnographers are open about the theoretical assumptions and cultural identity politics that give purpose to their work and tend to promote reflexivity (see Fleetwood, 2014).

However, for all that early feminism seemed to embrace ethnography, today stand-alone feminist ethnographies are relatively infrequent. Notable recent exceptions to the trend are found in the work of Jodi Miller in the US and Jen

Fleetwood in the UK. Miller focuses on female involvement in gangs, as well as victimisation experiences of urban African American girls. In particular, she calls for other feminist researchers to help contribute to the general study of gender and crime, particularly in under-represented or unexplored areas of research. Miller's challenge has been taken up by Jen Fleetwood who has used ethnographic approaches to consider the role and place of women in the international cocaine trade. Moreover, it might be arguable that while there are plenty of topics that feminists perhaps ought to be examining ethnographically as they reflect an increasingly global and unequal world that remains extremely patriarchal (such as forced marriage, sex trafficking, female genital mutilation) these topics are hard to access, with victims difficult to locate.

FEMINIST ETHNOGRAPHIES – SUGGESTED READINGS

- Fleetwood, J. (2011) 'Five kilos: penalties and practice in the international cocaine trade', *British Journal of Criminology*, 51 (21): 375–393.
- Fleetwood, J. (2014) *Drug Mules: Women in the International Cocaine Trade*. Basingstoke: Palgrave Macmillan.
- Miller, J. (2008) *Getting Played: African American Girls, Urban Inequality, and Gendered Violence*. New York: New York University Press.
- Welsh, M. and Rajah V. (2014) 'Rendering invisible punishments visible: using institutional ethnography in feminist criminology', *Feminist Criminology*, 9 (4): 323–343.

CULTURAL CRIMINOLOGICAL ETHNOGRAPHY

Cultural criminology is a theoretical, methodological and interventionist approach to the study of crime that seeks to understand crime in the context of its culture. Largely emerging in the USA with the likes of Jeff Ferrell and Mark Hamm, cultural criminology is in some ways a rejuvenation of the symbolic interactionist tradition, and has ties, particularly in the States, with the American Society of Criminology's critical criminology network.

Cultural criminology looks specifically at how crime shapes culture, and culture shapes crime, taking as its focus the contemporary mediated world and the complex issues of representation and reality. However, in methodological orientation, it has long championed ethnography as a resistant form of research, vital for gaining emic and etic understanding of the complex phenomena of crime. In this respect, it not only uses notions such as *verstehen* and 'edgework', but reconsiders how some crimes can be regarded as symbolic forms of resistance to socially dominant norms. Hence it views and conceives of both crime and the agencies of crime and social control as cultural products.

Cultural criminology seeks to highlight how power affects constructions of crime, such as laws created, laws broken, and the interplay of moral entrepreneurship, moral innovation and transgression. In both the United States and the United Kingdom since the mid-1990s cultural criminology has become something of a transnational US–UK meeting place, and perhaps has been the most important single movement in promoting ethnography among a new generation of critic criminologists. At a time when, on both sides of the Atlantic, an abandonment of concern with aetiology, rational choice and a default positivistic and quantitative methodological orientation were dominant in mainstream criminology, cultural criminology provided an important counter perspective (Ferrell and Hamm, 1998). Hence while cultural criminology draws heavily on the Chicago School of sociology and the 1970s Marxist and neo-Gramscian criminologists, it is also very much a theory of the present. However, some have criticised its understanding of culture, and criticised for its focus on lower-status crimes of non-conformity (O'Brien, 2005) whereas others, and particularly ultra-realists, have criticised its notion of resistance, questioning the extent to which any form of resistance is possible under the conditions of contemporary capitalism.

DEVIANT LEISURE ETHNOGRAPHIES

Straddling cultural criminology and ultra-realism is, arguably, an emerging 'deviant leisure' perspective, which shares a subject and focal concern with the former, but a theoretical orientation with the latter. This emergent perspective has claimed the ethnographic sensibility of criminology and set out to examine the nexus of leisure and deviance that is alert to the contradictions and damaging nature of global capitalism as it relates to forms of commodified leisure. Taking as its focus some activities that are linked to low levels of social harm being directly or indirectly criminalised – some forms of drug taking, for example, or engagement in extreme sport type leisure pursuits that bring individuals or groups into conflict with owners or guardians of private property, such as skateboarding or free-running – it has, like cultural criminology, already shown an ethnographic sensibility (Raymen, 2019). Yet the deviant leisure movement similarly questions why some forms of undeniably harmful leisure meanwhile are legal, or positively sanctioned – consider, for example, certain types of alcohol consumption which are tolerated, such as youthful intoxication (Smith, 2014), which also have close connections with the ultra-realist perspective (see below).

CULTURAL CRIMINOLOGY ETHNOGRAPHIES – SUGGESTED READINGS

- Ferrell, J. (2002) *Tearing Down the Streets*. London: Palgrave Macmillan.
- Ferrell, J. (2006) *Empire of Scrounge: Inside the Urban Underground of Dumpster Diving, Trash Picking, and Street Scavenging*. New York: New York University Press.
- Snyder, G. (2011) *Graffiti Lives: Beyond the Tag in New York's Urban Underground*. New York: New York University Press.
- Yuen Thompson, B. (2015) *Covered in Ink: Tattoos, Women and the Politics of the Body*. New York: New York University Press.

DEVIANT LEISURE ETHNOGRAPHIES – SUGGESTED READING

- Raymen, T. (2019) *Parkour, Deviance and Leisure in the Late-Capitalist City: An Ethnography*. Bingley: Emerald.
- Smith, O. (2014) *Contemporary Adulthood and the Night Time Economy*. London: Palgrave Macmillan.

ULTRA-REALIST CRIMINOLOGICAL ETHNOGRAPHY

Ultra-realist criminologists reject the notion that plural cultures are the bedrock of society. Instead, they argue that ethnographers can communicate with each other to construct plausible accounts of our shared reality that should be connected to a consideration of underlying political economy of advanced capitalism. Ultra-realist criminology, associated principally with the work of Steve Hall and Simon Winlow, broadly seeks to understand that the problems of generalisation and researcher bias have limited the effectiveness of the ethnographies that have dominated the field up to now, and that the philosophical and theoretical frameworks the researchers have used – such as pragmatism, symbolic interactionism and post-structuralism – are overly influenced by traditional and still dominant yet ultimately problematic political positions.

Succinctly outlining the ultra-realist position is no easy task, given that the perspective has several elements that work at various levels of explanation. It is far more complex than the popular concept of special liberty, by which Hall (2012) in particular encourages academics to look both up and down capitalism's contemporary social strata to consider why it is some individuals can imbue themselves with permission to visit harms on others. That tends to get more attention than Hall's working of pseudo pacification, essentially a challenge to the traditional notions of the civilising process encountered in the sociology of Norbert Elias, and instead considers how capitalism variously cultivated functional and useful sensibilities at points in history, with associated permissions or injunctions written large within that. For Hall, contemporary crime is no simple 'moral panic', and nor is it a reflection of the desire of street criminals to resist the totality of global capital. It is real, destructive and corrosive. Moreover, ultra-realists take issue with liberal-left discourse that has focused for too long on 'the barbarism of order' (the oppressive and potentially totalitarian state) and ignored the 'barbarism of disorder' that occurs daily on the margins of civil society and in the boardrooms of economic elites, while also discouraging much conservative and right realist branches of criminology. For ultra-realist's criminology needs to be unsentimental and resolutely 'realist' and fully capable of understanding the complexities of today's capital and its multifarious harms.

Ultra-realists advocate the establishment of ethnographic and theoretical networks within nations and across the world, using advanced ethnographic methods, collaborative data and new theoretical frameworks using concepts adapted from advanced philosophical positions (see Hall and Winlow, 2015). They believe that such data and theorisation can provide the degree of gener-alisability necessary to connect localised meanings and practices to the broad global structures and processes of history, economy and consumer culture. For instance, Winlow et al. (2015) used ultra-realist principles to gather data and construct a new theoretical perspective on riots that occurred in England, Spain and Greece after the recent economic crash and austerity programmes, and then, to understand the swell of the far right in England (and more broadly with the election of Donald Trump in the USA (Winlow et al., 2017)). The aim of ultra-realists is not to produce a single 'grand theory', but to move beyond yesterday's assumptions in order to craft collaborative research methods, net-works and new theoretical paradigms that have more incisive explanatory power in today's rapidly changing global world.

A vital element of ultra-realism, which maps to ontological and epistemo-logical understandings of research method, is to push beyond what is termed critical post-positivist ontology. For ultra-realists, criminology must begin to look again, through research, not simply at the empirical or the actual dimen-sion, but instead, to seek to craft understandings of the underpinning generative mechanisms and drivers of human action. Understanding all of these dimen-sions is essential, and as such ultra-realists seek to consider and acknowledge:

- the empirical dimension (phenomenological experiences of knowing subjects)
- the actual dimension (real events and subjective experiences)
- the real dimension (underlying generative mechanisms that cause the events that are open to experience).

In this way, ultra-realism at least in part champions a return to both theory and questions of aetiology but extends that concern between traditional interac-tionist ideas. That is why, with its interest in generative features and deeper drivers that may not necessarily be articulated, there may be synergies between ultra-realism and perspectives such as psychosocial criminology (Gadd and Jefferson, 2006) in seeking to craft a new approach that combines a clear understanding of the shape of contemporary global crime and harms with intellectual opposition to the currently dominant criminological paradigms of conservatism, neoclassicism and left-liberalism. What is more, the results of the interplay of new theory and ethnographic research are already crafting texts that will inspire a new generation of ethnographers.

ULTRA-REALIST CRIMINOLOGICAL ETHNOGRAPHY – SUGGESTED READINGS

- Ellis, A. (2016) *Men, Masculinities and Violence: An Ethnographic Study.* London: Routledge.
- Lloyd, A. (2018) *The Harms of Work: An Ultra-Realist Account of the Service Economy.* Bristol: Bristol University Press.
- Wakeman, S. 'Fieldwork, biography and emotion: doing criminological autoethnography', *The British Journal of Criminology*, 54 (5): 705–721.
- Winlow, S., Hall, S. and Treadwell, J. (2017) *Rise of the Right, English Nationalism and the Transformation of Working-Class Politics.* Bristol: Bristol University Press.
- Winlow, S., Hall, S. and Ancrum, C. (2008) *Criminal Identities and Consumer Culture: Crime, Exclusion and the New Culture of Narcissism.* Cullompton: Willan.

CHAPTER SUMMARY

In this chapter we have seen that criminological ethnography can be considered an important part of a more general social scientific ethnographic project, but at the moment quantitative research remains dominant in criminology, which means that the finely detailed meanings and practices that constitute human life are relatively marginalised.

I commenced by arguing that although the ethnographic approach to criminological research has to contend with some methodological challenges and, like all research, throws up some ethical problems, the rich data it can provide goes further than the quantitative approach as more broadly understood in providing an adequate descriptive and realistic empirical basis on which convincing theoretical explanations of criminality and its modes of control can be constructed. However, to perform this task the ethnographic approach requires a more established place in the sphere of criminology, and so must not sit back but instead must use the increased rigour and the further development of its methods that have been occurring in recent decades to begin to show its value. Despite the historical disciplinary marginalisation of ethnography in criminology, there is scope for optimism. Contemporary ethnographic methodology is advancing at quite a pace, and in recent years has been at the forefront in the new theoretical developments in criminology, providing innovative ways of understanding the rapidly changing world of crime, harm and social control we now face nationally and globally. If these criminological ethnographic methods can be practised in growing networks to produce generalisable data that can be combined with new theoretical frameworks based on concepts currently seemingly in the ascendency, the ethnographic approach could become the go to methodology and an empirical mainstay of a rejuvenated, new and valuable twenty-first-century criminology, but that can only happen if criminologists are willing to take a leap of faith and employ the methods to study crime and its control, and it is to that project I will next turn.

PART TWO
PREPARATION AND ACTION

4

PLANNING A CRIMINOLOGICAL ETHNOGRAPHIC PROJECT

LEARNING OBJECTIVES

This chapter intends to move beyond abstract and theoretical discussions regarding the framing of criminological ethnography as a research enterprise and as a means to inform theoretical perspectives, and to begin to consider the practicalities of doing criminological ethnography practically. By the end of this chapter you should have a better understanding of:

- how to develop and frame a research focus
- the practicalities of undertaking ethnographic research
- refining a research topic
- ethics and risk.

By now you will be familiar with some of the main ideas and concepts that help to shape the contours of criminological ethnographic inquiry, and some of the theoretical and conceptual framework that helps to explain its place, use and function. Criminological ethnography involves observation and participation. It involves watching, listening and asking questions about people's daily lives and experiences, and the meaning they attach to these and, specifically, doing this when the focus is crime and criminal behaviour and its regulation.

Yet for ethnographic researchers, a close and regular field engagement with participants raises both practical and ethical challenges related to intrusion, relationship boundaries and issues of 'attachment' on leaving the field. Research that has the added dimension of profound sensitivity may also present the researcher with the challenge of managing the impacts on them of emotional stress caused by watching people's discomfort and suffering, and this is even more apparent when the issue in focus is crime. I think that well-planned, well-conceived ethnography can assist in mitigating risks to researchers, participants and organisations, and for that reason, I have given over a chapter to planning and preparing for undertaking ethnography. Hence, this chapter will cover all the core considerations that should form the backdrop to undertaking an ethnographic project. It will offer an introduction to understanding the study of crime and control through the ethnographic lens and provide some discussion around how ethnographers select their subjects. It will consider the practical issues of getting into the field. The goal of this chapter is preparation; it is about equipping the ethnographer with everything they may need to start their project from the best possible place. Of course, even that cannot make ethnography a method that is without risk, ethical dilemmas and complexity. It is, after all, a messy business.

Of course, any plan will be tailored to the specific focus and aims of an ethnographic project. The range of methods to which an ethnographer has access, the methods selected for a particular ethnographic study, and the way those methods are used are dependent on the purpose of the research, as well as on the particular social settings upon which the research focuses, which will of course affect and impact upon any plan. I am certainly not suggesting that all ethnography should follow a checklist, as such checklist styles are, in many ways, the antithesis of the get out and try it out, 'fly by the seat of your pants' manner in which ethnography is often perceived. Certainly, I do not wish to standardise practice, or reduce ethnographic planning to a standardised to-do 'checklist' inspired by a desire simply to get the data. There is a danger that such a push for efficiency potentially narrows the opportunities to engender 'the unpredictable, the tangential and the creative', so that all that can remain is, 'methodological instrumentalism' (Mills and Ratcliffe, 2012: 152). This is by no means my intent.

That said, I also have some concerns about the way in which the various negative views of qualitative research and ethnography can be employed and utilised as a form of academic critique and censorship. As an ethnographer, I am not wholly aligned to extreme social constructionism which regards all representations of reality as mere social constructs, outcomes of the ability of powerful groups to utilise language to construct a narrative that comes to dominate what passes for truth. The fact of the matter is that criminological ethnography, while enjoying a resurgence in popularity in recent years, is still most often a maligned method. It occupies a juxtaposition in that it is often regarded by critics as either unscientific and available to absolutely anyone, or a dangerous method that is inherently risk laden and, potentially, much more unethical than any other method. In my experience, ethnography and qualitative methods can, and often do, face far greater levels of critical scrutiny than other social research methods, and that point perhaps is made when

I note elsewhere that recent arguments have sought to make ethnography subject to 'legal standards' (Lubet, 2018). Yet no such requirement has been mooted for regression analysis or random control trials, despite the fact that there is a long history of academic malpractice pertaining to those methods, and fabrication, falsification or plagiarism in proposing, performing or reviewing research, or in reporting research results is hardly the sole preserve of qualitative social scientists.

A symbolic interactionist focus on discursive self and the structures of symbolic definitional power has had a long lasting appeal in universities, where stories can be told and research represented (or ignored). The dominant perspectives in social science departments remain social constructionism and/or a commitment to large scale quantitative analysis and statistical analysis. While ethnography is sometimes popular with graduate students and practitioners, not least because of its ability to tell of and craft an image of reality that is authentic and born of an intimate relationship with the research field and context, it can also be a way that it is marginalised and devalued by some critics.

Descriptive ethnographic work immediately grabs us and demands we pay attention, unfortunately it can also be the subject of a cynical, snobbish dismissal from those who have shown no desire or ability to conduct it themselves, and that is undoubtedly the case when the focus is crime and deviance. It is considered 'macho' when studying any violent male cultures, and derided for the perceived machismo of the researcher, just as the motives of a female studying male crime groups will give rise to questions about her probity and quite likely her chastity, as for example females undertaking ethnographic work in male prisons can be derided as 'wanting to gaze at rough, tough men' or ethnographers studying criminal men derided as 'a bit Ross Kemp' by those who are resolutely unwilling to leave their own ivory towers. I have encountered and overheard such comments often enough in the academic community to know that such views are aired (sometimes unguardedly). Former drug users are regarded as lacking the objectivity or neutrality when studying drug cultures (as if former users are the only individuals who might form views on drug use). Almost all the ethnographers who conduct ethnographic work will have stories about the dismissive, critical and condescending tone with which their research can be and had been received and derided.

Perhaps the best way to avoid some of these criticism is to plan the project well, document the findings well, undertake careful, considered analysis of the gathered data, write it up in a considered manner that connects the empirical data with theory, and be able to defend it and any claims that are made. It sounds easy, but the reality is likely to be messy. However, that is where planning and preparation can certainly help.

LOOKING AT CRIME AND CONTROL THROUGH AN ETHNOGRAPHIC LENS

As I have thus far shown, ethnography is a lens, or a means of looking at the world, but before we can ever use a lens, we must decide what it is that we will look at. What confuses many students is that given that often ethnographers seek to stress how separate they are from the positivistic tradition of developing research questions or testable hypothesis, how is it possible to focus the lens on a specific research question?

Convention holds that ethnography is selected because it is the appropriate method of studying something, i.e. decisions to use it are about the appropriateness of the subject. While I fully understand and respect this, I also suspect that the reverse is often true, and that by the time a decision is made to use ethnography, it is often premised on an aspirant researcher's commitment to ethnographic and more generally qualitative methods rather than the appropriateness of the methods to a topic that they are interested in. While traditionally it has been suggested that ethnography be employed where the researcher's concern is socio-cultural activities and patterns of a group or culture, I suspect that today, many embarking on a PhD have more interest, or at least equal interest, in method that topic. That is why, at least in part, we should consider ethnography not just in terms of its appropriateness, but also its potentially innovative application, that is, if you know you want to use ethnography, how do you find an appropriate place to use it in an innovative way?

However, here I feel advised to give some words of caution. Many people decided upon their desire to use ethnography to study for a PhD, and its popularity is certainly rising in some fields linked to criminal justice, such as policing and prisons. Yet being in the field is time-consuming, demanding, frustrating and difficult, or it can be, and so considering what in a topic will keep your interest will arguably be an important factor in being successful in an ethnographic study, because you will be living it. With that in mind, it seems both obvious and prudent to ask some questions before you begin. Is this something I can do? Is it something I want to do? Will I be happy doing it? Here I am suggesting that a process of self-questioning and critical self-reflection (or reflexivity) should begin before you ever embark on an ethnographic study.

Put simply, while I believe that ethnography can be done by most people, criminological ethnography might not be right for everyone. If you do not feel comfortable in large crowds, it may not be wise to undertake an ethnography of a street protest movement. Many students like the idea of working in prisons but find the reality claustrophobic when they encounter them, because prisons can be intimidating, boisterous, threatening, violent, upsetting and unsettling places.

Ethnography undeniably has its shortcomings, and so will those who conduct it. In ethnography there are more questionable aspects around validity, 'objectivity' and issues of generalisation, but many of the issues of ethnography are issues of all social research. If we look across the academic vista of social research, we would quickly see that many of the greatest instances of malpractice are not the result of ethnographic researchers at the early stages of their academic careers. The debates about the validity and techniques of ethnography have now been discussed in depth elsewhere in this text, and therefore, I do not intend to re-hash them once again here in great length as these are arguments that may never be fully resolved (Ferrell and Hamm, 1998; Ancrum, 2013). Instead the spirit of this chapter is one that accepts that all research methods have their situated functionality and utility when applied appropriately to a correct topic or study, and hence here I am attempting to get the reader to consider how they make their aims appropriate to ethnography, or how they use ethnography in a manner that is appropriate to aims and objectives.

Although the terms 'aims' and 'objectives' are quite often used uncritically and interchangeably, it is worth spending some time clarifying the difference between these, as such clarification can assist in developing successful research proposals, making grant applications, compiling documentation for internal and external oversight and review, and developing a project that is likely to be successful. If you are seeking to undertake ethnography as a postgraduate student, it is inevitable that you will face such hurdles, and clarity about what you need to provide will likely assist you in managing the process is a timely manner. Most proposals will ask that you provide:

- **a title**: this is just a tentative title for your intended research, but with some funded research or schemes, this may be provided for you. You may want to think of this as the first step in helping draw interested parties to you, and use key words and terms to pull in an audience
- **an abstract**: the proposal should include a concise statement of your intended purpose. It will often be word limited, and hence is often an exercise in determining what most matters and what is the most pressing and pertinent issues in a research topic
- **the research context**: you should explain the broad background against which you will undertake your research, what the setting or settings will be, whether one place or several, in essence (and as far as it is possible to predict in advance) where is it foreseeable that the research will be conducted.
- **the research questions**: the proposal should set out the central aims and objectives of your research.

As the later point illustrates, aims and objectives will likely be part of any social research proposal, but differentiating what these are matters a great deal.

Several authors, including Spradley (1980: 34), have suggested that a funnel is a good metaphor for an ethnographic project, and I often tell students 'start broad and shallow, but aim to go deep and narrow'. What I intend to convey by this is the evolutionary nature of ethnography where the research shifts in the very process of its undertaking; the topic and focus of the study are defined with a greater precision in the project's undertaking. As the ethnographic field-work commences, the focus will evolve, and hopefully narrow, new topics and issues will come to the fore. While it pays for ethnography to be 'fluid and flexible' rather than rigid, all ethnography will need a focus, and as research it needs a question to frame the focus. In a qualitative and ethnographic study, researchers tend to begin with a research question (or questions) rather than objectives (i.e. specific goals for the research) or hypotheses (i.e. predictions that involve variables and statistical tests) though not all organisations will understand such distinctions and so it is not uncommon for students to be asked for their research hypothesis or objective when they plan. However, for me, what is useful in framing an ethnographic project, is the intent to explore the complex set of factors surrounding the central phenomenon and to present the varied perspectives or meanings that participants hold.

As Spradley suggests, the ethnographic researcher's central question is simply 'what is going on here' (1980: 12), and that question perfectly connects the detail of local meaning and culture to larger social forces (in specific relation to some field of human interaction). Criminological ethnography has a starting point that is decisively different from that of research 'in other cultures', the traditional stuff of anthropology. It is likely that criminological ethnographers do have vast implicit and explicit background knowledge of any field they are studying. Since criminological ethnographers are also, for the most part, knowl-edgeable of the groups that they study and issues of crime before they even start to enter the field, the traditional view that they cannot generate any hypothesis and should go in to observe everything may not hold. This pre-existing knowledge may constitute a methodological problem that must be controlled and considered reflexively, but it may also be used heuristically. Even if the researcher may lack the contextual knowledge of specific crime situations, he or she will typically know of these, the study may require a greater focus from the outset without having to stray so far as to develop a fixed hypothesises. Whatever the case, as the criminological ethnographer will look at how culture and behaviour are related, and conduct research while liv-ing and/or working within the environment they study, they will often have some time to plan for 'blending in' and being in the field that they have a knowledge of, and so can plan and adapt an array of aspects of the project. However, from how they will dress to how they communicate and engage in activities, most aspects of the field can be considered before the researcher enters the field, and such planning, preparation and forethought are arguably extremely useful in criminological ethnography. I therefore suggest that rather than seeing the process of planning research and overcoming bureaucratic and institutional barriers as simply a hurdle to be overcome, there can be merit in regarding it as the first stage of undertaking a successful and good quality piece of work. That stated, there may be merit in spending some time trying to craft a project and write a short research proposal, and this chapter culminates in an attempt to get you to use the guidance here to undertake the task of writing a research proposal as if you are proposing undertaking ethnographic fieldwork as a means of putting the discussions here into practice.

PLANNING THE CENTRAL RESEARCH QUESTION(S)

In some ways, the central aim in ethnography can be as simple as to seek to observe or understand a cultural group or phenomena, and it is perfectly accept-able for your aim to be to conduct an 'ethnography' of a crime or crime control phenomena. However, an equally important aspect when beginning the process of undertaking ethnographic work, more often than not as a postgraduate stu-dent, will be to convince a number of stakeholders or gatekeepers that such work is realistic, achievable and valid. While that instantly conjures the idea that such access negotiations will involve participants and subjects of research, the reality is that the process of gatekeeping the field begins well before this, and now more commonly involves, for example, convincing academics of the merits of the pro-ject, securing institutional support and ethical clearance, and convincing an array of people, including directors of studies and potential advisors or supervisors, that a project has merit. For example, here is an example template that shows how a central research question might be expressed:

> This project aims to provide an in-depth ethnographic study of the world of _____. Attention is given to the experiences of _____ in order to investi-gate the norms, values and behaviour that typify the social world of _____ from the inside. This qualitative investigation will draw on data generated by conducting fieldwork together with a number of in-depth interviews and suggests that _____ (describe the main argument of the research in one, salient sentence).

Several higher education organisations also now use Creswell and Plano Clark's (2007) (or an adapted version of) script to help students to frame a central qualitative research question:

> _____ (How or what) is the _____('story' for narrative research; 'mean-ing of' for phenomenology; 'theory that explains the process of' for grounded theory; 'culture/practice' for ethnography) of _____ (Insert the central phe-nomenon or practice under study) for _____ (Describe the participant group) at _____ (Describe the research site and place). (Creswell and Plano Clark, 2007: 130)

So for example we might get a rather formulaic, 'What is the culture and practice of dealing with street crime late at night for the police in Oldham city centre?' or 'What is the meaning of hate crime victimisation for gay men in the night time economy in Manchester?' However, as you will probably realise, such formulaic guidance should perhaps serve at best as inspiration and a very rough guide for framing research interests and questions rather than a means of generating a final project.

I ought to say, however, that I am not a supporter of such formulaic methods of writing a project specification at the outset. Indeed, in many ways it presumes that what will be known can be described at the start rather than at the culmination of the project. However, on a pragmatic level, I recognise that 'An ethnography of ...' title that simply describes a setting or group may not be sufficient to secure institutional support for a project.

While such templates are a guide that might help to describe the central focus, to simply adapt and use them can be somewhat rigid, and so other good practices exist. Using Creswell and Plano Clark's model and suggesting that the researcher propose a project with some of the same aims, but no more than 50 words or three sentences can be another useful strategy. Soo too, the use of templates like those above does not detail the level of participation for the researcher, the specific ethnographic approach that will be employed, or further clarify the researcher's epistemological and ontological stance. For that reason, having a clear idea of the aims and objectives of the research is perhaps the best way to begin to craft and develop a proposal that will assist you in securing support for an ethnographic research project, while remaining focused as that process plays out over the time that it will take to gather data, analyse it extensively, develop theory and craft a written document.

REFINING THE RESEARCH TOPIC

It might be true to say that some of the most notable ethnographic studies conducted on youth and crime in Britain, such as James Patrick's (1973) *A Glasgow Gang Observed* and Howard Parker's (1974) *A View from the Boys*, would probably have encountered difficulties in navigating the ethical approval process via university ethics committee if they were to attempt to gain the necessary clearance today. Yet we think it is important that while the increasing control of research and particularly ethnographic and qualitative research is subject to critical scrutiny, and in some instances, criticism, so too it would be remiss to pretend that some of the changes are necessarily for the worse.

It is not necessarily the case that the previously cited youth crime research was inherently unethical, but what is clear on reading it is that the structuring context was very, very different. Attitudes to ethnographic research undertaken in previous decades was *laissez-faire*, and many projects started out of the researcher's own individual interests and were incepted and undertaken with little real planning. Indeed, re-reading many of the seminal studies, such as Carl Klockars' *The Professional Fence* (1974), the projects emerged in an extremely haphazard manner, and it might be fair to suggest that the welfare of participants was not always at the forefront of the researchers' mind. That is arguably no longer the case, and some of this change is for the better.

A successful project will not just come into being, and the reality is that in a majority of instances, before any ethnographer enters the field, a huge amount of backstage work will be undertaken. Some of that is likely to be administrative and bureaucratic, for example, identifying the field, securing the funding, seeking institutional support, gaining access and the like. While there are examples of spontaneous ethnographic work being undertaken instantaneously and with little planning (Treadwell et al., 2013) a great deal of ethnographic fieldwork is, in reality, the culmination of a very lengthy process of backstage work that might not always be apparent in the first instance.

So, what makes a good project proposal? Well clearly, part of it is quite simple. If you are seeking formal approval or buy in of others for your project, you want to be able to clearly and coherently explain what the project is, what it will do, how it will contribute to the academic field, and explain that to an audience (and often now, an audience that may be unfamiliar with some of the core ideas that you take for granted). However, from the other side and from my knowledge of the process of seeing projects institutionally reviewed, I would suggest that two central questions come foremost to mind when project proposals are subject to oversight and scrutiny, and briefly they are: what is/are the potential harms that come from this project and are they justified by the larger public good to be gained from the research results? And how can researchers manage and where possible mitigate any potential harms? Of course, to be able to convey these central points, it is useful that the reader is given a context and understanding of some of the core issues and gets a clear, comprehensible picture of what it is that you will actually be doing, and they will largely ask those questions in light of information that you make available to them. For example, as standard any good research project proposal should:

- Define what your study is and where it will happen. Explain your logic (i.e. why you will conduct your study this way and not that way) and include descriptions of how you will collect your data ethically and safely. Discuss the benefits of your proposed study and why it is important to you. Complete and include all the necessary permission and release forms, and give you an opportunity to show that you understand the norms and requirements of undertaking social research.

- Show planning and the parameters of the inquiry. Include research questions and try to answer them. If you're studying prison life, you may want to ask about hierarchy regarding age, physicality and offence history, how can you show you can do this? Will you need security vetting and is this achievable? You may need to show you understand what is realistic and show that you have thought about fieldwork that is practicable and realistic in any research project.
- Consider the theoretical orientation. Academics generally choose personal theories based on which theory makes the most sense to them, but qualitative inquiry and ethnography generally are rooted in symbolic interactionism, social constructionism and social phenomenology, but these are not the only orientations, and the beliefs that academics have, both epistemological and ontological, will frame the research and should be properly acknowledged.
- Define the data collection plan. This section specifically describes what your research is and where you will engage in the study. Describe how you will conduct your research: do you have or need special access to the site? The practicalities and their justification are important: how many interviews, how many days fieldwork, for how long? While this may be aspirational and therefore hypothetical, having an aspiration for your project and a robust justification is key in convincing others that the project has merit and value.

Of course, ultimately doing the fieldwork of criminological ethnography can be very different from what features in the plan, and of course in fieldwork, it is often necessary to be fluid and adaptable and to go with the flow. However, how criminologists and ethnographers go about planning and coordinating research projects it is often quite similar and uniform. Whether the research is funded or self-started, often the pre-research phase involves intense labour. There are decisions to be made, lists to write, equipment to gather, travel to book and people to liaise with. How much of this is done in detail, in advance, prior to entering the field and how much is done spontaneously or at the last minute can of course vary considerably. Some researchers prefer to plan the basics and deal with the rest later and others like to plan carefully down to the minutia of detail, while the majority probably fall somewhere in the middle of these two extremes. What is certain is that the world and the governance of research have certainly changed substantially from the days where the likes of Fredrick Thrasher studied gangs (1927) or William Chambliss entered the field with dirty clothes or a few days growth of stubble for this book *On the Take* (1978) and spontaneously undertook ethnography free of any constraint and left to their own devices.

Certainly, ethnography historically thrived most when it was not constrained by the formal process of management of research. There was a period in the US and Britain between the late 1960s and 1980s when many ethnographies were published in criminology, socio-legal studies and the sociology of deviance about different criminal subcultures and the criminal justice process, but it is probably remiss to think of this as some halcyon phase, but rather a slightly different social world with different norms and expectations.

Today, the main criminology journals mostly publish quantitative studies. Some academics have suggested that there is a substantial neglect of ethnography and, perhaps more importantly, a lack of interest among mainstream criminologists in the methodological issues that arise when employing this research method and in qualitative research more generally. That does not help the novice ethnographer with planning fieldwork though, and there is much utility to proper planning of fieldwork. Time in the field will create a mass of rich and nuanced empirical data variously drawn from first-hand observation, in-depth interviews, life stories and institutional reports gathered over years of fieldwork. What is more certain though is that better planning and organisation help with getting the most out of that data.

CONSIDERING THE RISKS AND ETHICS

Before any course of academic research can proceed, it is now normal for it to be subject to various forms of review. For established academics that can involve peer review before acceptance in established journals, whereas for PhD candidates the culmination of the process, on submission of the thesis, will likely be a 'viva voce' oral examination, which literally means by or with the living voice, i.e. by word of mouth as opposed to writing. So the viva examination is where you will give a verbal defence of a thesis, and candidates are expected to demonstrate their ability to participate in academic discussion with research colleagues, showing that the thesis is their own work, that they understand what they have written and can defend it verbally, that they have an awareness of where their original work sits in relation to the wider research field and that the thesis is of sufficiently high standard to merit the award of the degree for which it is submitted. Essentially in either process peer reviewers are expected to ensure and maintain academic standards, and that will include research conduct.

Of course, research ethics are important in the field, but ethnography (and particularly criminological ethnography) is an area fraught with ethical dilemmas. In many ways all research is or can be, but the issues of ethics become much more acute and pronounced when the research involves immersive human interaction. Rather than seeing ethics as something to be done or a barrier to be overcome, a better and more productive approach is to see ethics as a core aspect of the process and a central issue for reflection, but ethical conduct does not begin and end in the field. It should be a process that is central to research at every stage from start to conclusion.

It is arguably that while ethnography has not been responsible for many of the worst instances of research misconduct in the last century (particularly falsification, fabrication and plagiarism) or harming human subjects (no ethnographer has reached the level of the Tuskegee Syphilis Study which ran between 1932 and 1972 and saw African Americans deliberately untreated to see the effects of the illness even when effective treatments became available) there is some merit in considering risks that researchers face. US criminologist Lonnie Athens was set up for an attempt to rape him while he was undertaking prison research (Rhodes, 2000) and Bruce Jacobs (1998: 160–174) was robbed at gunpoint. Of course, some risks are unforeseeable, others might be more easily prevented. While I cover ethics in more detail in the next chapter, understanding the way in which ethical misconduct has been historically understood and debated, specific to ethnography, is no doubt useful.

CASE STUDY

LAUD HUMPHREYS: *THE TEAROOM TRADE*

In the USA in the mid-1960s homosexuality was illegal. Laud Humphreys, an academic within the Chicago School of Sociology that specialised in studies of deviance, undertook an ethnographic study (involving covert participant observation, interviews and a social health survey) in order to explore the impact that the criminalisation of homosexuality was having on men who desired other men. Humphreys' study revealed that such criminalisation placed men in precarious and vulnerable situations and so they often engaged in clandestine and risky behaviours in order to fulfil their (illegal) sexual desires. Humphreys' book *Tearoom Trade: Impersonal Sex in Public Places*, based on his 1968 PhD dissertation, proved controversial immediately on publication.

The first phase of Humphreys' study involved covert participant observation (pretending that you are the same as those you are studying) for around 18 months (summer 1965 to winter 1968). Humphreys posed as a 'watch queen' in tearooms (public restrooms) where he observed sexual encounters between men (tearoom trade). Humphreys observed that there were several different roles for participants who attended the tearooms. One such role was the 'watch queen' (voyeur) who gained sexual gratification from watching others involved in sexual interactions. This was the role that Humphreys assumed, and he acted to warn participants if there was a threat of their illegal activities being discovered, which also legitimised his ability to observe the interactions taking place between men without disrupting the men's illegal activities (Humphreys, 1975: 25–26).

The second phase of Humphreys' study involved finding out about the kinds of men who were engaging in tearooms. Undertaking observations over 18 months meant Humphreys learned about the elaborate practices involved in such encounters, but he knew nothing about the men's backgrounds. Alongside his observations, Humphreys also recorded 134 tearoom participants' car registration plates. He then approached a 'friendly policeman' claiming he was undertaking a social health survey about men and the car registration plate details would allow him to compile a sample of respondents for this survey. The officer purportedly did not ask too many questions about the 'type of market research' he was engaged in and, through this deception, Humphreys was able to obtain the names and addresses of the men he had observed indulging in sexual encounters in the tearooms (Humphreys, 1975: 38).

Men who were engaging in tearoom trade tended to be heterosexual and married with children. Humphreys (1975: 41) surmised that tearooms were used for casual sexual encounters with other married men in the same situation to minimise the adverse consequences of their homosexual activities being revealed to the wider community. Exposure meant men risked earning a criminal record, acquiring a discredited identity that could end careers, bringing shame on their immediate and extended family, leading to a loss of respect and standing within the community.

Other avenues for seeking sexual pleasure with men were available (e.g. established gay bars and male hustlers) but these were not feasible options for Humphreys' participants because they had gained a reputation for being dangerous in terms of their potential for exposing illegal homosexual activities. Established gay bars were known to be frequented by homosexuals who were comfortable with their stigmatised identities and were subject to surprise police raids. Stories flourished about some of the less scrupulous police practices where officers were known to exploit the situation and resort to financial extortion of homosexuals found in these bars. Male hustlers who provided sex for cash also gained a reputation for resorting to financial blackmail, exploiting the stigmatised status of their homosexual clients.

Humphreys' seminal study is perhaps most famous for the highly unethical and questionable practices he used in his pursuit of knowledge about the men who were participating in tearoom trade. Key problems were the use of deception and the risks his research posed to himself and his participants. Such measures are unlikely to be tolerated in current research projects. At the time, he justified the deception as necessary. If he had disclosed that he was a researcher then he would never have been able to observe the 'highly discreditable behaviour' of his participants (Humphreys, 1975: 25). His research also posed extraordinary risks to himself and his participants, because his fieldwork contained detailed and incriminating evidence about the places those men were engaging in criminal acts, which could have led to the prosecution of his participants, had this information been seized by law enforcement. This is despite Humphreys' valiant efforts to protect his data.

Employing these methods, however, meant he was able to debunk powerful myths about the 'dangers and threats' of homosexuality. At the time, there was a lot of secrecy and ignorance around homosexuals and homosexuality as an identity, which allowed misunderstandings to circulate about the dangers that homosexual men posed to others.

(Continued)

(Continued)

QUESTIONS

- Why might Humphreys' work have faced challenges over ethics? Was it solely about his research conduct?
- Was Humphreys' study justified in any way?
- Could Humphreys have disclosed his researcher status?

Ethical principles and concerns are at the heart of criminological research and can arise at the planning, implementation and reporting stages. It is vital that researchers are aware of the issues involved so that they can make informed decisions about the implications of their actions, and while some ethical issues might arise wholly unforeseen, it is likely that others can be managed effectively if the researcher gives a good deal of thought to them before entering the field.

Indeed, academic institutions, like so many other bodies, are increasingly risk-averse and may wish to avoid the publicity and scrutiny that goes with examples like that of Laud Humphreys (or more contemporary examples to which we will shortly turn). Some academics have predicted a chilling effect of institutional ethical governance of research, regarding it as a potential 'death knell' for ethnography or 'risky' research (Fleetwood and Potter, 2017).

There is a great deal of evidence that PhD students, supervisors and researchers have nonetheless managed to defend their research, allay concern and produce a great deal of insightful, well-crafted, inspiring, innovative and influential ethnographic work. But that work requires determination, innovation, guile and a hell of a lot of hard work. It also involves two other things that are often in short supply for many people existing in today's world: time and money. When planning any ethnographic project, it is worth remembering that it will take longer than you think. Ethnography is time-intensive. Typically, a one-hour interview requires a minimum of three to four hours (or more) of analysis. When you add up the time to schedule, conduct and transcribe the interviews, as well as the time to organise, discuss and write up results, timelines can quickly extend past a project's original plan. However, time to reflect and think about the data collected is a critical component of a successful ethnographic project. Given these requirements, from beginning to end, even a relatively small study can take a lot longer than might be anticipated, and that is before we begin to acknowledge that knowing when to leave the field can also be a problem for ethnographers. It is therefore important to be realistic in your expectations regarding the amount of data that you can effectively collect and analyse. Additionally, it can be more expensive than you think. Ethnographic research does not require a great deal of expensive equipment (probably the most important tools in ethnography remains a sharp mind and the ability to talk and listen), and most of the equipment you will need is relatively inexpensive (a pencil and paper is relatively low cost). However, if we move into the realms of digital recording equipment, costs go up. So too, getting to the site of study and the cost of being in it can be significant, and few fieldworkers get paid for the time they are spending in the field, but it does not stop there. Ethnography can be expensive, in a myriad of ways.

CHAPTER SUMMARY

This chapter has sought to begin to consider the process of criminological ethnography. Most successful social research tends to have in common that it has been well planned and considered. However, some of the best ethnographic studies emerged at least partly from somewhat haphazard processes and it is difficult to foresee the moral, ethical and practical complexities that might arise in field research, and ethnography is arguably difficult to plan. It has also considered how to frame research questions, and considered some of the issues relating to research ethics. It is hoped that it will be useful as an initial aid to thinking about some of the practicalities and dilemmas that are concerned when it comes to ethnographic research, but as you might expect, there are excellent sources of additional reading covering both specific sites and settings of field research on crime and crime-related topics, through to a number of good texts offering guidance on conduct in the field.

FURTHER READING

Preparatory reading when planning an ethnographic project is normally focused on the subject area as much as the method. Ocejo (2013) *Ethnography and the City* is an excellent collection of short texts, though its focus is predominantly classic and contemporary US studies. Silverman (2017) *Doing Qualitative Research* is now in its fifth edition and is an excellent primer, preparing readers for wider qualitative research, and Flick (2014) *An Introduction to Qualitative Research* is also an excellent broader primer for fieldwork.

5

DOING ETHICAL CRIMINOLOGICAL ETHNOGRAPHY

LEARNING OBJECTIVES

The title suggests this chapter concerns ethics in criminological ethnography. However, at the outset, I ought to suggest that criminology is again distinct in that questions of laws, codes, morals and ethics are inseparable from it, on a broader level. In many ways, criminologists will be well familiar with the notion that questions of the right way to treat each other as human beings in a research relationship are not distinct from questions about the values which should prevail in a society, or the moral and ethical questions that so often constitute the topic of criminology. However, the aim is that by the end of this chapter you should have a better understanding of:

- the risks of ethnographic research
- the ethical issues inherent to criminological ethnography
- the difference between risk and ethics
- the contemporary debate surrounding how ethical and defensible ethnography should be constituted and 'evidenced'.

RISK, HARM AND THE NEOLIBERAL UNIVERSITY

While ethnography has its supporters as well as its detractors, its utility in considering the more shadowy aspects of society has meant that for scholars, it has long been suited to examining behaviour that borders on the illegal. Concerns that revolve around ethics are something of a more recent consideration – a great deal of the participant observation that built the framework for criminological ethnography today was undertaken in an unplanned, haphazard manner – and it is undeniable that the contemporary context in academic institutions is something that necessitates discussion if we are truly to understand the nature of contemporary criminological ethnography.

Ethnography is necessarily by its core methods normally a 'lone' process. While some projects involve team and collaborative working, and 'lone' researchers in the field will normally have people who will support them in the process, it is undeniable that the changing nature of academic institutions has impacted significantly on ethnography as a method. Today frequently academics will talk of the neoliberal university, a term that is shorthand for the idea of the university as a market-driven system, which employs modes of governance based on a corporate and marketised model where the university is increasingly placed as a business. For example, it is now over a decade since Kevin Haggerty (2004), claimed that scholarly research was experiencing a form of 'ethics creep' characterised by a dual process whereby the regulatory system is expanding outward to incorporate a host of new activities and institutions, while at the same time intensifying the regulation of activities (social research) deemed to fall within its ambit. Hence some academics are extremely critical of how they see the university increasingly impinging on academic freedoms.

A core focus of concern from the likes of Haggerty is what is termed the Institutional Review Board (IRB) in the US or the Ethics Committee in the UK (the terminology is varied depending on the country).

The roots of the IRB go back to the Nuremberg trials, where recognition of the need for guidelines dealing with human subjects in research emerged following disclosure of medical experimentation abuses by Nazi doctors. But the three guiding principles for IRBs were formally codified in the United States in 1979 as part of the 'Belmont Report' by the National Commission for the Protection of Human Subjects of Biomedical and Behavioural Research and these were:

- **Beneficence** (to maximise benefits for science, humanity and research participants and to avoid or minimise risk or harm)
- **Respect** (to protect the autonomy and privacy rights of participants)
- **Justice** (to ensure the fair distribution among persons and groups of the costs and benefits of research).

In the US, IRBs exist on a statutory footing, and the IRB process in US academe derives from a legal requirement. It is overseen by the US Department of Health and Human Services, although there is variation in so far as each individual academic institution is allowed to tailor the IRB requirements and the federal guidelines to its own specific model.

Some ethnographers and social researchers are highly critical of the regulatory regime that surrounds social research projects generally, and often ethnographic research projects can be (and have been) refused permission to proceed by Ethics Committees (UK), Institutional Review Boards (USA) or Human Research Ethics Committees (Australia). What happens as a result of this is complex. Certainly, I am aware that some ethnographers have reported that they have had no choice but to take unpaid leave and go it alone in their own time, and there are certainly instances of notable ethnographies being undertaken away from universities by self-starting researchers working outside of the university. Yet that is perhaps not an option for those looking to utilise ethnographic approach for a degree level study, and hence while research may not necessarily be unethical, if it is perceived as 'risky', it may be unlikely to proceed.

Perhaps the most prominent among these ethical quandaries that criminological ethnographers face relate not to ethics *per se*, but to issues of risk and liability, as arguably the terms ethics and risk have been conflated so as to become synonymous with one another. In essence, for the reasons suggested above, criminological ethnography can be risky research, replete with problematic issues with regard to researcher and participant safety and confidentiality. In contemporary academe, it is (understandably) commonly regarded as unethical to deceive participants, to put anyone involved at risk of psychological or physical harm, and to disclose any confidential information, and covert research or deception is increasingly frowned upon (Calvey, 2017). Yet what can seem simple and clear cut is often not. For instance, many ethics committees and review boards would rightly be concerned that it should not be permissible to withhold information from the police concerning crimes. This is understandable, but while it might provide the educational researcher with a dilemma, it is perhaps more likely a tangential one. For those who wish to spend a great deal of time immersed in a field setting studying crime, it is likely that some degree of self disclosure will be an absolute necessity if the research is going to be maintained for any length of time.

It can therefore be argued that the 'most serious problem for the criminological ethnographer is that the duty to disclose criminal activity often precludes ethnography's most fundamental method – participant observation' (Hall, 2018: 398) although some have suggested that research can be undertaken even if it involves some degree of law-breaking. For example, using his own research with football hooligans, Pearson suggests that in some settings the committal of offences can be unavoidable and that it is further guidance – but not regulation – that is required to protect academics carrying out this type of participant observation and ethnographic research (Pearson, 2009).

Certainly, it was once possible for researchers to accompany criminals as they committed non-violent crimes and that might be harder now, but we also feel that it would be remiss to suggest that it is now impossible, rather, it might be that a better justification and a more purposeful defence of the necessity of such a course of research is needed.

In Parker's classic Liverpool-based ethnography *View from the Boys*, he was only able to gain insight as he had previously met the boys he was studying at a centre for Liverpool's deprived children. He says, however, 'If I had not been young, hairy, boozy, willing to keep long hours, accept permissive standards, the liaison would never have worked' (Parker, 1974). Institutional control and oversight as part of ethical regulation has undoubtedly made work such as this much more difficult. However, it is arguable that the imperative to disclose knowledge of crime (what was traditionally termed guilty knowledge) is not necessarily enshrined in law, and this is a subject that is far more complex than might first appear.

For criminological ethnographers it is useful to be aware of ethical codes from key organisations representing criminologists such as the British Society of Criminology, the British Sociological Association, the American Society of Criminology and other professional bodies and scholarly societies in order to use these as guidance and justification for research practices.

So too, previous successful academic ethnographies can be used to help defend and justify practices, but most researchers recognise that the skill in some ways is often negotiating the narrative that is contained in official documents, and then regarding negotiating the field as an entirely separate experience. Even if some academics might have sympathy with the 'refreshingly lucid advice' that Gary Armstrong cites in the acknowledgements of his brilliant ethnography of Sheffield United's Blades Business Crew, *Football Hooligans: Knowing the Score* (Armstrong suggests that Dick Hobbs advised him that he should 'fuck the ethics and get on with it', 1998: viii), it is probably not wise to write this on an institutional ethics form. However, on a positive note, the recent number of good ethnographies produced by academics at the early stages of their careers suggests that there may still be either a willingness or an ability for academics to secure institutional consent to them undertaking ethically problematic and risky research.

Researcher safety in ethnographic fieldwork is increasingly foregrounded through the discourses and systems of an occupational health and safety framework and a regulatory framework that will be encountered through institutional guidelines and protocols. Such guidance and policy have framed the transdisciplinary travels of ethnography. Working across disciplines, ethnographic researchers are urged – through university lone worker policies, risk assessment forms, or ethical review – to plan for ensuring their safety when undertaking fieldwork.

It is undeniable that some classic works of ethnography, when considered with the benefit of hindsight, looks extremely ethically dubious, whereas others rightly raise questions of validity, accuracy and honesty (Lubet, 2018). While it is not uncommon to see commentators lament the decline in ethnographic criminological research, but we would argue that such a concern is overstated. While criminological ethnography faces a more cautious passage towards inception than once it did, it is possible for research to gain approval and to have an impact. That is not to suggest that all claims about the difficult terrain that researchers wishing to utilise the method complain about are entirely a fiction or exaggerated. Criminological ethnography faces challenges due to the risk governance culture of UK universities ethics committees and their rigorous ethical approval applications and risk assessment forms, as well as governmental demands that research findings are generalisable beyond the sample size of the study and, subsequently, the quite real governmental preference to fund quantitative studies over qualitative studies. If criminological ethnography is to assert its utility, veracity and application, it needs do so with a proper ability to assert its relevance, contribution and impact. While it is common to encounter the lament that criminological ethnography faces undue and undeserved scrutiny and restrictions, a counter contention is that it stands in a place where it offers unprecedented promise, has been undergoing something of a resurgence, and has increasingly been refined and professionalised, particularly in the past two decades. This is at least in part because criminology has begun to revisit some of the ontological, epistemological and theoretical underpinnings. For example, Winlow and Hall (2012) have convincingly argued that ethics committees are simply a bureaucratic replacement for what should rightly be an organic culture of ethics reproduced by the researchers themselves; and furthermore they aver that such processes have little to do with real 'ethics' but rather operate as a form of 'risk management', confiscating ethics and politics from researchers in order to minimise the financial and reputational risks and maintain the image and reputational brand of the university, whereas ethics are an embodied practice that researchers carry with them.

Of course, debates about ethics necessarily also begin with a necessary consideration of what the term 'ethnography' actually means, or how we might draw boundaries around the term. If ethical review makes ethnography hard to do ethically, then what happens if a researcher simply goes out to see, in their own time, what is going on and strikes up conversations with people? Is this ethnography? It may lack a long-term immersive element, but what if it is in a community in which the researcher has lived the entirety of their life? This is not just a silly abstract argument, because some things in life happen quickly. If you had been in Berlin in the days leading up to 9 November 1989, or walking in New York central on the morning of 11 September 2000 you may not have had time to seek ethical approval from a university to describe the events you would have witnessed. If you went out with a notepad, talked to people, described what happened, what it felt like, would that be unethical? When does ethnography commence?

The problem here is that, like many other methodological terms used by social scientists, 'ethnography' does not form part of a clear and systematic taxonomy, and this problem means that in the absence of a clear categorisation, what constitutes ethnography can necessarily be somewhat fluid and flexible.

As a result, the term 'ethnography' is used in different ways on different occasions to mark off work of one kind from that of another.

Obviously, a key dimension relates to the kind of methods employed. Ethnography is often seen as a specific form of qualitative inquiry, to be compared or contrasted with others, for example, with life history work or discourse analysis; though even the boundaries with these neighbours are somewhat fuzzy. Yet ethnographic work sometimes includes the use of quantitative data and analysis, so that it may not be purely qualitative in character.

The origins of ethnography lie in anthropology, so a good place to begin is with the criticisms that some anthropologists have made of what they see as other social scientists' misuse of the term 'ethnography' (Hammersley, 2006). For most anthropologists, ethnography involved living in the communities of the people being studied, more or less round the clock, participating in their lives and activities as well as interviewing them, collecting artefacts to bring back and discovering meaning through a process of intense connected interaction. Moreover, this fieldwork took place over a long period of time, at least a year and often several years. In contrast, much of what is referred to as ethnography in the other social sciences today, including much criminological research, does not meet with such engaged anthropological definitions or traditions. Most criminological ethnographers do not actually reside with the people they study, for example, living with them in the same place or spending time with them most of the day, most of the week, month in and month out. Instead, many sociological ethnographers focus on what happens in a social institution when it is in operation, so that in this sense their participant observation is often much more part time and time limited. Arguably, this has been exacerbated by the fact that criminological ethnography is often the preserve of PhD students, postgraduates and Early Career Researchers (ECRs), who are increasingly encouraged to complete a period of study, write up and produce findings in a much more time restricted manner than was traditional in social sciences.

There is perhaps a tendency to overuse the term ethnography in contemporary criminology, and it can too easily be used as shorthand for qualitative research, but there is the difference and the issue: these two methods are not one and the same. Can a criminological researcher who does some interviews in a prison with offenders escorted by an officer use the term 'ethnography'? To what extent can someone who spends three months in a police station or court really have been said to have captured the emic and etic understanding of that institution rather than a temporary picture? How many 'ride-along' sessions (accompanying patrolling police on shift work) would be considered necessary for an individual to have undertaken an ethnography of policing?

Such questions cannot be easily resolved, although here I would aver that good research and true embodied ethics perhaps ought to be at the core of academics working transparently, and I have something of a concern that the term ethnography can be used to confound and complicate just as it can be used to illuminate. Ethical ethnography must be built on ethnographic experiences in the field (and especially in the field of crime, control and deviance) and it is, in my mind, important that academics working in the qualitative and ethnographic tradition are responsible in the claims they make about their empirical engagement. Because their work is focused on sensitive issues and the hidden life worlds often of extremely marginalised people at the base of the capitalist class pyramid (for example, working-class drug users, policing communities, the underground night-time economy, state detention and incarceration of young people, and youth support community contexts supporting disadvantaged areas) and because they seek to bring out the voices of those experiencing a turbulent and dangerous urban life, it is vital that they are honest and open about what their engagement actually involves and that they do not over claim experience, engagement and knowledge. That includes careful self-policing and occasional self-censure to avoid the misuse of the term ethnography when qualitative research is clearly more appropriate.

A further challenge to ethical ethnography arises out of the common tendency to consider the focus of ethnography as the stuff of 'culture', that is, the shared beliefs, values, attitudes and behaviours among members of a group. Using such definitions, culture provides a sense of identity and meaning, the structure that guides how individuals are expected to behave and the ways in which individuals and those around them interpret experiences. Ethnographic researchers recognise the importance of examining the processes associated with the transmission of culture and its ever-shifting understanding among group members. In other words, culture to ethnographers does not constitute a fixed set of behavioural traits, as it is understood to be flexible, inventive, process-focused and contested, relative to ongoing historic trends and in terms of wider social structures. Good and ethical ethnography must recognise just such contested notions, and the very real nuances and constrictions that occur in social settings, and must try and give the most honest and representative view. This is especially vital if ethnographic findings provide an evidence-based foundation for the development of interventions.

DOING ETHICAL ETHNOGRAPHY – RESEARCH ETHICS

At best, abstracted ethics formulated from the comfort of a proverbial 'ivory tower' are a sort of anxiety reducing practice for giving the self the belief that dealing with the unpredictability of real world ethnographic life in the field is within the scope of abstracted reasoning nourished by immersion in appropriate canonical texts. At worst, the relevant ethical concerns are resistant to *a priori* resolution; the procedural logic characterising institutional audit-culture practices where group-thinking is difficult to evade offers false hope to the researcher and misleads by conjuring the ethical landscape as being easily amenable to conclusive and widespread consensus: instead the truth is this deluded mind-set offers nothing more than a tentative rationalisation of ethical dilemmas that cannot be solved by reason and extensive scientific citation. The customary reliance upon written ethical approval based upon appraisal of written documents submitted is also obnoxious to me on moral grounds because it obscures attention from the virtues of the researcher upon whose own ethical integrity any research revolves.

In other words, the actual relevance, meaning and difficulty of ethical issues can only be fully appreciated in the face of concrete, context-bound situations which challenge the researcher's own auto-biographical wisdom, often leading her/him to assent to pragmatic as opposed to ethical resolutions. Indeed, conformity to institutional research ethics board prescriptions may undermine the quality and originality afforded by autonomous researchers. The historical context of the neoliberal university and contemporary higher education indicates immense commercialisation tendencies, profound audits defining the value of research and evermore dependence on gaining financial resources outside of the state from capitalist enterprises. Capitalism contains a model of the virtuous person and models of research impact or relevance. It is foolish to overlook the ideology it advocates given the intensification of capitalist logics into the nature and operation of the university system in the twenty-first century. As a criminologists, I am sympathetic to the vision of Jock Young expressed in *The Criminological Imagination*, where he makes readers aware of how criminal justice is biased towards serving vested interests of the existing social class hierarchy (Young, 2011). In brief, if as researchers our ethical stance involves moral empathy towards the marginalised groups we work with, does this potentially puts us at loggerheads with the universal ethical orientation inherent in institutional ethics approval processes? If it does, how should we act?

Ethical principles and concerns are at the heart of criminological research and can arise at the planning, implementation and reporting stages. It is vital that researchers are aware of the issues involved so that they can make informed decisions about the implications of certain choices. The general presumption in academic research is that researchers have a duty to promote dissemination and advancement of knowledge, to protect intellectual and professional freedom, and therefore to promote working environments and professional relationships conducive to these aims. Researchers should endeavour to ensure that the methodology employed and the research findings are open for discussion. Yet the practicalities and difficulties confronted by students and academics conducting research into sensitive topic areas such as crime often mean that issues are complex, different people hold different aims and intended outcomes. Research in the social sciences presents a different set of issues than those say in pure scientific research. The academic research enterprise is built on a foundation of trust. Researchers trust that the results reported by others are sound. Society trusts that the results of research reflect an honest attempt by scientists and other researchers to describe their findings accurately and without bias. But trust in academic research can only endure if the research community devotes itself to exemplifying and transmitting the values associated with ethical research conduct. Ethics should frame every stage of research, such as planning, conducting and evaluating a research project and analysis. Ethics should also perhaps be regarded an area of debate and discourse, albeit one framed by a fundamental desire, so far as possible to do good and avoid harm.

However, it is also true that it is under the guise of research ethics that a greater degree of formal control has been exercised, and this has become discomforting for some academics. Basic ethical principles are largely accepted as given by academics (it is only a small minority that act negatively), and include that researchers should avoid any risk of considerably harming people, the environment or property unnecessarily; should not use deception to ensure people participate; should obtain informed consent from all involved; should preserve privacy and confidentiality whenever possible; take special precautions when involving vulnerable populations; should not offer significant inducements; should not plagiarise the work of others, skew conclusions based on funding or researcher views, or, as is perhaps often suggested in ethnography, 'make it all up' (I would suggest it is actually quite hard to make up ethnography, because fieldwork, even when anonymised, is traceable, as the case of Goffman below tends to prove). However, it is also true that when it comes to the more complex realities, we each have different morals, shaped by our individual upbringing, culture and life experiences. Although most people acquire their sense of right and wrong during childhood, moral development occurs throughout life and human beings pass through different stages of growth as they mature. Ethical norms are so ubiquitous that one might be tempted to regard them as simply given and uncontested. Yet on the other hand, if morality were nothing more than common sense, then why are there so many ethical disputes and issues in our society?

Although almost all societies use laws to enforce widely accepted moral standards, and ethical and legal rules use similar concepts, ethics and laws are not the same. An action may be legal but unethical (such as capital punishment in some people's view) or illegal but ethical (such as some forms of whistleblowing). In the social sciences and legal subjects, we also use ethical concepts and principles to criticise, evaluate, propose or interpret laws. Indeed, in the last century, many social reformers have urged citizens to disobey laws (civil disobedience) they regarded as immoral or unjust, for example Ghandi or Martin Luther King. Moreover, while research ethics are often framed by a discussion that suggests that what is being sought is good conduct, some academics have questioned to what extent research ethics are really concerned with ethical conduct at all.

Throughout higher education this obsessive concern with academic research ethics does not necessarily reflect a recently discovered fascination for the intrinsic merits of research and ethical justification, but instead it reflects an instrumentalist anxiety over potential and costly law suits leading to reputational damage, should research participants or others judge their rights to have been infringed. In this framing, regulatory research ethics are not really about ethics, but a risk management strategy that seeks to mitigate reputational and financial risks. To some extent I would endorse such a view. The question then for me as a realist and pragmatist becomes, how might risky unethical criminological ethnography be avoided? Perhaps the best way might be to consider some recent cases where ethnography and its methods have been called into question.

Social sciences (and criminology for that matter) throw up some examples where researchers' conduct has been called into question, although it should be noted that many of the worst cases of research misconduct in academe originate outside of the social sciences. However, because of the topic, the method and the proximity to the research subject, ethnographic criminologists have, on occasion, become embroiled in research ethics scandals.

CASE STUDY

ALICE GOFFMAN: *ON THE RUN*

When Goffman's book *On the Run: Fugitive Life in an American City* was published in 2014, it was instantly met with a very high level of mainstream US media attention. It had taken Goffman several years to finish and produce the book, following a format that other successful academics had, somewhat cast in the mould of Sudhir Venkatesh. In many ways Goffman already enjoyed a privileged position in sociology in so far as she is the daughter of Erving Goffman and socio-linguist Gillian Sankoff, and on publication of her book, she received high praise from eminent US criminological and sociological luminaries such as Howard Becker, Elijah Anderson and Cornel West.

On the Run is certainly something of an unconventional text and does not follows the format of the traditional academic monograph. That perhaps reflects the way that the text began as a research project Goffman started as a second-year student

(Continued)

(Continued)

at the University of Pennsylvania, when she immersed herself in a disadvantaged neighbourhood of Philadelphia with African-American young men who were subject to a high level of surveillance and police activity. She continued working on this project as a graduate student at Princeton, eventually turning it into her doctoral thesis and later, the text. However, rather than a traditional monograph, the book is written very accessibly, in a manner more reminiscent of true crime than most PhD monographs, a style that arguably owes much to the crossover success of some academic celebrities who have adopted a more market geared style of publishing looking to reach a wider audience.

The book uses a great deal of thick description and storytelling, eschewing academic references and normal structuring (a methodology appeared as an appendix at the end). Placed at the fore and centre is the ensemble cast of 'Chuck' and his friends on 6th Street, a group of Philadelphia-based criminal black men involved in violence and small scale drug dealing. Goffman makes a wider argument about the experience of how young, black men are treated and mistreated by police within the framework of the American criminal justice system, and how this reshapes the lives of families in America's impoverished and disadvantaged, black neighbourhood. In the book's introduction, Goffman highlights her central argument: that the intensified policing and imprisonment in poor black neighbourhoods is transforming community life in ways that are deep and enduring, not only for the young men who are the targets but for the entire communities.

Arguably much of the success Goffman enjoyed came because her work so perfectly chimed with a rising concern about punitive policies impacting upon black men in the US (while Goffman is far from the only ethnographer to register such concern, she was different by virtue of being white, female, privileged and from well-known sociological parentage). However, Goffman's text also undeniably chimed with the campaigning mood of US prison reformers and the Obama administration had turned attention to America's staggering prison incarceration rates, especially for black men, and that topic was arguably one where at the time there was a shared bipartisan political concern. In the year after publication, Goffman undertook numerous public speaking appearances, including a TED talk, and was becoming something of a sociological celebrity. And then the allegations of misconduct started.

Almost by the time that Goffman's TED talk received its millionth view, a rancorous backlash to the book had begun, some of it involving heavy criticism in the form of an unsigned, 60-page, single-spaced document of anonymous authorship, which was emailed from a throwaway address to hundreds of sociologists, detailing a series of claims casting doubt on the veracity of events as Goffman described them. As the document put it:

> Typically authors might have a few problems in their work due to errors of some sort and ethnographers might change a few facts to protect their subjects' identity. But the appearance of literally dozens of factual problems,

falsification of quotations, textual inconsistencies, improbabilities, and impossibilities as well as self-aggrandizing exaggerations in Ms. Goffman's work are too plentiful to be dismissed. Moreover, there is no sensible explanation (for example, protecting personally identifiable information) for certain implausible accounts she tells. Below, across more than fifty pages filled with careful substantiation, you will read about nearly four dozen problems in a (partially) arbitrary order. If even just a portion of the below problems are what they seem to be, then this will suggest serious research misconduct, possibly including data fabrication, data falsification, data destruction, sloppiness, and failure to protect her subjects' anonymity. (Pastebin, 2015)

Criticisms concerning factual inaccuracy mounted. Some were highly concerned about her alleged and self-declared felonious conduct (in the book's methodology appendix she admits to what could be construed as engaging in a conspiracy to murder) which became the foremost criticism from Legal Professor Steven Lubet (although it was far from the only one) who in reviewing *On the Run* for *The New Rambler*, claimed that Goffman had admitted to committing conspiracy to commit murder and 'involved her[self] as an accomplice in the evident commission of a major felony' (Lubet, 2015). He also questioned Goffman's claim, which he called 'outlandish', that she had personally witnessed police officers making arrests after running the names of visitors to hospitals. News reporter Jesse Singal located some of the anonymised subjects of the book and interviewed them. He concluded that Goffman's version was 'mostly true' but noted that Lubet's scepticism appeared well-founded and concluded that the most likely explanation for these discrepancies is that Goffman simply didn't heed her own advice about credulously echoing sources stories. While some academics and ethnographers have come out as strong defenders of Goffman, for others her work remains tainted and suspect. However, usefully, the episode did frame a useful discussion of what is ethical in criminological ethnography.

RISKS IN FIELD RESEARCH

There are of course risks in general that we encounter in everyday life. Crossing the road or driving a car are not risk-free activities, but there may be specific risks encountered in taking crime as a research topic. While those risks will are unlikely to be as extreme as the examples given, it is prudent to think carefully about what will be encountered in the field and what some of the risks may be in a sober manner.

Criminological researchers go into drug dens and crack houses (Briggs, 2011) are present during riots (Treadwell et al., 2013), brawls (Winlow, 2001) and in situations with volatile and dangerous men with established reputations for violence and volatility (Ellis, 2016; Treadwell, 2018). They spend time in prisons and on the streets in disadvantaged and high crime areas. Some forms of criminological perspective, such as cultural criminology, even advocate types of research that involve what is often called edgework, a type of research-based 'voluntary risk-taking' (Lyng, 1990). Others use the term 'edge ethnography' to describe researchers using covert or full participation methods to conduct research (Tewksbury, 2009).

Criminological ethnographers may not fully comprehend risk until they are in the process of research. However, there is a dearth of academic research that can serve as useful contextual background reading that helps to consider what the risks may be. Accounts of policing tell of how police ethnographers have dealt with malpractice. Of course, the pre-eminent risk that often comes front and foremost is the risk to the researcher, and this will necessarily be contingent on the topic, place and other cultural and situational factors.

Hopper and Moore (1990) had guns pulled on them one morning when they entered a bikers' camp while conducting research on motorcycle gangs. The bikers, sleepy and hung over from the previous night's party, thought Hopper and Moore were competing gang members. Bruce Jacobs was robbed at gunpoint by one of his informants during his research because the informant later disapproved of the researchers conduct and perceived disrespect for him (Jacobs, 1998: 160–174). Venkatesh (2009) also describes a gang shootout in which he was forced to take cover while watching others get shot, and Goffman claimed to be present at the shooting of one of her key informant's friends (Goffman, 2014). While of course firearms are more common in the States, they are not absent from the UK and can be encountered in criminal laden settings. Westmarland (2001) wore a bulletproof vest or anti-stab vest while observing police in England. On one occasion she was forced to hide behind a tree to avoid being shot by an offender. Calvey (2017) reports being in a threatening situation involving armed men while he conducted ethnographic research on door supervisors, often called bouncers, in Manchester, England. These anecdotal examples illustrate the very real danger of physical risk that can exist for researchers, but it is important that those risks are not overplayed or unduly exaggerated. In years of fieldwork on violent football gangs, Armstrong (1998) got a punch in the mouth and a thick lip on West Street in Sheffield. During his fieldwork on homeless families, Liebling (1999) describes how she had a pen plucked from her hand. The prisoner pointed out that if he had wanted to, he could kill her with it, indeed almost every fieldworker leaves the field with such stories to tell, and some have done so in an accessible manner that consider research ethics (Winlow et al., 2001).

Researchers may be at some risk when they enter the field, they can (and on occasion do) witness some extreme, unsettling and nasty things, and it is wise to be prepared for that potential. Emotional risks may be less apparent initially, and yet each person will have a different subjective view of what constitutes risk, threat or discomfort. For some people entering an unfamiliar environment can lead to feelings of stress and apprehension. Yet while risks may be common, people will experience different reactions and feelings to what they encounter in the field. Managing such risks then inevitably becomes something of an individual project. Wakeman talks of how biography and background can be useful in managing potentially risky situations and deciding when fear is ill or well founded (Winlow et al, 2001; Wakeman, 2014). Good supervision and support networks can also be vital, and this links back to the project planning stages and the positive protections that some degree of ethical oversight can bring.

However, risk can be overplayed, and as Treadwell (2018) has noted, while there are numerous texts stressing the risks of ethnographic research that can overplay its negative standing and actually make attaining permissions and support harder rather than easier, and that contrary to the often passed on adage that ethnographers ought to 'leave the field as they find it', and hence, not make it more difficult for others following to employ the methods in the future. Furthermore, Treadwell has noted that the problem of overplaying the 'risks' of ethnography is that it overlooks the other emotions it can entail, and he advises aspirant ethnographers to:

> Prepare to be bored, frustrated, angry, annoyed, disappointed, frustrated, upset, anxious and perhaps occasionally depressed and frustrated, the ethnographic adventure is often presented as very exotic and exciting, but a lot of it is repetitive, monotonous and well, just a bit dull. (Treadwell, 2018: 300)

Perhaps it is right that we should equally prepare people for that possibility, because rare events such as those detailed are just that. So before entering the field, ethnographers should consider what the potential risks of any specific project are, because they are likely to be different and encompass a range of:

- physical/health risks
- emotional risks
- personal and professional risks.

If these can be listed and identified, then many can potentially be mitigated. There are various strategies for this, but I have employed a range previously:

- have a solicitor (perhaps the university solicitor) briefed about the nature of any projects where arrest is likely and have a number with you to contact them
- manage items taken into the field (leaving smartphones and not taking excesses of cash)
- leave detailed plans and where the activity involves lone or isolated working a safe method of work must be in place, e.g. a buddy system, doubling up for first visits, calling in at pre-set time, having people drop you off and pick you up from field sites.

It is a positive that many universities are starting to adopt 'Safety Codes of Practice' for fieldwork, but these may not be a panacea and can be quite generic, and the better approach can be to have knowledgeable and experienced ethnographers familiar with the methods and dangers involved in mapping and assessing risks. Part of planning a good project may be to pre-empt criticisms, and we believe that good planning is vital for good ethnography.

ETHICAL 'EVIDENCED' ETHNOGRAPHY

Of course, many situations must be resolved in the field, and there may be no shield for some criticism, but akin to Lubet whose book *Interrogating Ethnography* (2018) provides much food for thought for criminological ethnographers I am convinced that ethnography is and should be defensible and robust.

Table 5.1

Issue	Lubet's suggestions	Problems and counter arguments
Accuracy	• Ethnography should rely less on unsourced generalisations • It should be clear in the text when generalisations about what is encountered in the field are being made, and it is the author's responsibility to clarify when this is the case • Descriptions of typical behaviour should be accompanied by explanations of frequency that are less general (perhaps numerical factors) • Composites should be avoided, if they are used, they should be clearly identified • Field sites should (where possible) be accurately described • Data should not be changed unless necessary • If assurances are given that minor details have been changed, these should be clarified • Pseudonyms should only be used where there is no alternative	• Hearsay and rumour are frequent in the field • Numerical descriptions may not work with the requirement to protect participants • Explanations of frequency may not be possible, and are just as prone to exaggeration and false claim • Composites are sometimes necessary • It can be vital to protect locations, and criminological work is different from other forms of ethnography in that there is sometimes a need for criminologists, who lack formal legal protections, to protect sources • What constitutes necessity remains subjective • Minor details are not changed for subterfuge • Without assurances of anonymity, criminological work may not be possible

Issue	Lubet's suggestions	Problems and counter arguments
Candour	• Clear distinctions should be made between what is observed and what is derived from other sources • Second-hand accounts should not be reported as statements of fact • Rumours and folklaw should be clearly identified • Scepticism about unreliable information should be clearly made • The argument of the text should be openly acknowledged • Contrary facts and inconvenient witnesses (those who disagree or confound arguments) should be prominently identified	• Most ethnographers make this distinction, but observation may be fallible • If the social realm can be differently viewed and interpreted, to what extent is it the authors responsibility to convey this? • Most ethnographers acknowledge rumours and information cannot be verified, and are sometimes an inherent feature of the field, for example, that active criminals are prone to deception need not be stated, it is implicit in all ethnography • What is reliable and unreliable is deeply subjective • Most ethnographic texts do, through a process of reflexivity, acknowledge inherent biases, indeed it is far more apparent in qualitative than quantitative data • Again, as the aim of ethnography is often to present the nuances and complicity in human life it is arguably already a domain expectation
Documentation	• Sources of information should be clearly identified, including the dates and nature of communications with anonymous research subjects • Fieldnotes should be provided to a third party and checked against text for accuracy • Dates and locations should be stated accurately, to facilitate verification • Ethnographers should routinely fact check one another's work • Re-visitation of field sites and attempts at replicability when feasible should be made	• Journalists are afforded legal protections that ethnographers are not, off the record may be a necessity especially in criminal and criminal justice settings • How can a third party who was not in the field ensure accuracy? • Can verification and protection of participants, the highest aim of social research, be compatible in criminal settings? • In criminology, fact checking already occurs largely as an informal process and via academic peer review. How can subjective experiences be fact checked? • Informally much ethnography has done this, increasingly the lone ethnographer is not the standard and there is oversight and peer monitoring of criminological ethnography broadly

Lubet has recently written *Interrogating Ethnography* (Lubet, 2018) which focuses on US urban ethnography (a field that is frequently connected to criminology) and asserts that as an academic specialism, it relies heavily on anonymous sources, often as reported by a single investigator whose underlying data remain unseen. In critically analysing a number of seminal US ethnographies, historical and contemporary, Lubet suggests that from his legal perspective, too many ethnographic assertions were dubious, exaggerated, tendentious or just plain wrong. Employing the tools and techniques of a trial lawyer (his background is as a legal scholar) Lubet looks to explore the stories behind ethnographic narratives. He concludes by suggesting that action is necessary to bring ethnography into line with other evidence-based disciplines and suggests three specific requirements. Hence in *Interrogating Ethnography*, Lubet ultimately argues that ethnographic social science would benefit from greater attention to the quality of evidence, and ultimately provides recommendations for bringing the field more closely in line with other fact-based disciplines such as law and journalism.

Lubet has provided a powerful critique of ethnography, and much of his criticism has a great deal to commend it and much should be taken in the spirit in which it is made, with the aim of improving the quality of social science. Yet I would also content that the challenges he advances are also made more complex when transported into crime and criminal justice settings. In many ways, Lubet's suggestions and recommendations are a form of legal and academic interventionism that takes his own view of knowledge and reasoning as a gold standard, with very little reflection on contexts and construction. Lubet, perhaps unlike many criminologists, seems to begin by arguing that the criminal trial process establishes 'truth' in a quite fundamental sense (whereas I might aver that socio-legal scholars like McBartlett have used ethnography to show that this is not in fact the real purpose). Lubet is arguing that in creating an assemblage of admissible evidence and accepted 'fact' and testing it in combative cross-examination, jurors and/or judges can determine 'what really happened', but this is also quite at odds with the traditional socio-constructionist view of qualitative research.

In essence, we might ask is Lubet reasonable in seeking to set qualitative researchers the aim of being more precise about how they actually collected their data and what it consists of? Perhaps, to revisit an established argument, the term 'ethnography' is now too loose and inconsistent to be regarded as a universal (but then all social research, indeed all research, is). Certainly, a counter point to his contention is that much ethnography is already held to a far higher standard, both prior to its undertaking and on its publication, than other material generated by equally questionable quantitative and qualitative methods, and its veracity in capturing the world and making sense of it is well established. Moreover, the networked nature of the world and the scholarly and peer community make 'faking it' much more likely to be detected and outed now than at any other historical juncture.

Qualitative researchers, and particularly criminological researchers, already know a great deal about the processes through which alternative and supplementary official reports and statistics or media reports are created. Does this necessarily lead to some scepticism about Lubet's claim that officially manufactured data is inherently more valid than observation or interviewing? Perhaps it ought to, as most criminology students learn reasonably early to approach statistics with a well needed degree of scepticism.

Lubet's fact-checking is, in effect, a version of triangulation, but the limitations and pitfalls of such a mode of accounting and verification will already seem very apparent to some ethnographic and qualitative criminological researchers. While some may already be working to the standards Lubet expects there are also numerous problems that can come of criminological researchers facing pressure from criminal justice agencies when it comes to both sharing and access information (see Ferrell and Hamm, 1998). Is it possible to have an asymmetric proof procedure? As an example, say you undertake a prison ethnography and prisoners complain tirelessly about use of restraint by staff when nobody is present to witness it. Lubet's response might be to say that use of force must be legally recorded, so write to the prison authorities and establish the number of recorded uses of force by staff. Say you then write to the prison authorities who assure you that no such behaviour occurs because there are no records of it. It may be accurate, that may be deceptive, it may well simply be that there is under recording as senior managers are buffered from reality as staff are not recording. But in denying the prisoner testimony because it fails to meet Lubet's standards, would you be invalidating the ethnographic method by reference to the second-best approach? Is this not a greater risk?

I am not here arguing that we should dismiss Lubet's criticism out of hand, for most ethnographers themselves see production of good quality, accurate data as a core value that they carry with them. However, whatever the stance on ethical conduct, perhaps the most pertinent point to take from this discussion is that ethnography is subject to a degree of oversight and scrutiny not common to many other styles of qualitative research, and invariably attracts a high degree of critical appraisal. When that comes, and when it is highly critical, sometimes it has some merit, sometimes it is baseless. Occasionally that criticism it is just cruel and ill informed. That is why it can annoy and frustrate. Reflecting on whether criticism is merited and can usefully be incorporated and used to improve one's work is perhaps the most important part of planning an ethnographic project, as planning is rarely undertaken on one's own or without the opportunity for peers and mentors to give feedback. Criticism is inevitable, how and whether you take it on board is not. Just like criticism, in ethnography, moral and ethical problems will come, they can be anticipated, but like the criticisms those challenges must be faced, and that is why my attitude is perhaps best surmised as 'go in with anticipation and a plan with one's eyes and ears open'. In both instances, planning can help.

Usually when people think of carrying out ethnographic research, they think of studying a specific human community or cultural group. Ethnographic studies have, however, been carried out among families or domestic units, kinship and other social networks, groups characterised by a common trait (e.g. drug use, mental illness), institutional and organisational structures (prisons, police stations) and local communities and neighbourhoods with high crime rates. Ethnographic methods have also been used in the study of dyads (two people) and of single individuals with extensive life histories, sometimes woven together to form several life accounts. Ethnographic methods have also been used to study social events (e.g. an international football tournament), as well as the activities included in such events. The wide range of social or cultural settings, the short- to long-term continuum, and the ability to capture an account of what is going on means that ethnographic methods can be used (and arguably should be the method of choice) in any setting in which humans are interacting. That does not make ethnography wholly beholden to the symbolic interactionist tradition (a point to which I return). Yet I hope this overview will help you to think about the possible benefits and drawbacks of using a method, and help you think about which type of project will help you to really get what you want out of the field-work and make your precious time more valuable. Obviously, these are not comprehensive, and you need to think about what method will be best for you and your project but take this as a starting point for reflection on what you want to get out of an ethnographic project, and realities of doing that.

Many texts on ethnography will talk about the multifaceted nature of reality (though here again there is a deeper philosophical discussion) but whatever one's ontological and epistemological orientation, research design requires a degree of planning and foresight, and while I want people to get out into the field and start researching, it is better that they do it in an informed and considered way, and one that not only protects themselves, but recognises that they are also responsible for protecting a method that many of us hold very dear. So put simply in the words of an anonymous colleague and respected ethnographer, 'Don't be the one to mess it up for the rest of us'.

CASE STUDY

BRADLEY GARRETT: *PLACE-HACKING* AND PROSECUTION

Garrett is the author of *Explore Everything: Place-Hacking the City* (2013), based on his PhD thesis, which is an extensive and engaging ethnographic account of the activities of the London Consolidation Crew (LCC), a group of 'urban explorers' or, as Garrett terms them, 'place hackers', of which he was a member. The book describes the exploits of the LCC, as they trespassed into hundreds of locations over five years to reveal and reclaim the hidden city. Garrett claims the goal of this work was to re-map London by opening out vertical urban imaginations and exposing the ways in which surveillance and control are embedded in modern spatial and control practices. In 2011, four of his project participants were arrested inside the London Tube at Easter, and later Garrett himself was also arrested at Heathrow Airport by British Transport Police. All were ultimately charged with criminal damage and his case referred to the Crown Court. Garrett maintained that his ethnography was legitimate and the only appropriate way to understand a culture is to become fully immersed in it. The charges against Garrett eventually concluded with a three-year conditional discharge and a £2,000 fine being issued by the court, yet there was, at one stage, the very real risk that he and his participants faced custodial sentences if convicted, and some of the evidence against Garrett's co-accused came from his research notes.

Now consider:

- If you were asked to advise the police on research ethics with a view to prosecuting Garrett, would you do it?
- What about advising his defence, would you do it? Why? Why not?
- Is there ever a justification for a researcher to break the law?
- Did the fact that criminal charges were brought against subjects of Garrett's research, based on material he created, make that research unethical? Why? Why not?

CHAPTER SUMMARY

This chapter has sought to introduce the concepts of risk and ethics and begin to consider the way criminological researchers look at issues of ethics and legitimacy in research conduct. It has attempted to assist readers to consider classic and contemporary discussions on research conduct and research ethics.

FURTHER READING

There are an array of good books on research ethics. Cowburn, Gelsthorpe and Wahidin (eds) (2016) *Research Ethics in Criminology: Dilemmas, Issues and Solutions* is a great edited collection. Some fantastic sources deal with specific issues such as the signing of consent forms, for example Coomber (2002) 'Signing away your life? Why research ethics committees (REC) shouldn't always require written confirmation that participants in research have been informed of the aims of the study and their rights — the case of criminal populations', and Yates (2004) 'Criminological ethnography: risks, dilemmas and their negotiation' is excellent on field research with young men. Classic ethnographic studies should of course supplement this reading, and Winlow (2001) *Badfellas*, is an excellent example.

6

ENTERING THE FIELD

LEARNING OBJECTIVES

Having spent some time discussing the background of ethnography, both in terms of theoretical perspectives and the practicalities associated with the method, this chapter now moves into the phase of considering the very 'praxis' of being a field-worker. It therefore seeks to set out and discuss a range of issues, and by the end of this chapter you should have a better understanding of:

- how to negotiate access to the field
- how to recognise the key figures in a group or organisation
- how to manage image and identity in the field.

Additionally, it will touch on issues such as the management and negotiation of research in the field. However, I have kept separate issues of writing and recording in the field and more practical issues such as keeping notes, field documentary and recording data for the next chapter. Also, having established and debated what constitutes ethical criminology in the previous chapter, I suggest here that it is in the field that some of the most complex and fraught ethical situations are encountered and negotiated, and I consider issues of safe and ethical conduct in praxis and describe accessibly some of the realities and complexities that might be encountered, negotiated and resolved.

CRIMINOLOGICAL ETHNOGRAPHY: THE ANTHROPOLOGICAL APPROACH?

While ethnography has enjoyed a resurgent popularity in social sciences more broadly, and in criminology specifically, rather curiously, the issue of accessing the field often seems under-represented. This is odd, considering that gaining access to the setting is essential for a study to begin. Of course, in criminology, for a long time, the ethnographer's presence has sometimes been covert or mingled with the role of practitioner or full participant, and in classic studies it is not uncommon for ethnographers to have been fully involved in the scene that they study or to have gone back to a setting where there is great familiarity.

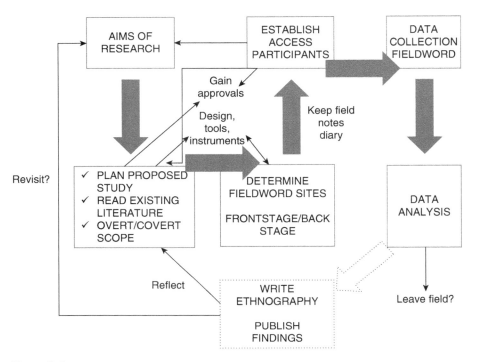

Figure 6.1

The anthropological creed and the classic view of ethnography (i.e. the traditional/classical period for ethnography) casts it as research that is undertaken in foreign lands by a lone ethnographer, primarily men, and those whose objective was to study exotic cultures, languages, customs, beliefs and behaviours of 'natives'. It was through the systematic collection of observations, interviews and cultural artefacts that the lone ethnographer would hope to come to understand and explain these bounded cultural systems and ascribed meanings therein while remaining detached, both physically and emotionally, from both the setting and the individuals studied. The admonishment of not 'going native', which was typical for ethnographers, was instituted to preserve anthropology's tacit commitment to objectivism and its parochial stance concerning one's role in the field. However, today's researchers reject that view of the degree of formalism promoted by anthropological ethnography and have increasingly sought to implement a form of fieldwork, in street and urban ethnography, that encapsulated the socio-cultural milieu of neighbourhoods and its residents. A careful reading of some of these earlier works reveals that the vestiges of interpretive ethnography remain in place, and still do today, and yet fieldwork today is very different from that of the early phase of anthropology, and criminology now takes its guide much more readily from social science and social science guidelines than it does from anthropological groups, especially in the UK and Europe.

American sociology (much of which was long concerned with crime and deviance) has always had an interest in the marginalised, a 'sociology of the underdog' (Becker, 1967) and of the so-called 'underworld'. Talk of urban ethnography originated in the United States based on a natural curiosity about certain aspects of urban social life and its participants. Urban ethnography's interest in the early part of the twentieth century focused on marginalised groups, or 'outsiders', such as the drug user/addict, the prostitute, the juvenile delinquent and their gang, the pick-pocket and their 'fence', the dance-hall girl, and so on, with an expressed objective of developing a theoretical-cultural framework based on an inductive approach to social research while maintaining the often delicate balance between an emic (insider) and etic (outsider) perspective, a balance that over the years has been more a matter of the degree to which it reflects academic politics and culture rather than empirical reality. Moreover, as I have already argued, this research thrived against a backdrop of not only social change, but academic attitudes, general permissiveness and flexibility and freedom that were also underscored simply by 'academic curiosity', time and freedom, which made it perfectly possible to simply go out into the field with little formal backing and commence a project of study freely and wholly unhindered.

For criminological ethnographers, fieldwork is about working inside often marginalised, neglected, disadvantaged and forgotten communities, giving prominence (a voice) to people who are often devalued and characterised by outsiders as nothing more than street people. The street became the early ethnographer's sociological environment and laboratory, it was a place that holds specific yet dynamic cultural systems, meaning and practices. The traditional criminological ethnographer's working attitude in the field was often described as that of an intimate or 'professional stranger' (a term used by Michael H. Agar (2008) in his classic reflection on the ethnographic craft that drew extensively from his own research experience using ethnography, particularly among drug users). The ethnographer may come to be regarded as a 'friend', a personal confidant to the many people he or she befriended in the field (the street), yet is always an outsider because of the research objectives and specific aims that guide him or her.

Whereas many people view social life conveniently through partitions such as the legitimate and illegitimate ('under') world, the legal and illegal ('underground') economy, the criminal offender and the law-abiding citizen, from early on, criminological ethnographers were arguably more attuned to the nuances and complexities. Early symbolic interactionist street ethnographers recognised and entered a social world that defies linearity in terms of how such worlds are created, practised and sustained. The encountered social life is more a constellation of behavioural norms and expectations, a social system of differing styles, methods and modes of communication, all of which reveal a high degree of convergence between seemingly opposing social worlds and its members. Throughout diverse, 'hidden' social worlds, for example, sex workers, drug dealers and users, armed robbers, homeless families, street children, migrant workers, hotel chambermaids, doormen, political dissidents, bouncers, taxicab drivers and female gang members, to name a few, could be accessed, and their culture documented and brought to life. Hence from early on, criminological ethnographers were well attuned to the contradictions and complexities in lifeworld's which could be highlighted. What was needed was no more than a little desire and a will to go out and discover in situ, as they unfolded, these groups' lives, values and meanings in and throughout urban social settings.

In addition to an intellectual commitment to building a theoretically and culturally driven understanding of street cultures and a profound, sometimes personal, commitment to providing a voice to the individuals often socially, politically and economically disenfranchised therein, early criminological ethnographers purposively embraced the complexity inherent in studying people in their natural social settings.

Fieldwork has typically been conducted in an open or public space; the empirical milieu of a criminological ethnography was traditionally any setting, physical or social, where people would socialise or hang around. Indeed, this trend continues, for example in the work of Philippe Bourgois (2003) on the crack cocaine dealers operating out of the game room or Gary Armstrong (1998) on Blades football hooligans in Sheffield and Simon Winlow (2001) on bouncers, which all play out in 'public spaces'. However, in the study of deviancy and criminal behaviour, fieldwork has always focused on the kinds of communities, environments and people connected with illegal and deviant activities and their concomitant lifestyles. Although the history of deviant/criminological fieldwork has been diverse in terms of settings and research participants/informants (e.g. street corners, brothels, housing projects, methadone clinics, criminal justice training academies, adult video stores, halfway houses, drug smugglers, psychiatric hospitals and jails/prisons), an enduring methodological link in the field has been the systematic use of observation and interviewing. It also more frequently straddles and crosses the public and private space divide.

It has long been acknowledged that, when studying non-mainstream groups in society such as the marginalised and the stigmatised, researchers must tailor their data collection methods to both the sensitivity of the research topic and the vulnerability of research subjects. Because observational research does not necessarily intervene in the activities of the people being studied, ethnography can be suitable to investigating sensitive issues because it can provide rich, detailed descriptions about the unknown or the little known, the less overtly acknowledged, the secret and the unspoken.

As the only field method that allows researchers to observe what people do in real life contexts, not what they say that they do, ethnographic participant observation can supply detailed, authentic information unattainable by any other research method. As participant observation and ethnographic observation have the greatest potential to uncover contextualised, honest data, which is otherwise inaccessible, it ontologically and epistemologically underpins human quests for understanding multiple realities of life in context. Yet that observation is contextually specific, as in, the ethnographer has to be there to see it. So while ethnography can be extremely useful both in allowing a framing of a description of what happens (the events) and in revealing what lies beneath (the motives, drivers and even subjectivities), ethnographic research can empower the very people being studied, transform the 'public consciousness', challenge misperception and misinformation, dispel everyday 'common sense' about the disadvantaged in society.

ACCESS

In conducting any qualitative research, it is important for the researcher to think about how to go about gaining 'access', by which social researchers essentially mean the process of convincing people to talk to them. Once a researcher has decided upon who should be the informants or participants that would provide information required for a study, they often seek to talk to as many people as possible by developing rapport with them and to be in a position to learn from them. Therefore, gaining access is not a simple task, it requires some combination of strategic planning, hard work and luck. This is often ill considered from the very outset though, and I will give an example of how this might be the case.

Many criminologists, including quite established academics, will build their research on talking to those who have been involved in policing and law enforcement, others on crime and criminality, and a smaller number on both, but we might ask, how might a research project potentially flounder or be impacted by the order that people are spoken to? Take for example, a research project on street drug dealing in a small English market town. It might be that an ethnographer wants to generate as comprehensive picture as possible, so seeks to speak to drug suppliers, users, drug workers, police officers, police managers and probation staff, all as part of the ethnographic work, but where should they begin? It might be simply acceptable to turn up on the street or in a drug drop-in charity, once ethical approval is granted, and start asking to speak to people, but how might the very order in which people are selected as participants impact upon the project? If the first sources used and spoken to are users and dealers, how might this shape later interactions with police officers, police managers and probation staff? What if that group were the first to be spoken to, is there a potential for that to impact on how drug users or suppliers might perceive the topic and the researcher? Might there be an impact upon the data that can be collected and the findings that might be produced.

TASK

When ethnographers are seeking to enter the field or gain access, it is important that they consider the order in which they contact people, and how they explain their purposes, because it is often suggested that groups may be concerned about researchers because:

- they fear potential repercussions of the research
- they are concerned about what the study might find
- they are concerned about the potential for the research to be disruptive and cause them inconvenience
- they believe that the research might harm an already tarnished reputation (for example, criminal justice practitioners such as youth justice, police, prison and probation staff can develop a 'siege mentality' where research is not regarded as positive or likely to yield good outcomes)
- they do not understand or are sceptical about who the researcher has loyalties to, knows or is allied to.

Gatekeepers and key informants can be useful in acting to help build access, but they too may have their own agenda, social circles, views and attitudes that may impact upon the research process. What is more, it is often the case that people, even those in the same group of organisations, may not trust one another, and so researchers need to be alert to the fact that the contacts and connections that they make with some individuals may close possibilities to gain access to others. It is worth remembering that both crime and criminal justice networks can be very political arenas.

Thinking about some examples of criminological ethnographies, consider:

- Who is the work representing?
- Who might use it to make arguments in terms of policy?
- To what extent is it possible for the researcher to control the use of research once it is written?

Here perhaps the suggestion is that it may be time to move beyond Robert Park's suggestion, found in the quote that opens this book, that ethnographic research can simply be commenced where there is a will, and recognise that there is a lot more that perhaps ought to be considered now. While on one hand, I am keen to suggest to readers that criminological ethnography is eminently more accessible and available to most researchers than is sometimes suggested, and yet similarly, I believe that one of greatest pitfalls in successfully conducting ethnographic criminological research is the inability to obtain 'access' to a research field or the fieldwork site.

Researchers often spend a considerable amount of time on this task, especially when the research requires an in-depth study of their respective research field and this task can be even more complex when (as is frequently the case with issues of crime and victimisation) it involves a sensitive topic or processes involving powerful actors. Indeed, the literature on crime frequently promotes it as being secretive, hidden, sensitive and specialist. This, I would aver, can be the case. And yet additionally I would also highlight that crime is ultimately a human process involving people, and that the tendency to suggest that all crime exists with a normalised Omertà that acts prohibitively to close down the potential to study it is deeply problematic. While criminological ethnography might be hard to do well, it is often presented as if it is something that is just hard to do, and frequently that view is underscored by a popular mythology which seemingly suggests that crime takes place in places and settings that are hidden or inaccessible. This is not necessarily the case.

FRONTSTAGE AND BACKSTAGE PLACES

While the crime might be perceived as inaccessible, the perception is slightly different when it comes to criminal justice organisations. While notionally these often provide a justice function that is driven by and underpinned by notions of transparency, the realities can often be very different. There are some places that are largely and normally open to the aspirant criminological ethnographer, such as, for the most parts and in most places, the criminal courts. However, there are also settings and places that are more difficult to access, and these are often described as 'backstage' places.

The concepts of 'frontstage' and 'backstage' in social sciences were used to differentiate forms of everyday behaviour, and are associated particularly with Erving Goffman (1959), forming part of the dramaturgical perspective within sociology that uses the metaphor of the theatre to explain individuals' social interactions and the 'presentation of self in everyday life', where social life is a 'performative' and carried out by 'teams' of participants in three places: the 'frontstage', 'backstage', and 'offstage'.

The idea that as social beings, we perform different roles throughout our everyday lives, and display different kinds of behaviour depending on where we are and what we are doing, is familiar to most people. Most of us, whether consciously or unconsciously, behave somewhat differently as our professional selves versus in our family roles. In Goffman's theorising, the 'frontstage' behaviour is that which we do, when we know and are conscious that others are watching or observing us. In other words, it is how we behave and interact when we have an audience. Frontstage behaviour reflects internalised norms and expectations for our behaviour, which are shaped in part by the setting, the particular role we play within it, and our physical appearance. How we participate in a frontstage performance can be highly intentional and purposeful, or it can be habitual or subconscious. Either way, frontstage behaviour typically follows a routinised and learned social script shaped by cultural norms.

There's more to Goffman's notion of backstage conduct than what we do when no one is observing, or when we think no one is looking, but this example illustrates it well and helps us to easily see the difference between backstage and frontstage behaviour. How we behave backstage is freed from the expectations and norms that shape our behaviour when we are frontstage. Being at home instead of out in public, or at work or school, is the clearest demarcation of the difference between frontstage and backstage in social life. Given this, we are often more relaxed and comfortable when backstage, we let our guard down, and we might be what we consider our uninhibited or 'true' selves. We cast off elements of our appearance required for a frontstage performance, like swapping work clothes for casual clothes and loungewear and maybe even change the way we speak and comport our bodies. Often when we are backstage, we rehearse certain behaviours or interactions and otherwise prepare ourselves for upcoming frontstage performances. We might practice our smile or handshake, rehearse a presentation or conversation, or plan the elements of our appearance.

However, even in our backstage lives we often have a small team with whom we still interact, like housemates, partners and family members, but with whom we observe different rules and customs from what is expected when we are frontstage. This is also the case in the more literal backstage environments of our lives, like the backstage of a theatre, the kitchen within a restaurant or the 'employee only' staff areas of retail shops. The notions of frontstage and backstage can also perhaps be added to an ethnographic dichotomy that separates the public from the private realm, and the open from the closed, especially when considering fieldwork sites and settings. While this binary is obviously a sketch, and does not hold wholly true (as many settings and places are, in actuality, better conceived as being on a continuum that ranges from open to closed, public to private).

However, the dichotomy of frontstage places and backstage places breaks down frequently when we consider that many settings are a blend of both. Certainly, when conducting ethnography, it is the aim to gain a comprehensive

Table 6.1

	Characteristics	Examples
Frontstage places (frontstage performances)	Public and accessible spaces, open to all, democratic	The street, public places, public court rooms, shopping malls, work corridors
Backstage places (backstage performances)	Largely private, less controlled/ observed, performed in front of privileged access	Prisons, CCTV control centre office, private offices, private homes

picture, rather than be subject to a stage-managed performance, and to do this, it is vital to be able to gain the trust and acceptance of the participants in order to conduct one's research. This will normally involve some combination of strategic planning, hard work and opportunity, and frequently a little luck. This is undeniably the case for most ethnography, but where criminological ethnography is arguably different is in the nature and character of the central topics of crime and control with all the inherent moral ambiguities and tendencies to blur the lines between what is truly criminal. As Dick Hobbs has suggested, when it comes to winning the will of offenders to speak to them, academics can be in a hard place. Criminals often have far more to lose than anything to gain by opening up to academics, and much access depends on trust, which is perhaps not the overriding quality in many proto-criminal environments. Academics asking a lot of questions can be a hindrance, a nuisance and a threat to business, but that is not simply true of criminals. Almost all of those involved in an ethnographic research project are managing presentations of themselves. Indeed, one of the most frustrating things when it comes to access is that we do not recognise the structured power that bodies have to control and manage the representation of organisations and actors relative to their place in a socially stratified system, whereby the more powerful the actor, the more ability to stage manage the impression. In any setting, researchers who are considered outsiders of an organisation are often not welcomed, especially if they ask questions that are sensitive and awkward. Often many academics face numerous obstacles in trying to gain access to various organisations where they would like to carry out their research. The hurdles are often neglected, or it is seen as merely a tactical issue. Organisations (and perhaps particularly powerful criminal justice organisations and statutory bodies) are usually very sceptical about the role of outsiders, and concurrently, may not value academic studies, especially academic studies that may raise problems, bring little reward, paint the organisation or body in a bad light or raise controversies and make life difficult. In addition, many organisations deny access due to academics' failure to provide answers about what, how and why they are carrying out the study, and whether the study would provide value to the organisation itself. For example, the prison service in England and Wales will only grant research permissions through its National Research Council (NRC), a process that is allied with the aims and objectives of the Ministry of Justice and its strategic priorities, and such an instrumentalisation of research is quite counter to what some academics will suggest is the intellectual curiosity that should be the dominant guiding principle of academic inquiry.

While access is a vital issue, many researchers do not even describe their fieldwork practice in their research report. It is only in ethnography-based research that access to the research field is described explicitly. There are numerous different ways that researchers have gained access to the field, two classic examples are presented as case studies below.

CASE STUDY

PHILIPPE BOURGOIS: *IN SEARCH OF RESPECT*

In Search of Respect, Philippe Bourgois' now classic ethnographic study of social marginalisation in inner-city America, won critical acclaim after it was first published in 1995. In 1997 it was awarded the Margaret Mead Award, and it was subsequently re-published as a second edition. Bourgois, a medical anthropologist, managed to gain the trust and long-term friendship of street-level drug dealers in one of the roughest ghetto neighbourhoods in the United States, East Harlem, whose activities largely centred around a place termed the game room from which Ray, their leader, ran the trade. Yet Bourgois states that his fieldwork was largely generated fortuitously and resulted simply from the fact that low income meant that he took up an apartment and lived, for five years, with his family next to a crack house in East Harlem during the mid-1980s through the early 1990s. The crack dealers he encountered there, such as Primo, Caesar, Luis and their families, became his associates and friends, and allowed him to craft a sympathetic and yet honest and grounded account that reveals both the structural barriers that marginalised men and the minority group of Puerto Ricans, but also the nasty and violent street culture that further isolated them from mainstream society. Bourgois uses honest reflections of mistakes made in the field, such as regrettably placing himself in conflict and confrontation with Ray early in the research project where, by one thoughtless act, he jeopardises his very standing among the entire dealer group.

Bourgois discusses how, while showing off his article in the *New York Post* newspaper and attempting to get the main dealer Ray (who is responsible for a large amount of the drug dealing in El Barrio) to read it, not realising that Ray was illiterate, he could easily have destroyed his very access to the field. Yet he also reflects on how the men he is studying both liked the status of hanging out with someone who is 'legit' and use him as a resource themselves, enjoying the fact that they can impress him with their stories and supplement their usual and limited experiences interacting with white people, which have largely been constrained to welfare settings or subordinate and subservient positions in employment. It is clear there is affection, at least from some participants, for the fact that they have an academic professional reliant upon on them for information.

The main characters of the work are Primo, who manages the local crack house; Ray, his boss; Caesar, who is Primo's friend and employee; and Candy, who is the most prominent of the women who spend time in the crack house. These people's stories meander through Bourgois' interviews: we watch them try to find legal jobs, discuss their childhoods, engage in brutal and senseless acts of violence, explain their hopes and fears, all the while doing a consistently high volume of hard drug against a backdrop of pervasive violence. Beneath it all, they, like all human beings, are 'in search of respect', but many are isolated from the formal economy and have found that while they would welcome the opportunities for legitimate work, such avenues are simply closed to them. Bourgois explains the circumstances that have brought his subjects into such desperate circumstances. All of them are immigrants from Puerto Rico, an island that may have born a more difficult burden of colonialism than other places in the Americas, and past racism continues subtly to exert influence on their lives now. The dealers in Bourgois' monograph are all constantly looking for legal work but find their skill set unsuited for the jobs available to them. Bourgois repeatedly questions how a highly successful drug dealer like Ray could not hold down even the most basic of legal jobs. But he comes to suggest that the required skill set is wholly different between the two milieus. Ray, with his quick mind and unstable emotions, had repeatedly failed to establish a foothold in legitimate business – he simply cannot surpass the necessary bureaucratic hurdles. Despite Ray's power on the streets, his ability to function against mainstream norms is sadly deficient. The only place his participants feel a semblance of respect afforded to them is in the illicit economy.

Bourgois' portrayal is one that perhaps undersells his method and skill, he simply avers that being acceptable to his subjects suffices. Yet the evidence in the form of photographs and rich thick description and the way he manages to contrast, and yet be alert to, the violence his subjects engage in, while also remaining sensitive to the desperate situations they can find themselves in, makes this a criminological ethnography that remains for many the seminal study of illicit drug dealing.

QUESTIONS

- Bourgois lived in the area where he undertook his research in an apartment with his wife and young child, what implications might that have had for the research that he undertook?
- Bourgois talks of his participants 'internalizing institutionalized violence?'. As a university professor how is he able to adjudge his participants' interaction with racism and oppression?
- At several points Bourgois hears stories of extreme violence including one participant Candy committing a shooting and an account of the rape of a homeless man by participants. Do you feel that ethnographers have any duty to report such information? What are the risks and problems of doing so?

HOW DO YOU GET ACCESS?

In order to conduct research, or to undertake observations, it is normal that the researcher must negotiate access to the fieldwork setting. When considering access, there are two specific issues that the aspiring researcher ought to pay heed to: first, the researcher must consider the degree of openness of the research setting in which they are seeking to research, and second, whether the research will be conducted overtly or covertly. Traditionally, ethnographic research was associated with covert and undercover studies, including of criminal groups. While this is becoming less frequent now, the justification for that was at least partly premised on openness.

Openness refers to the power that any group has to exclude those who wish to enquire into or observe its behaviour, practices, norms and culture in order to attempt to generate emic and or etic understandings. Groups that can wield power to deny outsiders and strangers access to a considerable extent are often termed 'closed groups' and while criminals have long been held as an exemplar par excellence of the closed group (because much criminality is perceived as being secretive and hidden away), closed groups do not only take the form of those involved in illegal or marginal and deviant behaviours. While football hooligans or outlaw bikers are easily regarded as closed groups, so too, elite groups, and particularly those performing core criminal justice functions, can be particularly adept at denying researchers access. For example, police, prisons, court judges and probation agencies, as well as all sorts of commercial ventures and charities and NGOs can be closed to research for a range of reasons, just as they can be welcoming and receptive if, for example it brings them benefits or will paint them in a good light. So too, the openness of an individual or group to a researcher may be tied to a range of other factors that are not always immediately apparent. The researcher's personality and character or appearance (for example, the clothes that are worn and how you look might matter, prisoners are often reticent to talk to those that they think look like police officers) alongside a range of other factors, such as gender, race, religion, sexuality, background, biography and social class, may all have a bearing on the research and negotiations towards access. For example, it is probably not too controversial to claim that a group of women who have experienced domestic violence might demonstrate a greater degree of openness to a young female researcher than to a man, so too it is probably the case that there are an array of factors that will influence judgements. If one wants to gain access to talk to senior prosecutors, it would probably be wise not to turn up to meet them wearing tatty jeans, trainers and a t-shirt, although that look, and a knowledge of designer trainers (or Sneakers), might be far better if the target group is young offenders. The main point here is that what Goffman termed 'presentation of self' (Goffman, 1959) can be an important feature in cultivating openness.

How you gain access is, of course, very much dependent upon what it is that you seek to study and the focus of your ethnographic work. Some frontstage ethnography, as a result of unexpected and unplanned opportunities – for example, recent ethnographic work on public disorder such as the English Riots in 2011 (Treadwell et al., 2013) or the phenomena of Black Friday shopping and the violence sometimes associated with it in the British context (Smith and Raymen, 2017) – has resulted from more opportunistic, short-term or instant ethnography. In contrast, large scale ethnographic works that occur in prisons (Crewe, 2009) are unlikely to be possible without institutional backing, and will have a long lead up and lead in.

Access is always a power process and it is always negotiated, and then re-negotiated in the field. It should always be remembered that access is not so much a one-chance process that results in successful immersion, rather what is detailed as access involves deciding where to study and when, introduction to participants and recruitment, persuading participants, negotiating around sensitive topics, as well as considering how to present oneself. Indeed, these small things can become big in the mind of students, and I have known of countless examples where the things that concern new researchers are not necessarily the more practical aspects of what to do, but rather how to dress and appear, because some worlds that can be normal for the familiar ethnographer such as the police station or prison are intimidating for those less familiar with them.

TASK

It is often suggested in criminology that because crime tends to be a covert activity and offenders have every interest in keeping it that way, crime in action can rarely be observed, let alone in such a way as to allow for systematic empirical study.

Is this the case? Is it not true that a great deal can be observed in the right places, with the correct will, but too many criminologists just accept this simplistic and one-dimensional narrative and lack enough will?

Imagine that you have been tasked by a charity organisation with discussing the problems with being released from a short-term prison sentence for ex-prisoners.

- How might you go about explaining access?
- How might you explain what you want to find out?
- What might be the barriers that stop people talking to you?
- Who might want to talk to you and why?

There are multiple ways you could examine such a topic with an ethnographic approach or sensibility, but do you think there is a best approach that you would recommend taking?

There is no single way that criminological researchers gain access, and most successful projects are the culmination of trial and error. Those that come to fruition are the successful ones, and we know far less about failed ethnographies. Some researchers, such as Patricia Adler and her husband Peter, are very honest about how they gain insight. In *Wheeling and Dealing* (1985), a study of community drug dealers and smugglers, Patricia Adler describes falling into the research project as result of an inquisitive mind, useful neighbours and her own (quite honest) use of recreational drugs. Friends and contacts can be useful, but so too can family members. Employment or association with a 'scheme' can be useful, so for example Alistair Fraser used just such an approach to help smooth his access for ethnographic fieldwork carried out over four years in Glasgow with young people (Fraser, 2015). Employment can be another useful avenue. Famously, Simon Holdaway (1983) used his employment as a police sergeant as part of his ethnographic work on policing, while Winlow (2001) described how he used his size, build and physicality, and a close friend who was a 'bouncer' involved in nightclub door security, in order to examine crime and violence in the night time economy in the north east of England, and Ditton used his employment on a bread van for his classic study on fiddling and pilferage, *Part-Time Crime* (Ditton, 1977). A similar approach has recently been resurrected by Lloyd to examine workplace harm within low-paid, insecure, flexible and short-term forms of 'affective labour' through an ultra-realist lens using data from a long-term ethnographic study of the service economy (Lloyd, 2018). That role was both similar and yet slightly different from Rachela Colosi, who worked as a lap dancer and agency stripper, and notes: 'It did not occur to me when I first started working in the sex industry that I would one day both research and write about this occupation' (Colosi, 2010: 2). Similarly, it did not occur to Armstrong to support Sheffield United as a means of following and observing their football hooligan group, the Blades Business Crew, but had he not, he would probably not have been able to generate a study with anything like the appreciative quality or depth of *Football Hooligans: Knowing the Score* (Armstrong, 1998). Janet Foster talks of the benefits of joining a pub darts squad to ease her into acceptance among her research subjects (Foster, 1990) whereas much of Treadwell's work talks of the importance of biography, fighting, drinking and friendships cultivated in a large urban setting and with peers in boxing gyms and at football as useful for the criminological ethnographer (Treadwell, 2018). Similarly, Wilson's previous participation in the Northern Soul scene was brilliantly appreciated both at the time and in hindsight in his methodologically innovative and hugely engaging text which uses knowledge based on decades of immersion in the scene (Wilson, 2007). Even family members can be useful, for example Ellis eludes to a close relative with an intimate knowledge of violence and criminality as being a useful contact in his ethnographic study of male violence (Ellis, 2016). It seems fair to suggest that the ways into a field are potentially numerous, varied and complex. Goodey has noted that much criminology, as a social science discipline, has never embraced the idea of research that is based on the study of the individual. There remains an unhealthy intellectual suspicion of what 'the individual' or, more damningly, 'the personal' has to offer criminology' (Goodey, 2000: 474) and yet, the starting point for the aspiring criminologist might well be the personal and that which is already close. Criminologists must, by virtue of the sensitive nature of crime and social control, contend with the politics of gaining access and trust with either the study population or the gatekeepers of the data. These methodological realities manifest themselves in culturally defined ways and shape the nature of the research enterprise. So perhaps the questions that should guide are:

- Who? – Who do you want to speak to? Who do you know that might help you?
- What? – What is the purpose of the research? What is the benefit to you? To your subjects? What are you willing to do to gain the opportunity to undertake research?
- Why? – Why do you want to undertake this research? Why have you chosen this field? How will you articulate that to an individual in that world?

So while the purpose of your ethnographic project is important, so too are the practicalities of how you might gain access. To that, there is no simple answer.

SHOULD ETHNOGRAPHERS PICK SIDES?

You may not have thought about it yet, indeed, you may not be reading this text and planning an ethnographic project at all, but a useful exercise that is well worth trying is to think about how ethnographers go about re-negotiating access in every day field interactions, and just how different this is, or can be, from the usual early phases of explaining purpose and access, focus and scope in more conventional and formal academic language.

Often those who are seeking to undertake an ethnographic project commence their planning from this very point, considering how they will explain their aims and scope, the core interests and purpose, to an informed body, given that oftentimes the early part of securing an ethnographic project is to make a formal application, perhaps for financial support to a research council, as part of an application for funded doctoral studies, as a means of securing IRB or ethical clearance, or as part of a justification on a project. Yet this process of describing research to peers and colleagues, or to other informed academics, is very different from describing and detailing it to other stakeholders, or even to likely participants themselves. In criminal justice settings, such as courts or around police stations, it is likely that this will be expected early, as invariably an outsider will often be politely asked what their purpose is, and in many settings, there is understandable scepticisms and anxiety about strangers. That too can be true of other settings, even if a researcher is being covert it is likely that new faces will quickly be asked what they are doing.

Of course, there are some exceptions, for example, it is easier to maintain one's anonymity in the online world (Hall and Antonopoulos, 2016), as it is easier to build face profiles, and perhaps easier to justify covert research. However, there is a long tradition of covert research in criminology, especially as most academics will have some sympathy with the argument that certain forms of criminal conduct are only possible to research via covert means (Scheper-Hughes, 2004). However, any such justification is also based on complex debates about the purpose and function of research. As I have already suggested, criminological research has long faced the question of whose side the researcher is taking, as in whose side we are on. Interestingly, the classic variation of this commenced with a consideration of values, and the complex issue of value neutrality set against the often more complex and messy reality that human life is rarely value free.

Howard Becker's article 'Whose side are we on?', published in 1967, has been very widely cited in the literature of the social sciences. Furthermore, there is considerable consensus about its message. It is generally taken to argue that sociologists are inevitably partisan, and that they should be explicitly so. Galliher (1995) describes the message of Becker's article as arguing:

> that since some type of bias is inevitable in all research on human subjects, to gain a full understanding of the world it is essential that we consciously take the perspective of the oppressed rather than the oppressor. (Galliher, 1995: 169)

It is apparent from the outset that Becker's labelling theory of deviant behaviour is consistent with his view on representation in 'Whose side are we on?', which seems to advocate partisanship. The title itself assumes that we are forced to choose sides. And this is reinforced in the opening section of the article where Becker rejects any notional value freedom as impossible, and explicitly states that: 'the question is not whether we should take sides, since we inevitably will, but whose side we are on' (Becker, 1967: 239).

Moreover, against the background of Becker's work *The Outsiders* (1963) and advocating a sociology of deviance, the implication seems to be that we should side with those who occupy a socially subordinate position, that the sociologist should take on the role of the champion of the underdog, those who are denied power. Such a view has long informed many who are advocates of ethnography, which becomes a form of outsider sociology, and indeed, the ethnographic method has often similarly sought to portray itself as a maligned and outsider method, marginalised much like those whom it studies by a dominant force of quantitative positivist empiricism. It was for these reasons that Gouldner

(1975) labelled Becker's position as 'underdog sociology', a standpoint that was elected to highlight that it could be regarded as politically radical, even though Gouldner argued that it was ultimately not radical enough and still functioned to ultimately support the liberal establishment (Gouldner, 1975).

Of course, it is not only Becker who advocates social research taking sides. Labelling theory transformed the field of research on crime and deviance in several ways. Most obviously, it expanded the focus of inquiry to include the processes by which particular types of act, and particular people, come to be labelled as criminal or deviant. In this way, the 'labellers' and those in socially privileged positions, and the processes that underscored this, as well as the groups and individuals that they labelled, became objects of study. More fundamentally, on some interpretations, deviance as traditionally understood was no longer to be treated as an simple, objective or given feature of the world, the character of which could be taken for granted or assumed as fixed. Rather, what counted as deviance was contested and contestable, and hence now treated as a matter of social definition, so that the labelling process came to be regarded as constitutive of deviance rather than as merely identifying independently existing offences or 'crimes' accurately. In other words, deviance was defined as 'behaviour labelled as deviant', with labelling as a process of social construction open to both sociological study and social contestation; and this sphere, it was suggested, must be studied if work in the field is not simply to take over the common sense perspective promulgated by powerful interest groups in society.

TASK

Thinking about some crimes, for example, theft from shops.

- How do you feel about such crimes morally and ethically?
- Do you consider them worse than other forms of crime, say damage of public property or recreational drug use?
- What would you say it is that frames your viewpoints and moral stances?
- Are there any things that you find intolerable that you would have to speak up against in the field?
- How do you think your values, attitudes, biography and background might influence you as a fieldworker and ethnographic researcher?

Becker's viewpoint on the social construction of deviance is still strong in some forms of contemporary criminological perspective, for example, it is more foregrounded in works of criminologists who describe themselves as working in accordance with a cultural perspective, who tend to look more specifically at forms of 'resistance' to dominant culture than it is in works of those who regard themselves as criminological ultra-realists. However, it is worth remembering that Becker's call to choose sides came about during a period when there was a growing acceptance of the counterculture of the 1960s, which was an anti-establishment cultural phenomenon that developed first in the United Kingdom and the United States and which then spread throughout much of the Western world between the mid-1960s and the mid-1970s, with New York City, San Francisco, London and Paris being hotbeds of early countercultural activity. The aggregate movement gained momentum as the Civil Rights Movement continued to grow and would later become revolutionary with the expansion of the US government's extensive military intervention in Vietnam. As the 1960s progressed, widespread social tensions also developed concerning other issues, and tended to flow along generational lines regarding human sexuality, women's rights, traditional modes of authority, experimentation with psychoactive drugs, and differing interpretations of the American Dream.

THE POLITICS OF ETHNOGRAPHIC RESEARCH ON CRIME AND CONTROL

Of course, with the rise of the countercultural movement came also the shift in the purpose of some academic research, and debates surrounding the place of politics in academic inquiry. Today, where an academic stands in terms of their ontological and epistemological views will determine how they view research processes and what these can reveal. Is the world something that is constructed; that is, it is socially and discursively created rather than objectively 'out there' waiting to be found or discovered? While a mathematician might seek to find the answer, the qualitative social scientist, arguably, largely does not.

We might have opinions, but as ethnographers most researchers have developed neither fixed hypotheses requiring testing nor standpoints on the nature and character of reality, as most ethnographers remain social constructionist and iterative, just as social scientists now accept that the way that we use language and description is both imbued with and creates meaning. They accept that when we speak, or write, we cannot and do not do so purely 'objectively'. Arguably, we cannot escape the predilections, values and cultural assumptions that we bring about with the very words that we select and use. Therefore, as qualitative researchers and ethnographers, what we learn in the field and report back in the academy is not (for most at least) regarded as 'objective fact', but perspective based on informed opinion. As Altheide and Johnson (1994) suggest, 'all knowledge is', and for them, this 'perspectival nature of knowledge' must, it follows, be considered 'an obdurate fact of ethnography' (Altheide and Johnson, 1994: 490).

Yet as Hammersley notes, an increasing number of ethnographers have come to see their work as involving political or practical commitments which link back to the issue of 'how far ethnography is a theoretically neutral technique or involves epistemological and ontological assumptions which may be tied to particular political or ethical commitments' (Hammersley, 2006: 10). He notes that while, '[r]ejection of neutrality is most obvious in the case of critical and feminist ethnography, but it is also involved where ethnographers want to make their work serve the requirements of policymaking or professional practice' (Hammersley, 2006: 10–11).

The combined influence of feminist and postmodernist thinking has led to the slow-growing recognition of what Naffine terms the 'partisan' nature of criminological inquiry (in both quantitative and qualitative form) (see Naffine, 1997). This view has arguably moved from the margins to being commonly recognised in the social sciences but can accord with the view that Denzin has expressed that 'in the social sciences, there is only interpretation' (Denzin, 1998: 313). Of course, not all ethnographers agree with this standpoint, if there exist no 'objective truths', and value neutrality is an outdated concept, then we might ask, do we now need the term 'subjectivity', created and fashioned as an opposite? If all knowledge is subjective, what allows the ethnographer to present privileged knowledge? This is not simply an abstract or irrelevant question, but one which came to define debates regarding the theoretical validity of more traditional 'realist' ethnographic fieldwork during the late 1980s and early 1990s. This was brought about as social science was exposed to postmodernist thinking, and 'anti-realist' scepticism emerged regarding the validity of what the academic value of social science and ethnography was and what allowed it to claim a privileged academic (or scientific) grounding. How could ethnography make truth claims or claims to reality if there was no objective reality?

'Realist ethnographers', and particularly those who were working in anthropology departments (a subject which had arguably faced some of the most fierce and mounting criticism for its presumed colonialism, imperialism and inherent racism and sexism), were to attempt to advance a view that they were reporting neutral fact (Brewer, 2000). The problem was that by the late 1980s, such claims to objectivity, accuracy and truth brought about by thick description were being challenged by scholars who argued that such accounts did not represent reality as it is. These critics of realist ethnography (often termed anti-realists), argued that thick description was often selective and subjective, presenting only one version of reality from 'the various competing versions of reality that could have been produced' (Brewer, 2000: 42). In addition; and buoyed by the growth in popularity of the concept of postmodernity, this anti-realist challenge to the realist notion of the objective nature of ethnography became increasingly influential in the social sciences. By the early part of the 1990s, and the emergence of postmodernist populism, realist ethnographies and the notion of thick description, particularly those in anthropology, were increasingly criticised for being 'theoretically naïve and no different from those produced by ordinary people as part of their everyday life' (Brewer, 2000: 42) and hence less entitled to claim a scientific or privileged knowledge status. It was argued that ethnographers, particularly those with realist leanings, occupied no unique position of privilege in terms of the knowledge or theory that they produced. Those who were anti-realist and social constructionist increasingly sought to overtly assert the partisan and political nature of their research, rather than its ability to create objective truths. This resulted in a far more overtly politicised form of social research, and an ever greater taking of sides. Indeed, it was to become increasingly familiar to see ethnographic research borne out of activism where the political biases of the researcher were overtly acknowledged. Ethnography seems to be employed especially (though not only) and increasingly by critical and activist scholars with the intention to support constructivist ontological perspectives.

Activist ethnography, the participative observational study of social movements and alternative political and grass roots organisations, is now an established method of critical knowledge production. The epistemological turn towards practice as knowledge has allowed activists of alter-globalisation protests (Juris, 2007) or eco-sabotage (Plows et al., 2004) to legitimately present their experiences as relevant knowledge on politics (Polletta, 2012) and organisational strategies (Maeckelbergh, 2009). Activist ethnography is the formalised method of turning experiences into accepted knowledge through academic writing, which draws especially on feminist standpoint epistemologies by prioritising situated experiences. Activist ethnographers have used academia as a leveraging power to tell counter-stories from the margins (Plows et al., 2004).

Yet ought we ask whether the more we steer towards polarised understandings, the easier it is to lose sight of the everyday ambivalences that underlie our ways of making sense of the world? Is ambivalence better attuned to complexity and contradiction? Can attending to the dilemmas posed by deciding 'whose side we are on', as Howard Becker (1967) asked us to do, alter the character of social and criminological inquiry in and of itself and hence reposition the objects of our interests as inherently and clearly moral? If taking sides does this, is there a risk that it may set limits on how we see the world? What are we willing to see or consider, and do such choices restrict our analytical possibilities? Can such actions make invisible the intricacies of social practice and mistreat matters of concern as matters of given fact?

Fassin (2008; 2013) argues that the moral turn in the discipline thus requires a more demanding methodology that forces us to become more conscious and critical of our own moral presuppositions. This, he suggests, will help us to respect the epistemological grounds of our work while simultaneously preserving its political engagements. In other words, it helps to avoid the trap of conflating anthropological interpretation with moral evaluation. But Fassin is vague on what this more demanding methodology might entail, beyond general exhortations about the need to consider 'moral reflexivity as part of our research activity' (2008: 341).

The traditional injunction invoked against this is set out by the likes of Didier Fassin (2008) who argues that the moral turn in anthropology (and social scientific research using ethnography more broadly) requires a more demanding methodology that forces us to become more conscious and critical of our own moral presuppositions. This, he avers, will help us to respect the epistemological grounds of our work while also preserving its political engagements. In other words, it helps to avoid the trap of conflating social research interpretation with moral evaluation (Fassin, 2008: 341).

CASE STUDY

VICTORIA CANNING: ACTIVISM IN QUALITATIVE RESEARCH

Dr Vicky Canning is a critical criminologist who is happy to admit that her deeply personal interest in her research is borne out of political activism and political commitment. Her research interests are at least in part framed by her political involvement in pro-asylum activism, and lie with gendered harms, state power and violence, specifically in trajectories of violence in the lives of women seeking asylum.

Canning has undertaken extensive research relating to gendered harm and asylum in Europe, with focus points include everyday violence, sexual violence and torture support, temporal harms, immigration detention and destitution. Her PhD (2008–2011) investigated barriers to support for women seeking asylum in Merseyside, who were subjected to sexual violence during conflict and civil unrest, and this became the foundation of her book, *Gendered Harm and Structural Violence in the British Asylum System*, which won the British Society of Criminology Book Prize for 2018.

In that text, Britain is often heralded as a country in which the rights and welfare of survivors of conflict and persecution are well embedded, and where the standard of living conditions for those seeking asylum is relatively high. Drawing on a decade of activism and research in the north west of England, this book contends that, on the contrary, conditions are often structurally violent. For survivors of gendered violence, harm inflicted throughout the process of seeking asylum can be intersectional and compound the impacts of previous experiences of violent continuums. The everyday threat of detention and deportation, poor housing and inadequate welfare access, and systemic cuts to domestic and sexual violence support all contribute to a temporal limbo, which limits women's personal autonomy and access to basic human rights.

(Continued)

(Continued)

By reflecting on evidence from interviews, focus groups, activist participation and oral history, *Gendered Harm and Structural Violence* provides a unique insight into the everyday impacts of policy and practice that arguably result in the infliction of further gendered harms on survivors of violence and persecution.

Canning's book brilliantly uses a case study of a participant she calls Hawwi to consider and bring to life the types of disadvantage people seeking asylum face and which, she shows, affects asylum seeking women's capacity to engage in sexual or domestic violence services. However, while not directly a criticism of Canning's work, ought we to ask some questions about the interplay between activism and claims to science? There are and can be genuine scholarly problems that may arise from bias or agenda-induced research myopia – as there most certainly have been in the past and could be again in the future. It is problematic to position activism and scholarship as if they are invariably and inevitably mutually antagonistic. Arguably, the very act of selecting a topic of study and arguing for its significance is implicitly activist. Adhering to the field's standards of research, citation and professional rigour can or could be conceived of as acts of activism. Yet we also should not simply retreat to a relativist subjectivity, where anything goes and all is equal. In many sciences, any link between a scientific researcher and a body that profits from positive representation are, or ethically should be, clearly elucidated, and it is only right that we ask critical questions regarding activist research agendas, as we should ask critical questions about the construction, objectivity, validity and representativeness of all research.

Some questions for consideration:

- In what ways might activist research be less objective than other forms of social scientific inquiry?
- Are activist researchers attuned enough or expressive enough of instances where they neglect or ignore counter perspectives, or examples that confound or undermine their own political stance or objectives?
- Can good social science be reconciled with activism? If a researcher has already been involved in activism around a subject, how willing are they to consider counter perspectives? Should they have to? What would failure to do so constitute in your eyes?

SIMILARITY, DIFFERENCE OR AMBIVALENCE – WHICH MATTERS FOR A QUALITATIVE RESEARCHER?

Of course, an issue that remains for ethnographers in the field is what is being recorded. A simple answer may be data, or observations, but this belies a complexity, and is linked to the above discussions concerning how ethnographers filter and make sense of what they encounter in the field.

A conventional view is that this is not the stuff of fieldwork, because field-work is only the collection of data, and it is at some later point that this data will be considered, coded and made sense of, but the process of doing good ethnography involves sense making throughout, because every encounter is laden with data, and every moment brings the potential for understanding. To what extent is the ethnographer an open channel reporting what they encounter? What makes their field experience useful, both for their own theorising and for the building of critical intellectual capacity and under-standing for others?

While some such as Fassin (2008) are keen to assert that ethnography needs to become more reflexive as a guard against simply becoming moral evaluation, a slightly different starting premise may be to consider what it is that fieldwork is seeking to cultivate. For example, is it possible to assert that a better meth-odology is achieved not by becoming more conscious and critical of our own moral presuppositions, but by more actively seeking to cultivate ambivalence as an orientation in ethnographic work? Essentially, ambivalence, or the state of having mixed feelings or contradictory ideas about something or someone, might be a better end aim than alternative approaches that seek to find a better central ground.

Methodological ambivalence is, therefore, a call to explicate phenomena, to not take bipolarities for granted as simply descriptions of the way things are. An orientation towards ambivalence is an orientation towards complexity and nuance, contradiction and complexity, and hence it prevents the criminologi-cal ethnographer from operating according to fixed positions which can dis-tort his or her understanding of social phenomena, or the theory that can be built or tested from the fieldwork practice. Take, for example, prison and imprisonment. As an ethnographer who has worked in numerous prisons across the prison estate in England and the US, I have frequently asked pris-oners, 'What is this prison like?' as an opening question in conversation. Almost universally the answer comes back, 'It is shit'. From a moral position, this could be taken as indicative that prisoners do not agree with retributive and carceral punishments, but such a statement would also be shit, for prison-ers can be some of the most conservative, punitive and vindictive individuals going. So too, to say a prison is shit does not mean it is as shit as other prisons, or that it is shit compared to experiences in the world outside. If the aim of ethnography is to gain rich, holistic insights into people's views and actions, as well as the nature (that is, sights, sounds) of the location they inhabit, of course, a single line can tell us nothing, and this is why more questions always follow, but let us take that prison is 'shit': what is shit about it, the lack of legitimacy, the staff prisoner relations, the inmate relations, the physical con-ditions? Is it shit all the time? How can you adjudge the claim that a prison is shit? What is the opposite of shit?

In much research, the aim is to gain both emic and etic understanding, or to cultivate insider knowledge and understanding, and how we arrive at our understandings of meaning is vital. Some of the best criminological ethnography does not arrive at easy or clear-cut findings, and arguably not all ethnography is about working out which answer is right or deciding on a side in an uncomplicated binary. Indeed, in some ways much ethnography is in reality a process of promoting oneself and the interests of the researcher above that of the participants and subjects, even if that is not so frequently acknowledged. For example, as Hobbs has noted:

> Machismo, as well as a veil of eccentricity, is responsible for the cult of field work, as some of the grime of real life is brought back to the office … fleeting acquaintance … often shapes the master status of the academics as they grow paunchy on their six months or a year spent in the recess of what is sometimes referred to as real life. Those they leave behind on the streets, who experience real life every day of their existence find heroic status eluding them in the daily grind of survival, while the ethnographer, who was nearly arrested, almost beaten up and didn't quite go crazy builds a career on a youthful flirtation with the terrible uncertainty of life amongst the lower orders. (Hobbs, 1993: 62)

Mark Fleisher makes a similar argument about the exploitative process that ethnography can be in his chapter 'Ethnographers, pimps, and the company store' (1998) where he notes that there is much similarity between criminologists and those who act as pimps around the sex trade, in so far as both act as intermediaries. Moreover, Fleisher observes:

> I am a pimp, of sorts. I sell a product (tales about criminals) to those who have never seen a criminal up close … will I create loathsome characters? Or will I remain neutral, offer facts about their lives, but conceal their awful behaviour from public view? (Fleisher, 1998: 60-61)

Yet might we need to ask whether such binary choices as Fleisher is proposing are necessary? Indeed, perhaps a better way to conceive of the role of the ethnographer is as a conduit and interpretive lens that seeks to make sense by considering the grey areas, rather than the black and white, and by considering similarity and difference, employing both as a heuristic device towards arriving at a more nuanced understanding. What the ethnographer is not trying to do is to take sides or craft a simple story, but instead to seek out the ambivalence. Indeed, by regarding ambivalence as a heuristic device, might it mean that the aim of the good ethnographer is not to seek simply a surface reading, but to look at the paradoxes, contradictions and complexities? Working with and towards ambivalence might mean that in the sphere of crime and control there is much that we have to accept which is not clear cut, black and white, where the taking of sides is vital, and we need to learn about the conditions under which something may get called an atrocity or an outrage. Following people who take sides isn't a problem, but might it also teach us as ethnographers something more fundamental about the nature of the human world, that things are rarely so black and white, good and evil as they are in simple iterations, and hence, it is when the researcher predicates his or her research on a side taken that problems of validity might arise?

Certainly, when Jock Young criticised positivist criminology in the later stages of his career, and particularly in the criminological imagination, he was particularly attuned to how the cannon of positivistic and quantitative criminology was so utterly unreflective of the way it created only a problematising lens, that is, almost in universality, it made the stuff of lived experience numerical and ever abstract, whereas qualitative methods were better attuned to the variety of motivations and rationalities associated with the criminal act with all the inherent contradictions and paradoxes that often came connected to those lived experiences, individual subjectivities and a sensitivity and appreciation of perception, belief, attitude and values (Young, 2011).

It is often suggested that ethnography necessarily has a lack of validity and legitimacy on the very grounds it is unsystematic and unscientific, at least if judged from the traditional perspective and the classical experimental model. Ethnography, and data gathered in specific micro settings, cannot prove any sort of scientific validity for wider trends and practices, because the specifics of micro communities are so varied. The results of ethnographic research often are regarded as unreliable, lacking in validity and generalisability. Some ethnographers ignore such criticisms; others, recognising the potential threats to the credibility of their findings that such criticisms bring, have looked to develop mechanisms and techniques to address the issues (I discuss these in Chapter 9). However, too great a focus on the problems also hides what is a unique aspect of ethnography that is not apparent in traditional positivistic science, and that gets to the heart of the social sciences, which is the fact that ultimately, ethnography and ethnology (the branch of anthropology that compares and analyses the characteristics of different people of different nationality or place, and the relationships between them) are concerned with the human subject, and it is that emotive quality that they should be well attuned to.

Many past and present ethnographic studies in criminology have developed out of engaged and often illegal field research – that is, field research in which the researcher of necessity crosses over into the world of criminality and seeks to understand that world from participation and life lived within it. A variety of contemporary cultural criminological studies and perspectives highlight the importance of the meanings and emotions that emerge inside criminal events, and thus confirm the need for methodologies that can situate researchers to some degree inside illegality to form that emic understanding.

CRIMINOLOGICAL VERSTEHEN AND EDGEWORK

The concept of *verstehen* was traditionally associated with Max Weber, and for him involved the process of gaining a deep, empathetic understanding of social behaviour. When studied further, it represents both an interpretive and systematic understanding of both the meanings and motivations that underscore an individual's purposive acts and actions. In the mid-1990s, that concept was appropriated by cultural criminologists who were keen to rehabilitate the symbolic interactionist, critical and engaged perspective better attuned to the emic and internal elements of crime, and the wider socio-political and cultural context that crime played out against, and where laws are enacted and enforced. Cultural criminologists, such as Jeff Ferrell and Mark Hamm in the United States, were keen to rehabilitate and look afresh at the meanings, frameworks and emotive feelings that were associated with crime and control, and following the direction of researchers such as Jack Katz in his seminal study, *The Seductions of Crime*, sought again to encourage US scholars to rediscover qualitative (and particularly qualitative methods), interpretive-based research and ethnography (Ferrell and Hamm, 1998). In particular, Ferrell suggested that this new commitment to methodology should situate an understanding of verstehen at the forefront of ethnographic criminological research, with Ferrell suggesting that:

> Criminological verstehen denotes a researcher's subjective understanding of a crime's situational meaning and emotions … implies that a researcher through attentiveness and participation, at least can begin to apprehend and appreciate the specific roles and experiences of the criminals, crime victims, crime control agents, and others caught up in the day to day reality of crime. (Ferrell, 1997: 10)

However, it was not just in attempting to find situated emotive meaning that cultural criminology imported new ideas and looked afresh for theoretical stimulation. In perhaps a reflection of broader social theories becoming prominent and influential, cultural criminologists called for emic insight as a central part of a more critical and yet emotively attuned criminology. This is perhaps important, for while good qualitative methods had long been producing ideas that proved foundational in disciplines such as social psychology, the traditions of ethnography and early ethnography are arguably far better at describing events, processes and contexts than at documenting people being people. A number of traditional qualitative studies simply did not do too much when it came to participants' emotive lives.

In recognition of this, from its early inception, cultural criminology turned not simply to verstehen, but also began quickly to look to better accommodate both feelings and emotions. To that end, early cultural criminology also drew extensively on the work of Stephen Lyng (1990), a sociologist who had been concerned with the process of voluntary risk taking, which he described using the concept of 'edgework', which explores the reasons why people take risks as part of leisure activities. The concept of edgework incorporates the notion that voluntary risk-taking activities are about exploring the edges that exist along cultural boundaries. These boundaries may include those between sanity and insanity, consciousness and unconsciousness and life and death. Lyng suggested that 'edgework' involves skilful practices combined with emotional intensity. But the emotional dimension of voluntary risk-taking is more complex than simply involving the desire to incite intense emotions. Emotions such as fear, excitement and anxiety are central to edgework, but so are their control. Mental toughness – the ability to control fear and the physical symptoms associated with it – is an integral aspect of edgework. When risk-takers can exert mastery over emotions that are viewed as negative, they experience heightened feelings of control. While much of Lyng's work was applicable to extreme sports such as base jumping or riding high performance motorcycles at extreme speed, clearly conceptually the notion has some purchase for crime, from armed robbery to joyriding, football violence to shoplifting, and doing some forms of policing and law enforcement are similarly relevant, as is doing ethnography in criminology. Yet while engaging in 'edgework' can bring emic understanding, can it also be ethically problematic for those who wish to conduct fieldwork? For example, Lumsden suggests that, '"Edgework" blurs the line between insider and outsider status, thus threatening the researcher's ability to step back from the field and critically reflect on their experiences. The researcher can find themselves unwittingly drawn into the deviant activities of youths, as "deviance" slowly becomes "the norm" through prolonged immersion in their social world' (Lumsden, 2013: 285).

MANAGING IN THE FIELD

Through fieldwork, you incorporate everything you have learned behind your desk and put it into practice. It allows you to 'step beyond the known' and enter into the field world of your research participants, in order to see and experience the world from their perspective, although it is perhaps always best to remember that the role of the academic is to provide a bridge between two worlds and to stay alert to both. Apart from learning about the 'other', through fieldwork, criminological ethnographers also inform their knowledge, understanding and insight into certain phenomena they wish to study by observing and witnessing and recording. This requires careful preparation, and the importance of preparing yourself for fieldwork, and not just planning the practicalities of the project, should not be underestimated. Fieldwork has its own way of unfolding, and while much can be anticipated, it is a process where fluidity and adaptability can be important too, depending upon the context and what is being studied. Because ethnography is so often heavily dependent on both the context and the people you encounter, and often does not pan out according to plans, it is virtually impossible to create a research plan and timeline that you will be able to stick to perfectly. Yet, preparation is necessary, so how do you go about it?

PREPARATION FOR ETHNOGRAPHY

PLAN FOR THE UNEXPECTED

The most general tip I can give aspirant ethnographers based on my extensive experience of fieldwork in different criminal justice settings is to plan for and expect the unexpected. While it is useful to have a rough outline of what your fieldwork period will look like, it is even more important to keep in mind that you will most likely not stick to this plan, and that any plan, however well-made, might quickly need to be revisited when in the field. Mentally preparing yourself for a research period during which you feel like you have little control over what is happening and when, can help you deal with these more chaotic moments and the unintended and necessarily difficult issues that might arise. Furthermore, in combination with a rough outline of your research, you will still be able to find structure in it. However, ethnographic research as a method perhaps best suits those who are adaptable, less anxious, more spontaneous and who can 'go with the flow'. If the character of ethnographic research is fluid and flexible, then the best approach to take is to be just that. However, effective planning and practice can help, and as I tell all students, when it comes to ethnography, practise makes better (rather than perfect).

That said, a negative can also be borne of complacency, and while all research can be ethically complex and risky, in the case of ethnographic and criminological research this is undoubtedly the case. Planning and preparation can help guard against complacency and serve as a useful safeguard against taking unnecessary or ill-considered risks. Someone should always be able to contact you in the field, but are you comfortable giving out a mobile number or taking a high value phone into the field? Is it worth considering having a specialist fieldwork phone? Have you got an emergency contact who can get to you quickly if needs be. Does someone know where you are? Who will you call if you are arrested? Students sometimes do not consider the basics, and if they do not, the experiences of fieldwork can jar or be more uncomfortable. The following serves as an example.

In undertaking fieldwork in a prison in England, I became involved in a lock down situation where it became impossible to leave the prison. Obviously, mobile phones are not permitted in prison, and so, caught up within an incident, it became impossible to simply withdraw from the field. Fortunately, I was able to use a phone to contact apprehensive family members on the outside, but this point is worth making. In some settings, life does not play out in the normal way. I have supervised students who have spoken of the discomfort they feel undertaking work in a prison where they are removed from the normal way that outside interaction and contact can be managed, for example, adapting to being without a mobile phone can be liberating, but some find it very difficult. What happens if my child is sick and someone at the school needs to contact me? This might be a question that quickly arises. In many ways, one of the very clear and obvious features of criminological ethnography is the lack of safety in the setting, and not all people feel comfortable in high crime areas or high crime estates, whether they are working alone or with others. Some people do not like physical confrontation, and so even accompanying police officers can be a traumatic experience if the result is exposure to some of the nastier realities of their working lives.

LEARN FROM OTHERS' EXPERIENCE

A second step to take is to become familiar with some of the feelings and challenges other people face. As Amy Pollard (2009) has written for *Anthropology Matters*, many students experience feelings of anxiety, frustration, loneliness and isolation, stress, powerlessness and guilt both while in the field, and sometimes even after leaving. While life goes on while in the field, it can also change, and few academics write candidly or honestly about how fieldwork often negatively impacts on those around them, who must put up with the prolonged absences, the unpredictability, the anxiety and uncertainty. While certainly not every anthropologist will experience all these feelings, or will experience them to the same extent, most of them are very common, at least at some point during your fieldwork. Simply preparing yourself that you might encounter these feelings and that they are thus normal, can already help in working through them while in the field. All those undertaking ethnographic research will experience some emotional responses during their studies, and I have experienced the emotions of coming out of the field after my own doctoral fieldwork and, having completed it, recognise that the doctoral study process can be a difficult one. Often those highlighting the complexities and difficulties in the field, like Pollard, are recent doctoral students, and I would caution against embracing a tendency to overplay the hardships of the field, not least by criminological ethnographers who have both the choice to be there in the first place and the option to leave.

That might not be so available to the police officer with a family to support policing violence in the night time economy or the prisoner serving a substantial custodial sentence.

Yet too, I am not naïve to the fact that the rigours of fieldwork are usually greater in any social science, and that is undoubtedly the case when it comes to criminological ethnography not only because of the subject matter, but also because the burden of then undertaking analysis is much greater due to the mass of unstructured data that a long participant observation stint can produce, the emotive topic of crime and control which is morally and ethically charged, and the relative lack of a clear, well-defined method for writing up, certainly compared to more administrative branches of criminology and crime science which utilise positivistic models. Further, there is often a lack of transparency in ethnography, and PhD students (perhaps the group most likely now to spend a sustained period undertaking ethnographic fieldwork) are often dependent upon supervisors for support, and by no means do all supervisors have relevant fieldwork experience, and few have recent experiences. Also, there is not always a great deal of transparency to how people have experienced the process.

It is something of a shame that often, the good and bad emotive stories from the field tend to not be written up, and that many academics do not reflect all that openly or transparently about their good and bad moments in the field, although this is something I and others have attempted to do (Williams and Treadwell, 2008; Wakeman, 2018; Wakeman and Treadwell, 2018). The stories of hardships, and many are full of humour, tend to become informal accounts that never make it into formal presentations and publications but become the stuff of bar talk at conferences.

Of course, not all the failings of the ethnographic process or the hardships that come of it will necessarily be down to the individual, and a point that should be made about ethnography is that its solitary and individualistic nature is, arguably, one of its greatest features yet similarly, its biggest problem. That said, ethnography need not be an individual process. There is no reason that it has to be the preserve of one researcher alone in the field of discovery, although it is often romanticised and fetishised in that way.

GETTING ON WITH PARTICIPANTS

When undertaking ethnography in the field, the main criteria for success of failure is likely to be the management and maintenance of relationships, and yet this is the one element that will be taken largely out of any textbook and spoken of only incredibly superficially. Yet this is really and truly the core stuff of ethnography. Good ethnographers will like people, they will likely be people who are sociable and outgoing, and who are able to set people at ease and learn from them. That is often a reciprocal process, and in any ethnography, it is also likely that participants will learn from the ethnographer. That point made, how do we explain, for example, why Bourgois was so readily tolerated by the crack dealers he studied, or why Goffman was successfully able to document the lives of young black men? Was it simply about them and their skill in the field, or something more? Research is a reciprocal process that both sides found a beneficial arrangement. Approval of access to a setting may not mean that all participants have given their informed consent to be involved in research or wish to partake. Yet what happens may not be universal. When undertaking research with football hooligans in the north of England, I found that the process was complicated by the fact that some core faces liked me, others did not, and hence not all would give consent to be interviewed or involved. Elsewhere in the criminal justice arena, for example, access permission may be granted by managers or head office, rather than all workers. In large scale participant observations, it is unlikely that all individuals subject to observation will be informed or give consent.

Commonly it is recommended that researchers make their role in the setting clear, ideally by seeking explicit verbal, if not written, consent from all participants. There may be practical difficulties, however, in achieving this with every individual who is encountered in a research setting and repeated requests for consent may be unduly disruptive of the activities being observed. This may be particularly the case in participant observation where the researcher seeks to act as an ordinary member of the research setting in order that, as far as possible, events that occur during their observations do not differ significantly from those which occur in their absence. Practical problems may also arise where participants in a research setting are not in a state to provide informed consent. This may be an issue where observations may include, perhaps incidentally, vulnerable groups (young people, people with mental disabilities) or those who are using drugs or alcohol, but even here we might ask, even if we are going through quite a detailed process of attempting to give potential participants in an ethnographic study a full and clear understanding of the research process, how many in actuality will be making a very clear informed choice? How well is anyone able to make an informed judgement to participate in research based on what they are told and subjective judgements about how data may be used at some future point when that is a decision which is largely out of their control? A common means of protecting individuals' and organisations' concerns about disclosure is to guarantee anonymity. In practice this may be difficult to ensure. For example, individuals or organisations may be sufficiently distinctive that they may be potentially identifiable even when anonymised.

Therefore what is often really important is the true ethical conduct of the field researcher long term as a form of embodied practice and as a real and true commitment to ethics. Arguably, ethnography, given its frequent lengthier engagement in the field setting and the researchers' proximity to subjects, carries different risks than qualitative research more generally that are related to the long-term nature of the contact and the familiarity that this brings, which comes with challenges in terms of maintaining boundaries and ethical conduct. It therefore becomes beholden on the field researcher to consider the ethics of their own everyday conduct, and their own place in the world. Then the researcher can at least avoid putting themselves in a position where they might be regarded as having committed a violation of trust. It is not possible to always articulate your thoughts, feelings and ideas in an open and honest manner in the field, but generally it is not bad advice to try and be fair and balanced in how you interact with people. It goes without saying, to be a good social researcher is normally to be a good listener, as listening to people and giving others a voice is one of the core aspects of ethnography, taking time to listen to people is an important skill in life generally, but it is absolutely core for ethnography. But listening is an active process and ethnography is a conversational discourse, so being willing to talk and listen are both vital in ethnography, and the process is rarely one directional. Not all ethnographers will get that. If you were to ask ethnographers what makes a good ethnographer the answers you will get will doubtlessly vary, I suspect, even if you were to restrict the focus from anthropology to social science, or to stipulate criminology more broadly. I am sure some of the answers would be flippant, ability to swear and capacity for alcohol consumption might feature on some peoples list, as might the qualities of being non-conformist or maverick. That said, the effective criminological ethnographer:

- has a sociable personality and gets on with people
- is curious
- is open-minded
- is flexible and can adapt to changing situations
- is good at delving deeper into cultural phenomena
- can probe and question for deeper meaning/understanding and understands theory
- does not rigidly stick to discussion/observation guides but uses them as guides
- has empathy, compassion and understanding
- is adventurous and is not afraid to take risks
- can establish rapport and maintain relationships
- is a good listener and a good conversationalist, can sit back and let others talk or ask questions and solicit information when necessary/timely
- has excellent data collection and analysis skills
- is a good storyteller and is good with words and writes vivid description
- understands the implications of findings within organisational or other contexts
- can explain their methods to others
- can pull the meaning out of the mundane and every day
- is self-reflexive and self-aware
- a good ethnographer will know themselves.

With all this in mind, an ethnographer needs a few good qualities, but they do not need to be a paragon of virtue, rather, they ought to be able to work with people, in situations that might sometimes be challenging, but will often also be mundane, dull, repetitive and boring.

TIPS FOR FIELDWORKERS

Yet there are lessons that can be taught that are useful, and I would like to highlight the following:

1. Use your background and biography heuristically but be alert to the field and do not get naïve and complacent, in any criminal justice setting. It is not only the physical risks in the field, but the wider risks that you ought to be continually alert to, and if reflexivity is anything then it is questioning yourself and what you are doing in a way that is not self-flagellating. Be open to the fact that you are doing a research project, it is in a field that for other people is not research but is real life, and just try and keep that in mind.

2. Second, while I have talked about the art of listening, listening is a two-way process and should be done in a probing and respectful manner. Therefore, as I have suggested elsewhere, 'Don't be afraid to call bullshit on your participants: you do not have to be aggressive or disrespectful, but a lot of people will have pre-set narratives, and it would be remiss to just take these on face value and accept them. Do not be afraid to challenge people or dig deeper in terms of what they are saying, sometimes people will get a little animated, or even possibly angry so as and when you do this, tread carefully and you might want to be respected in the field, but ethnography is not about just hearing what people tell you' (Treadwell, 2018: 301).

3. On the theme of listening and generating field data, it is always worth remembering that you have two ears and one mouth, normally best used in that ratio, but don't be afraid to talk about yourself. In reality, you will be a part of any ethnographic study, and now it is common to see people recognise that and write themselves into ethnography, but it is also important to recognise that a research project can benefit from a little reflexivity and knowing the author's standpoint, placing oneself too central, smacks of narcissism, which is not what good social research is supposed to be about. So in the field, be nice, don't be naïve or let people walk over you or take advantage, but if you expect people to open to you, you must be willing to do them the same courtesy.

4. While the ethnographic adventure and the fieldwork process are often presented as very exotic and exciting, a lot of the work is repetitive, monotonous and just, well, a bit dull. Be ready for this. It is worth always having a book and a pen and paper around, but also a mobile phone can be a useful way of typing and recording fieldnotes. Beyond that, think about how you present yourself in the field and what information you share. Think carefully about your conduct at all times, monotony can lure researchers into a false sense of security and make carelessness more likely. For example, be careful what information encountered in the field you share with others. The practical

and ethical challenges surrounding research into serious abuses and dealing with vulnerable populations are not wholly dependent upon the ethnographer, but the field researcher can certainly make situations better and worse. You should also be prepared to not like some or all of your participants: some ethnographers have a habit of overstating their ability as researchers to build rapport or form close bonds or relationships with their participants, but while being on good terms with participants can be useful, it isn't the ethnographer's task to make friends.

5. It can be useful for any aspirant researcher to be aware of the SRA Code of Practice for the Safety of Social Researchers (http://the-sra.org.uk/wp-content/uploads/safety_code_of_practice.pdf) and the BSC Code of Ethics for Researchers (www.britsoccrim.org/docs/CodeofEthics.pdf), and always be contactable and take safety seriously. Public settings are generally less risky, but it your inter-personal skills and good judgement that are the most vital safeguards in all situations.

6. While you might find people that you like or can relate to in the field, you may also find people who you don't. You will think this about research participants just as you do about colleagues, family members, and friendship groups. As Treadwell (2018: 301) notes, not having a close emotional connection with your participants does not make an individual a bad ethnographer. Certainly, spending a lot of time in the field and get used to it. It is time that is spent in the field that builds familiarity, but the point is to build that familiarity with a critical eye. In essence, while in the field, you may well act as if you are not, but remember the ethnographer's role is constantly to question, to continually ask the question, 'What is going on here?' (Spradley, 1980: 12).

7. The most important aspect is that you are there and there consistently, and that by being there you get the chance to speak to people. Sometimes it is better if you just go with the flow. Don't waste your time and energy defending what you do to doubters and detractors, critics and naysayers. The best ethnographers have spent plenty of time dealing with these folks, but then they also come to realise that not only are their opinions unwarranted and unneeded, they are also unsolicited. To spend too much time dealing with critics is time lost that you will never get back. If they want to challenge you, tell them to do it in print. You might get a citation that way. Instead, get out into the field: lots of people can offer you advice, but the best way to get better at anything is through practice.

I have now imparted what I think are the core considerations for those looking to undertake ethnographic fieldwork in crime settings, and have tried not simply to impart advice, but to use the discussion to raise some wider questions and debates aimed at facilitating better ethnographic fieldwork, or at least, better critical engagement with existing ethnographic research when it is encountered.

KEY INFORMANTS

Key informants, sometimes termed key participants and sometimes acknowledged as gatekeepers (because they serve as an entry point to the field and can also facilitate access to other individuals who might be useful to the ethnographer), are really people who become a vital part of the fieldwork process. Often ethnographers will spend a disproportionate amount of time with some core individuals because these participants appear to be particularly well informed, articulate, available, willing, interested or just well liked. Often these figures become the central cast in the written ethnographic work, and it is often seen that researchers will use key informants to generate a snowball sample (that is, they will use key informants to find other contacts willing to be observed, accompanied and spoken to or interviewed). Particularly in ethnographic studies, key informants (such as Gordon in Armstrong's study of football hooligans, Armstrong, 1998) are simply part of the study in their own right, but often times, the fieldworker's relationship with them means that they are the people whose life histories appear, and who come to dominate the data and study. There is nothing inherently wrong or problematic with this, but it is worth the fieldworker being ever mindful in considering the extent to which the perceptions, views, attitudes, values and ideas of key informants are espoused by other individuals and are reproduced more generally in the setting overall. For example, a charismatic and forceful police officer who acts as a key informant might be a good indication of the shared values of response car officers, but it is also equally possible that his attitudes are different from the rest of the team generally.

GOING NATIVE

Going native is a rather strange term, for one, it has rather unsavoury colonial and imperialist overtones (a throwback perhaps to ethnography's anthropological origins). The term refers to a researcher who becomes an active member of a group that they are studying and hence lose their ability to reflect on their researcher status and retain their objectivity. Recently, that criticism was made of Alice Goffman's work in *On the Run* (2014), but there are better historical examples. In his ethnography, *Vagrancy, Alcoholism and Social Control*, Peter Archard admits that his work went off track as he became alcohol dependant (Archard, 1979). Clearly there can be problems caused by a wholesale loss of objectivity and preventing this from happening is vital in good ethnographic research. The ethnographic criminologist is clearly being called upon to walk a fine line between being accepted by those who they study and maintaining a degree of detachment and an analytical mindset. However, we might legitimately ask, given that the whole point of ethnography is to see the world as one's participants do, how appropriate is it to criticise ethnography on the basis that the researcher has got very close? Certainly, we should be concerned about the researcher's potential to lose objectivity, but then that also assumes that the researcher entered into the field with that to lose.

THE HAWTHORNE EFFECT

Adler and Adler (1998) have argued that a central feature of observational methods such as participant observation is that it is 'non-interventionist', meaning that as far as they are concerned, the fieldworker should act so as not to manipulate or stimulate participants. For example, their view holds that the researcher should not ask the participants the research questions, pose tasks for them or deliberately create provocations. The reason for this is to ensure that the behaviour and interaction continue in the presence of a researcher just as they would normally. However, there is a debate to be had about whether or to what extent the presence of a researcher automatically changes things, because the presence of the fieldworker has an inevitable and unavoidable impact, and hence, the researcher's presence cannot be mitigated. The presence of a researcher impacting upon and altering participant behaviour is known as the Hawthorne effect (which is sometimes referred to as the observer effect). The term was coined in 1958 by Henry A. Landsberger when he was analysing earlier experiments from 1924–32 at the Hawthorne Works (a Western Electric factory outside Chicago). The Hawthorne Works commissioned an academic study to see if workers would become more productive in higher levels of light. The workers' productivity seemed to improve when changes were made and slumped when the study ended. Landsberger suggested that the productivity gain occurred not as a result of light levels but because of the motivational effect on the workers of the interest being shown in them, and hence the term became one that described how the observed individuals modified an aspect of their behaviour in response to their awareness of being observed.

TASK

QUESTIONS

- How can a researcher guard against 'going native'?
- In the field, how can you account for individuals acting to impress you? How might you take steps to verify how they behave? Are you aware of situations in which people have acted for you or put on a specific performance because they have a knowledge of your research interests?
- To what extent do you agree with Adler and Adler's (1998) notion that field researchers should actively be limiting their involvement or impact on the field?
- Given Adler and Alder's above view on researchers' limiting impact, what do you think their view would be of activist research?

CHAPTER SUMMARY

This chapter has sought to consider the advantages and pitfalls of doing criminological ethnography as fieldwork. I have introduced much of the core terminology required for fieldworkers and debated and discussed effective empirical work in ethnography.

FURTHER READING

There are so many good things to read on academic fieldwork that comprising a succinct list becomes a real challenge. A favourite pre-ethnography task I set students is to read John Van Maanen's article 'The asshole' (1978) based on the meaning of the word 'asshole' among the police officers he studied during his now classic ethnography in the 1970s. Van Maanen went through the police academy, rode along with them on patrols and was otherwise embedded with them for a year or so. This text perfectly demonstrates empirical, methodological and theoretically innovative work that stands the test of time. For some time now, criminologists have been calling for a 'reversal of the ethnographic gaze' and this has started to happen in some excellent texts that show how established ethnographers deal with the complexities of doing fieldwork. A longstanding favourite has been Ferrell and Hamm (eds) (1998) *Ethnography at the Edge: Crime, Deviance and Field Research*. Recent years have seen many compelling accounts of 'the self' in criminological research (e.g. Liebling, 1999; Ferrell, 2006; Phillips and Earle, 2010). However, for me, Jewkes (2011) 'Autoethnography and emotion as intellectual resources: doing prison research differently' is a refreshingly honest, candid and readable piece of reflection on researching prisons, whereas Wakeman (2014) 'Fieldwork, biography and emotion: doing criminological autoethnography' considers the world of drug use and crime in the community. Finally, Gary Armstrong's chapter 'Like that Desmond Morris?' in Hobbs and May (eds) (1993) *Interpreting the Field: Accounts of Ethnography*, on his time in a football hooligan gang is excellent, as is the book generally.

PART THREE

THE FOLLOW-UP

7
WRITING CRIMINOLOGICAL ETHNOGRAPHY

LEARNING OBJECTIVES

The aim of this chapter is to get readers to think about the process of recording ethnography, from the writing of fieldnotes to the presentation of ethnographic material. By the end of this chapter you should have a better understanding of:

- what information should be contained in fieldnotes and how they should be constructed and structured
- the processes of undertaking and recording information in and from interviews.

This chapter concerns the process of developing criminological ethnography and turning the process of fieldwork into a product. Although convention dictates that sections are separated and often processes are described in a linear, sequential manner, the reality of ethnography is absolutely nothing like that, and much of the writing of ethnography will occur in the field. Fieldwork is a difficult process, not only because it involves long days of interacting and observing, but also, at the end of that process it involves extra time writing, because convention holds (and it is good advice) that good, comprehensive fieldnotes that describe time in the field should be compiled as quickly and as contemporaneously as is practicable. To suggest that a criminological ethnographer will do the fieldwork, leave the field and then write up is not necessarily the case (few people would possess the memory to be able to do so) and hence fieldwork and writing are ongoing processes. Yet it also seems right that a text on ethnography should give some specific attention to writing, because the 'grapho' (to write), remains a vital aspect of the craft, even if more generally research and social research are placing perhaps less emphasis and stock on the traditional research-based monograph, and are becoming more accepting of how ethnographic fieldwork can create representations and data that are far wider than simply the words on a page.

Visual ethnography, performative ethnography, ethnography as film work and data gathered in ethnography that goes beyond mere text are becoming more common, although, this again reignites the potential for ethical issues and dilemmas. Of course, this was not traditionally the case. Few early social science and criminological works fully employ the term ethnography, but rather preferred the anthropological term participant observation. That situation is now commonly reversed and arguably, ethnography is employed more frequently whereas few academics now talk of participant observation in criminology. Of course, participant observation in social science research has a longstanding history as an unobtrusive method (there were exceptions, and more intrusive applications, but for the most part it seems fair to suggest that its practice had little impact on participants and subjects). In fieldwork, participant observation, however, has had a much shorter yet controversial existence. Its legitimacy as an appropriate data-gathering technique and a methodological approach for creating more ethical dilemmas in the field has been reviewed, debated and at times vehemently defended throughout the social sciences, in the field of anthropology. Yet critical debates around participant observation occurred until the 1940s, with a significant text concerning participant observation not published until the 1950s.

For fieldworkers, the central issues have always been defined around the meaning, practice and utility in making participant observations in situ. Therefore, participant observation is as much a personal orientation for the fieldworker as it is a professional approach for studying social life. Raymond Gold's classic 1958 article 'Roles in sociological field observations' exemplifies the near-obsessive nature of fieldworkers in their contemplation of the myriad social roles required of the participant observer. Gold suggested an observer role typology (complete observer, participant-as-observer, observer-as-participant and complete participant) based on a model developed working with Burford Junker at the University of Chicago in the early 1950s. It is not uncommon to see academic texts and textbooks on ethnography still use distinctions and categorical demarcations based on these distinct categories. Yet I would suggest that Gold's classic typology should be interpreted, and not used as a static categorical template, but rather as a barometer that enables fieldworkers to make informed choices concerning their own tolerance level for inherent ethical challenges. These challenges are especially heightened when fieldworkers are studying deviant and/or illegal communities and their members, according to the degree of their involvement in the lives of participants, and in relation to other tangential field decisions (e.g. access, reciprocity, time, confidentiality, personal biography, rapport, resources, etc.) that may impact the scope and duration of the study. Moreover, and this is a vital point, because criminological ethnography deals with participant observation of issues, settings and processes primarily involving issues of crime and its control, the notion of the ethnographer as some neutral observer who cannot have an impact on participants is naïve, and should be arduously resisted.

What I am suggesting is that because criminological ethnographers are dealing with the topic of crime, they must always be attuned to, and considerate of, how the very research that they do forms part of that process, and how it can be used in that very process. There is no such thing as the neutral, outside observer, because even if that is the embodied value that the researcher wishes to have, they can never simply be complete observer.

Participant observations are primarily recorded using fieldnotes, a tradition of note taking used for contextualising field events, meanings and social interactions. The recording of fieldnotes is a method for preserving the social-physical environment of a study's setting and its people and their respective behaviours. It facilitates both the immersion of the fieldworker in the local culture and an understanding of human relationships, in terms of both the researcher and research participants, unfolding in the setting. From jottings to more formal entries consisting of analytical memos, taxonomies, social network mapping, journals, blogs and video, fieldnotes facilitate the systematic collection and analysis of participant observations. They also offer a medium for preserving the nature of informal, often unscripted field conversations, a rather common occurrence in the field. Field conversations are just another form of interviews that are part and parcel of the fieldworker's toolkit.

FIELDNOTES AND RECORDING OBSERVATIONS: WHAT MAKES GOOD FIELDNOTES?

There are numerous ways of recording observational data and the process of fieldwork, and what is certain from the outset is that there is no right way, but more accurately, there is a way that is right for you. Most commonly in ethnographic fieldwork people will write fieldnotes, but there is a great deal of variation in how, when and where people will do this, what they will write and record. That point made though, fieldnotes perhaps should not be described or adjudged good simply because of process, because it is possible to imagine someone diligently recording fieldnotes in an administratively efficient and organised way, yet never having truly got to the real point of the process. What makes fieldnotes good is an understanding of what is being observed, and then including what is relevant. Textbooks on ethnography more generally, such as Hammersley and Atkinson (2007), argue that fieldnotes should consist of relatively concrete descriptions of social processes and their contexts. For example, in a research project carried out on prison violence, every witnessed incident of use of force or violent incident would be recorded in fieldnotes: what the

offenders were doing, what the staff where doing, what time of the day, where
the violence occurred, what was said, what happened, where the incident was
witnesses from, what feelings were elicited. The purpose is to give someone
who was not there, who did not see things, as contemporaneous and as holistic
a picture as it is possible to give. It is perhaps for that reason that some ethnographers have started to capture data in the field in the form of tape or video
recording (see below) although, again, such actions are context specific.

CASE STUDY

DICK HOBBS: *DOING THE BUSINESS*

If ethnographic criminologists were asked to select several ethnographies as favourite texts, we think it is a safe bet that quite a number would opt for Dick Hobbs
monograph based on his PhD research and published in 1988 as *Doing the Business*. Hobbs' book remains an accessible, utterly readable, wonderfully empathetic
yet theoretically rich portrayal of the cultures underpinning, and arguably uniting,
'entrepreneurial' police detectives and criminals in the East End of London during the high years of Thatcherism. Hobbs' ethnographic study involved participant
observation of the policed (petty criminals) and the police (the local CID) in the East
End of London. He pre-empts the text by talking about his own biography, utterly
rooted as it is to the milieu and the context that he describes. For him access came
in several ways, from friends and associates, where having trained as a teacher and
taught a youth football team were as important as kin networks and contacts cultivated through immersion in the field.

The central argument of Dick Hobbs' book is that a unique working-class and
entrepreneurial culture which stressed the individual role in being able to create
new opportunities had developed in the East End of London and, contrary to police
practice elsewhere, this distinctive culture also characterises the forms of social
control in the locality. The book, Hobbs (1988: 1) argues, is 'about both formal and
informal control strategies and the coercive regulatory power of the market place'.
Although it may be shelved alongside the growing number of studies on the police,
Hobbs is anxious to point out that it is not an analysis of policing. Rather, the activities of the police and the Criminal Investigation Division are studied from 'within
the urban milieu', which Hobbs (1988: 2) describes as 'a view of policing largely
from the point of view of the policed: policing from below'. The research, therefore,
is simultaneously a study of the policed and the police, both of whom are firmly
located in the East End and its culture. Yet Hobbs' book is so much more: tales of
late night drinking sessions with detectives and villains, one of criminology's best
and most memorable lines on the place of alcohol in some criminological ethnography, descriptions of phone calls from Sammy the Snout taken by his young
children, to recollections of curry paid for with stolen luncheon vouchers abound

in a book that now is perhaps more social history than it is sympathetic portrayal of the realities and complexities of policing crime in working-class locales. But Hobbs' text is also a brilliant reminder that while what is studied may have a high degree of congruence with the author, the best ethnographers make the familiar appreciable to an unfamiliar reader and do so in such a way that facilitates the construction of a clever and well-made argument more generally on how socio-economic, political and cultural mores shape individual practices. This world may no longer exist, but the principles and mores identified by Hobbs continue in any community where crime constructs the values below the surface, and *Doing the Business* remains a truly inspiring work that stands as a timeless vindication of how the ethnographic method can be used to consider crime.

QUESTIONS

- In *Doing the Business*, Hobbs is extremely overt about his own background and upbringing in the East End of London as a working-class male and how he came to academic work late having worked as an office boy, labourer, dustman and schoolteacher. Clearly, familiarity with a social milieu is important, but what specific advantages might it bring in terms of making the writing feel 'authentic'?
- Are there disadvantages to being a participant and ethnographer in a field that one has been born and raised in rather than entered into? If so, what do you think these are?
- In *Doing the Business*, Hobbs talks about drinking as part of the research, and gives a classic line that at times, with villains and detectives the next day he did not know whether to 'write it up or bring it up'. What are your thoughts on consuming alcohol while doing fieldwork?
- McAuley (2007) in *Out of Sight* goes a little further and admits to purchasing and sharing cocaine with the young people that he studies as well as acting as a chauffeur for them. What are your thoughts on this?

When writing fieldnotes speech should be recorded in a form which is close or as close to verbatim as possible. In this way, the ethnographer is seeking to capture the actual words that people are using, or what Hammersley and Atkinson (2007) term the participants' 'situated vocabularies'. In doing so, the researcher can comprehend and convey a sense of the setting as it is for the participants. If ethnography is writing about people then it should be that fieldnotes and field quotes evoke a sense of the field, so vivid descriptions that capture the social world well are the order of the day. In this way, when writing fieldnotes ethnographers might also want to record raised voices, when participants become animated or excited, again adding to the task of understanding the setting as it appears to participants. An injunction to reproduce, in a verbatim way, the sounds, sights, smells and feel of the field often mean that the researcher can take limited notes in the field, and it is best to write up full fieldnotes as soon as is possible and practicable, and this injunction has created some novel practices. For example, in *Part-Time Crime*, Ditton suggests that he retreated to the toilet in order to make contemporaneous scribbled fieldnotes (Ditton, 1977). Studying the Blades, Armstrong used a note pad, but noted that the taking of brief notes while with the lads in such a way did little to dampen the fears of a small minority that he was a 'copper's nark' (a police informer) (Armstrong, 1998). It ought to be remembered here that, as Yates (2004) has suggested, gaining a good enough level of immersion in the research site means that data can also attract the interest of the police. Indeed, several researchers have argued that the risks and dangers associated with researching crime primarily come from law enforcement agencies rather than from respondents (Polsky, 1967; Ferrell and Hamm 1998) and it ought to be remembered that it was the fieldnotes that academic Bradley Garrett made that in part were used to build a criminal prosecution against him, and also some of his participants.

Fieldnotes should not only include records of conversations but also details of the setting in which conversations took place. Such details should arguably contain information about:

- space: the physical place or places involved
- actor(s): the people involved
- activity: a set of related acts, what people are doing
- acts: single actions people do
- event: a set of related activities that people carry out
- time: the sequencing that takes place over time
- goal(s): what it is that people are attempting to accomplish
- feelings: the emotions felt and expressed
- exteroceptive senses: smell can be important, as can sound.

However, with fieldnotes, researchers and particularly those new to the field can find that they try to record everything, when only some details are actually important. That the carpet in a bar is sticky with spilled larger and that the duke box works only intermittently can start to set a scene perfectly, so too can unwashed glasses and a description of the barman, but what the researcher should be doing in initially compiling fieldnotes is gaining an aide-memoire. Too much in the form of fieldnotes can create an impossible burden for the researcher to subsequently deal with, and what might be important from the bar example above is only a little bit of conversation in the course of a day that talks about the general community and its permissive attitude to stolen property. That might be captured and detailed from all of five minutes in a full afternoon spent among people.

INTERVIEWS

By far the most popular methods in ethnographic research are participant observation and unstructured interviewing, as these tend to be the main stuff of ethnography. Ethnography is not only 'writing about the people', but it is all of the steps one takes, from asking questions of humanity and human social relations to observing, interacting with, interviewing, and in other ways documenting humans as they live their daily lives. It is the jotting of notes on everything one notices, the expanding of these notes each night into thicker descriptions and accounts, and even includes the analysing and writing up of one's findings. Ethnography is a multi-method research sensibility, a human-conducted examination of what humans do and say and think and believe, what they mean by what they do and say and think and believe, and why any of this might matter. Interviews are commonly the best way of finding out what people think and feel.

TAKING IT FURTHER

A surprisingly frequent question that is asked by students when embarking on qualitative research studies involves the practicalities of how much data to gather, and specifically, I am often asked 'how many interviews' by criminology students embarking on empirical work for undergraduate dissertations and as part of postgraduate studies.

The answer to this does not often please, but I often refer students to the National Centre for Research Methods review paper, 'How many qualitative interviews is enough?' (Baker and Edwards, 2012) as a starting point. They elicited answers from influential figures such as Patricia and Peter Adler, Les Back, Howard S. Becker and Norman Denzin. The text is freely available and makes useful background reading.

The riposte to the question of 'how many' from most the experts they sought out was largely, 'it depends'. In considering what it depends upon, however, the responses offered a range of guidance on the epistemological, methodological and practical issues to consider when conducting research projects. However, the general feeling is that such issues are not simply about attaching a numerical threshold.

When it comes to students, however, I point out that interviews can give far more depth than some people consider, and I certainly know of PhDs built on relatively few interviews, such as those using the life history method and only around a dozen participants. However, in such circumstances, there are often several lengthy interviews transcribed verbatim, and each participant is revisited on three or four occasions. The point is, the base must be appropriate to the claims being made and must be robust and defensible. Therefore, rather than 'how many interviews', perhaps the question needs to be reframed as 'what should I do to ensure a robust and representative data set?'

There are principally normally said to be three interview styles that interviewers conform to depending on the type of research, the expectations of participants (or access gatekeeping organisations, including universities, ethics committees and IRBs), and the external circumstances of a project. Most textbooks distinguish between structured, semi-structured and unstructured interviews:

> **Structured interview**: where approved questions that are pre-determined or ordained are put to the interview participant in a similarly ordered manner. The researcher does not add, amend or change questions, but rather follows the formal layout with the wording and the ordering of the questions as scripted preserved, usually to ensure a degree of standardisation across different interviewees.

> **Unstructured interview**: a much more free flowing and unconstrained exchange that tends to be the opposite of the structured approach, allowing the interviewer a degree of freedom in guiding the discussion. The interviewer may have a rough guide of topic or themes that will be covered in the course of the interview. The interview itself is likely to be more conversation like with the researcher inserting questions and following potential interesting emergent lines of inquiry.

> **Semi-structured interview**: can contain elements or a blend of both structured and unstructured interviews, so the interview may commence with a set of preliminary questions that attempt to elicit demographic detail, for example in a prison it might involve establishing someone's age, offence type, length of sentence, antecedent history, before moving to a less structured discussion of opinions and views and hence allow themes to be explored in more depth (for example, tell me what it is like in here?).

Academic discussions on interviews often describe them as either structured or unstructured, from fully structured to semi-structured to completely unstructured (it is normally the latter of these that are the stuff of ethnography). While a structured interview follows a prescribed list of questions, and a semi-structured interview is structured in so far as it designed around a loose set of questions and minimally guided, an unstructured interview often is nearest to an unguided process that merely commences with an opening question, 'So tell me what your role is?' or 'Tell me all about yourself'. For example, Crewe (2009) has noted the richness of the data he gathered from lengthy hanging around and interviewing prisoners in HMP Wellingborough in just this way, asking about the individuals' lives, and so such questions might, for example, be appropriately asked of prisoners in police custody or prison settings or those in criminal justice roles. Comparing structured and unstructured interviews, we can observe that while structured interviews aim to explain behaviour within pre-established categories, unstructured interviews aim to understand the complex behaviour of members of a society without imposing any *a priori* categorisation that would close down or limit the potential field of inquiry. Hence, unstructured interviews adopt an emic approach whereas structured interviews follow an etic approach.

However, while several texts on ethnography discuss interviews and conversations, perhaps a core difference in ethnographic interviewing is how the field setting and the context should properly determine the quality of interaction and how in-depth conversation that arises out of the context of well-established, longer term relationships is different from interviewing people based on other forms of access. It is the depth of conversation in field settings that can give 'ethnographer and respondent time to delve more deeply, to express their feelings to reflect on events and beliefs, and to expose their ambivalences' (O'Reilly, 2009: 125). In the places participants live their lives there may be all manner of cultural cues that open up new sources of understanding, and that perhaps is one of the traditional differences separating ethnography from qualitative research more broadly

The important element then in ethnography is that, for the most part, interviews are built upon a more sustained and developed relationship and knowledge about the interview subject than might be expected in the normal style of qualitative inquiry. This is undoubtedly the case in criminology as a subject more broadly, where there is, for example, sometimes a reliance upon qualitative approaches generally, but not the immersive requirements that are held as standard for most criminological ethnographers. It is not uncommon for criminological researchers to employ qualitative methods in pursuit of data, and yet, there is a great deal of difference, for example, in interviewing a drug user arrested and held in police custody and undertaking an interview with someone who has been known for several months through the process of getting close to them and spending time with them. For example, there is a stark difference in the level of understanding that is conveyed in brief qualitative studies when contrasted with, say, Daniel Briggs work on crack cocaine users in south London. Briggs is clearly a skilled ethnographer, and his account gives us a real understanding of the lives of the participants in his study, which does not condemn or romanticise, but gets to grips with the realities in a manner that can only be gained in a range of settings and contexts, including giving some fairly harrowing descriptions of the physical impacts of hard drug addictions (Briggs, 2011). This is why it becomes difficult to draw the line between interviewing and ethnography, because ethnography must be more than participant observation and conversation alone, as Burns notes, true ethnography aims to examine and explore socio-cultural activities in a particular group and culture, and to meet these aims ethnographers as a necessity ought be involved in both observing and interviewing. Moreover, as O'Reilly (2009) notes, the core differentiation between ethnographic interviewing and other forms of interviewing is it is built on the context of established relationships (or what we would call established commonalities) rather than merely the normal interviewer–interviewee power imbalance.

TASK

Read either of the following articles:

Ancrum, C. and Treadwell, J. (2016) 'Beyond ghosts, gangs and good sorts: commercial cannabis cultivation and illicit enterprise in England's disadvantaged inner cities', *Crime, Media, Culture*, , 13 (1): 69–84.

or:

Contreras, R. (2008) '"Damn, yo – who's that girl?" An ethnographic analysis of masculinity in drug robberies', *Journal of Contemporary Ethnography*, 38 (4): 465–492.

Now consider these questions:

- How do you think that the researchers are able to make judgements of the veracity of the statements being made by informants?
- Do you think that the same level of veracity could be gathered from individuals held in custody, or as part of a qualitative project that sought to interview offenders on probation with their consent?
- To what extent is the researchers background and biography likely to have been important in allowing them to elicit information in interviews?
- To what extent do Ancrum and Treadwell or Contreras reflect their subjects' views? Which views are their own?

LIFE HISTORIES

Life history allows the researcher to explore a person's micro-historical (individual) experiences within a macro-historical (history of the time) framework. Life history information challenges the researcher to understand an individual's current attitudes and behaviours and how they may have been influenced by initial decisions made at another time and in another place. Life history as a qualitative research method has been used intermittently as a part of criminology but is often linked with ethnography. As quantitative methods more generally gained popularity in sociology of the 1960s and 1970s, the life history method fell into disrepute as a research method in academia. That has again shifted because at heart a core element of the approach is repeated interviews, with the aim of building comprehensive data which seeks to convince the subject to tell the story of his or her life, in their own words. This is also called the 'narrative' research method, and hence, it is arguably reprieved somewhat as part of the aims of contemporary 'narrative criminology'.

Narrative criminology adopts a constitutive approach to the relationship between stories and crime, that is, the narrative itself, as opposed to the events and circumstances reported in the narrative, where the fact that people's stories may be fabricated, in part or whole, poses less of a dilemma. For narrative criminologists, individuals' stories need not recall actual lived experience in order to motivate storytellers and mobilise those who hear their stories. Narrative holds a particular meaning within narrative criminology and narrative studies generally. This is, however, arguably slightly different from the understanding of life history in ethnography where issues of veracity and accuracy are important because ethnography is claiming, at least in part, to give voice to reality; narrative criminology conceives of a world where experience is always storied and where action advances or realises the story (Presser and Sandberg, 2015: 289).

However, narrative criminology does not hold the monopoly on life history. Others such as Presdee and Goodey have argued for the importance of biography for the discipline's interpretation of people's (and in Goodey's case essentially men's) criminal lives and identities, proposing that criminological research can be usefully developed from the single 'life story accounts' of the individual's relationship to 'crime' within broad socio-structural contexts (Goodey, 2000: 473). The use of life history continues to greater and lesser extents in criminology, although arguably a retreat from considering the aetiology of crime from the 1970s onwards has meant that the life history method is perhaps one that is less used today. Occasionally ethnographies are built around central figures such as with the case of 'Vincent' in Carl B. Klockars *The Professional Fence* (1974). Also, British oral historian Tony Parker, whose work was dedicated to giving a voice to British and American society's most marginalised figures, including *The Unknown Citizen* (1963), *The Twisting Lane: Some Sex Offenders* (Parker, 1969), *The Frying Pan: A Prison and its Prisoners* (Parker, 1970), *Life After Life: Interviews with Twelve Murderers* (Parker, 1990) and *The Violence Of Our Lives: Interviews with Life-Sentence Prisoners in America* (Parker, 1995).

CASE STUDY

CLIFFORD R. SHAW: *THE JACK-ROLLER*

Shaw's book *The Jack-Roller* (first published in 1930) tells the story of 'Stanley', the pen name Shaw gave to Michael Peter Majer, who was sixteen years old when he first met Shaw in 1923 (when Shaw was twenty-six) (Shaw, 1930: 1). Shaw's book is essentially the autobiography of a teenage mugger at the centre of a

(Continued)

(Continued)

sociological casebook. Shaw contributed just three chapters to the text and implemented a five-year social treatment programme to reform the young man. The autobiography was the centrepiece of an urban ethnological research project that was funded by a state agency but published by the University of Chicago Press, a private university: 'The case is published to illustrate the value of the "own story" in the study and treatment of the delinquent child' (1930: 1).

The delinquent author signed an agreement with the sociologist to receive 7 per cent royalties and to retain the copyright to the life history. *The Jack-Roller* is the most well-known offender and the text is a classic in criminology, which initially claimed reformation of Stanley had been achieved. Interestingly, *The Jack-Roller at Seventy: A Fifty-Year Follow-Up* (Snodgrass, 1982) reveals more of the history of 'Stanley', who had by then been re-imprisoned for attempted armed robbery one year after the publication of the original study in 1930. He was institutionalised in a state hospital, on and off the violent ward, for five years during the mid-1940s and twice escaped. While it is now controversial, not least because of lingering questions about the ethics of the project, the accuracy of some claims, and the questions concerning the level of exploitation of socially vulnerable subjects in the research process, *The Jack-Roller* helped to establish the life history or 'own story' as an important instrument in sociological research. The fact that since its publication it has never been out of print is probably indicative of how significant it was and remains in criminology. Moreover, how it should be read and theorised continues to inspire criminologists, for example, Gadd and Jefferson have revisited the text as a means of attempting to test and assert the value of their psychoanalytically informed psychosocial criminology (Gadd and Jefferson, 2007).

RECORDING IN THE FIELD: TO TAPE OR NOT TO TAPE?

Sometimes researchers record fieldnotes, but taping interviews has the potential to chill the scene and impact directly on what the researcher might be able to generate. That said, tapes can be useful in so far as a good transcription service can turn tapes around very quickly, and the time investment to tape record and then transcribe interviews can be a substantial part of any project. Some researchers would never have others transcribe their works, believing that listening to tapes brings a better familiarity with data, whereas some criminological ethnographers would never entertain introducing a tape-recording of the topic, especially given the complex ethical issues involved in dealing with offenders. Some criminological ethnographers, recognising data are negotiated in the research setting, would prefer that recordings of data are not made as part of the guarantees that they give participants, but that does not mean that some of the most interesting ethnographers researching the most sensitive of topics do not tape, and sometimes covertly (Contreras, 2013).

CHAPTER SUMMARY

Researching and writing ethnography is an experiential and embodied practice, and in Clifford Geertz's classic phrasing, we expect it to be composed of 'thick description'. Of course, what counts as thickness shifts over the years and across different decades and across theoretical and methodological approaches, but one thing that remains constant in criminological ethnography is a deep commitment to realism. Whether non-fiction or fiction, prose or poetry, ethnography is a realist genre that comes to life through the presentation of written text that is made in the field and in interaction. Wakeman's term 'lyrical criminology' (Wakeman, 2014) evokes this, in that great song lyrics create an image in the reader's mind, and what ethnographers are seeking to do is to be a bridge into the field for those who were not there, but wish to know more.

FURTHER READING

A useful anthropological account of ethnography is George Marcus and Dick Cushman (1982) 'Ethnographies as texts', in which they review the state of ethnographic writing at the time of and following the discipline-changing work by Geertz (1973) *The Interpretation of Cultures*. There are great writers and great descriptions in all sorts of genres, from true crime and journalism to written fiction. The more you read the better you will be at writing. A good ethnographer is not just a good fieldworker but someone who presents the realities evocatively with a clarity and a good turn of phrase.

8

IMPACTFUL CRIMINOLOGICAL ETHNOGRAPHY

LEARNING OBJECTIVES

This chapter considers the impacts of ethnography, but in doing this it seeks to better understand the process of evaluating field data and making sense of data that is gathered. By the end of this chapter you should have a better understanding of:

- how criminological ethnography contributes to and impacts, in the broadest sense, debates on crime and crime control
- how criminological ethnographers analyse field data
- the concepts of grounded theory and reflexivity
- the notion of longitudinal ethnography against instant ethnography, and debates about how meaning and understanding come together.

By now you will be alert to many of the debates and controversies that surround qualitative research methodologies. With roots in sociology and anthropology, criminological ethnography is one qualitative approach and is concerned with learning about people, in contrast to studying people, through immersion. Traditionally ethnography is characterised by in-depth observation of groups of individuals, being cognisant of the influences of historical and cultural contexts on social interactions. Hence it is a longstanding argument that the process of ethnographic immersion in the real world context and detailed analysis it generates enables the researcher to discover and describe the complexities and shared cultural nuances of the social world, and to interpret the meaning of the phenomenon under investigation. Yet that misses perhaps a final point, and a place where debate is most vital, for traditionally those ascribing themselves to and promoting the practice of ethnography did so in a way which was clearly mindful of the criminological ethnographer's place only as a source of meaning. Those, like Polsky (1967), sought to be not an agent for law enforcement or a driver of social change, but simply a documenter of social practices. Yet if doing ethnography in criminology is a process of 'discovery through fieldwork' (Rice and Maltz, 2018) then a further question arguably remains. Discovery to what end? Do we have to ask, what is the point of ethnography?

This I would aver is not some exercise in academic navel gazing at the end of a project where I have already taken much of the readers time with what are quite complex and difficult debates and perspectives, but rather, is a vital question, particularly at the present moment. On one hand, qualitative methods more broadly (and ethnography specifically) seem to be undergoing something of a resurgence in popularity in the social sciences and specifically in a buoyant and growing academic criminology. It is partly for this reason, and because of a raft of studies and publications that have shifted ethnography from peripheral and marginal pursuit to one at the very centre of the discipline and discourse, that I elected to use the term 'criminological ethnography' and craft an introductory text. Yet at precisely the very moment that happens, I also ought to ask whether there is the very real possibility that making the argument that there is a criminological ethnography starts to undermine the unique quality of ethnography, as a social science and qualitative research approach. On one hand, there have never been so many good, reflexive accounts of ethnography being produced, and yet, by extension, what specifically constitutes ethnography and separates it ontologically and epistemologically from a raft of qualitative techniques becomes ever more questionable as the approach gains ever greater acceptance across a broad criminological community.

WHAT IS IMPACTFUL ETHNOGRAPHY?

In UK universities, the assessment of research quality and effectiveness, the Research Excellence Framework (REF), is increasingly focusing on research impact alongside the more traditional appraisal via publications in the top-ranking academic journals. In this quest for international and ground-breaking contributions in all subjects, adjudged by an internationalisation agenda and a quest for originality, significance and rigour and adjudging value based on continuous advancement, one might think ethnography very valuable. Clearly it can tell us much about the real world and what is happening. However, against that general trend the tendency to see ethnography as restricted to local cultural and small-scale material contexts, rather than being generalizable, means that it also is at risk of further marginalisation against perhaps more conventional large scale statistical and quantitative projects.

As part of the assessment and grading of research encountered in exercises such as the UK's REF the appraisal of research in terms of its impact, or impacts, is becoming ever more common. The term 'impact' in academia is one that has been selected to describe the notion that it is possible to consider the benefit of research to society, outside of academia and simply in terms of the creation of academic knowledge. It is interesting, however, if we consider this emerged agenda against the history of a participant agenda with simply the desire to ask broadly 'what is going on here?' (Spradley, 1980). 'Impact' as conventionally understood in higher education in the UK is the heading that seeks to consider how academic research contributes to the world, such as 'improves our health and wellbeing', 'creates economic prosperity', 'enhances our cultural lives' and 'improves environmental sustainability'. Moreover, the rise of concern with impact was also unarguably linked with a drive in the UK for a notional accountability for public spending on research (whether impact in any way secures this is a different question, given that for the most part what it ensures is a distribution of funds where most goes to the established and richest universities) but notionally, given that around £1.5 billion per year of taxpayers' money goes to fund research in higher education institutions, the idea and notion of impact attempts to pose the question: what is the return on that investment, for the taxpayer and the public?

It is now common for those seeking research funding to be asked to show that their research will have some form of 'impact', in short that research has some societal value, that it will impact upon policy, or the economy, or that it will have some wider value or benefit. It is now difficult to conceive of those in higher education being able to transcend these concerns, as the impact agenda has increasingly become centralised in UK higher education. Academics have been increasingly expected to demonstrate their broader engagement with the world and the evidence-related outcomes of their work. This change has profound implications for our universities and for the staff within them. Research impact undeniably now constitutes a significant section of the grant application processes for major UK funding councils. Today, obtaining core research funding (largely distributed based on REF scores) and project-specific research funding through making research bids are now both strongly dependent on researchers' abilities to respond adequately to questions about the broader (non-academic) value of their work, and similarly all manner of factors from university league table positions to individuals job retention can come to depend on it. The world of going to look at something because you are interested and think it worthwhile are largely gone. Instead, before you ever set out to undertake research you are likely to have to predict what future impact it will have, and plan pathways to best recognise that goal.

How social science research contributes to solving real world problems has always been a concern for researchers. Few people study social ills like crime or poverty without wishing to contribute to policies and programmes which help those so affected. Ethnographies are works of deep research based on in-depth, open-ended interviews and keen observations of how people go about their lives in different contexts. Researchers often spend years in their research sites to get to know the people and places they study in a way that can't be done using other methods. Classic ethnographies are (or arguably were) the most visible and relatable research products that academics have to offer the general public. The best tell stories about our social world backed up by rigorously gathered data. But ethnography is not always well supported by the emergent research agenda, which is increasingly instrumental, focused, bureaucratic and risk averse, and if this is true for ethnography generally, it is undoubtedly the case when it comes to criminology.

While ethnographers are very much expert in their research domains, their work is increasingly subject to public scrutiny. It is important for sociologists to develop and maintain professional standards that allow them to conduct the best research without compromising quality in the face of potential criticism and controversy. A conversation about the proper form of ethnography has emerged (Lubet, 2018) and a number of important issues have featured in this conversation, but I do not intend to revisit this topic here. Instead, I contend that the strength of ethnography, and its criminological and deviance focused variant, is how in-depth interviews and participant observation obtain real, textured insights into social phenomenon. However, despite this, it is fair to suggest that some ethnographic researchers try to invoke the reliability of quantitative methods by shrouding themselves in numbers as a way to legitimise their work. They offer up the number of interviews, the number of hours, weeks and years spent in the field and they propose bigger and bigger samples. Even as qualitative researchers assert that they have carried out in-depth qualitative research, they often revert to the language of quantitative research, of numbers, to defend, justify and legitimise their work. The nod to numbers as a way of claiming trustworthiness and, importantly, scientific expertise, which is usually equated with quantitative methods, is odd, and perhaps the really important issue that gets lost here is what is good data and what is good ethnography? Is good ethnography dependent on large sample sizes? Is this seeking of legitimacy through quantification simply a distortion of where the value of qualitative research truly lies? I say largely that it is a distortion, just as the notion of planned impact might be valuable, so too the predictability of impact and social benefits is hard to quantify on occasion. So perhaps we need to return to a consideration of what makes for good ethnography, and what good ethnography can do.

Instead, it is the depth of qualitative data that determines the quality of the work. Qualitative methods have the capacity to illuminate meaning – particularly the micro level nuances of attitudes and daily behaviours. Qualitative research can highlight the impact of large scale social structural forces on the rituals of daily life as well as many other spheres of life. This depth may in fact be linked to a larger number of interviews, or to more time spent in the field, but it should not be reducible to this. Besides such 'participant observation', most of what ethnographers do is writing, writing, writing. Not just finished books or articles, but field-notes, be they scrawled notes in mobile phones, in a jotter pad or typed on to a laptop, with the end aim of producing a study that will give understanding to others. Ethnography, then, is straying out of our comfort zone in order to understand another social world. It is a messy, fuzzy, tough and a sometimes risky and danger-prone line of business. Arguably in telling these human stories about the realities of crime, criminological ethnographers share something that is not wholly dissimilar to journalism and particularly investigative and new journalism (and it ought to be remembered that Robert Park was once a journalist) and if the lines between journalism and ethnography were ever and always slightly blurred, then the 'Gonzo' journalism of the likes of Hunter S. Thompson (1967) in Hells Angels has blurred the lines between the two further still. Yet ethnography is not a jour-nalistic exposé, and ethnographers may be better placed to avoid simplification and sensationalism that can serve as imperatives in the sale of mass media. Rather than search out facts in the story, good ethnographers aim to uncover something deeper about how a society or subculture works – and it does so by changing perspective to that of the insider. We must suspend disbelief and shift our gaze: what is the world really like when you experience it? How did it look, feel and seem? What truly matters is that emic and etic understandings frame the topic.

Yet in introducing ethnography and returning to writing, I make an important point: writing, good writing and good story telling, is at the heart of good ethnography. Another clear distinction between academics and journalists is that only journalists truly get paid to write for a living, though many academics forget this and use the description 'journalistic' as if it is an insult (I know, I have had it happen to me, but I take it as quite a compliment). Perhaps good journalism can positively influence ethnography or academic ethnographers, who must increasingly exist in a world where the accessibility and 'impact' of their work are likely to be key considerations.

DATA ANALYSIS IN CRIMINOLOGICAL ETHNOGRAPHY

In ethnography data analysis is sometimes described as 'the messy business of making sense of it all' (O'Reilly, 2009: 13). However, perhaps the term 'messy' is the most overused descriptor of the sometimes untidy or inconvenient reali-ties of qualitative research. Quantitative research can arguably be just as messy, but it is rare to see such metaphors employed there. Additionally we might want to ask whether continuing to stress the messy nature of data analysis in qualitative research contributes to the marginalisation of qualitative research, for equally why should data analysis in ethnography not be significant, rigorous, systematic, comprehensive and convincing?

While some advice textbooks on the topic of qualitative methods and ethnography regard data analysis as a distinct phase in its own right, others discuss it alongside interpretation and presentation of ethnographic data (Brewer, 2000). While every social science will involve a range of data, the ethnographer will collect a great deal of data in the field simply because conversational and field data tend to be so extensive (thick in detail and description). In a prison-based project I undertook with a colleague each tape recorded interview we undertook lasted between 1 and 2 hours, but transcribed this can generate anything between 30 to 50 pages of verbatim transcripts. If there are 40 or 50 interviews, it can quickly become apparent that there will be a lot of data to analyse. For example, Brewer suggests that he collected over three thousand pages of typed fieldnotes in [a] study of routine policing by the RUC, contained in over half a dozen large box files, and over 92 hours of tape recordings in [an] ethnography of crime, plus other fieldnotes and material. He goes on to note that 'Bulk and complexity thus both characterise ethnographic data' (Brewer, 2000: 105). Indeed, in this way ethnographic data is unlike that gathered in other social science because:

- data come in the form of extracts that use the language and terminology found in the field
- data are personal in terms of making sense to the researcher
- data can be generalised, although those generalisations are regarded as limited in scope to specific macro context
- data tend to be extensive and potentially overly detailed.

While most ethnographers work from an interpretivist standpoint, and tend to regard analysis as subjective and inductive, what unites most good ethnography as good research is that it is both systematic and rigorous. While few ethnographers accept a scientific standing for their analysis (although it ought to be noted, there is a growing drive to see the methods of qualitative data analysis made more transparent and scientific – see Lubet, 2018).

Good data analysis is, of course, dependent on good data collection. While it is common that these elements of an ethnographic process are regarded as distinct stages, again, this is simplistic. Data is analysed throughout the fieldwork process. As the first data emerge, researchers often tend to read over fieldnotes and interview transcripts to search for emerging themes. Throughout the data collection process, researchers often consider the research questions, reflecting on them and trying to figure out what interesting themes are surfacing. This analysis is almost always a pattern of discerning a focus (and letting go of other, interesting questions). Again, while ethnographers may have entered the field with concerns and a focus, this may be refined as they continue in their studies.

However, while there are numerous texts dedicated to the subject of data analysis of qualitative data, and the different approaches that may be taken to it, that range from quite generalist to extremely specialist, I am aware that a frequently asked question is: if a study aims to be purely an ethnographic study, what explicit modes of analysis must be used (if at all)? And relatedly, should researchers include an element of computer-assisted data analysis?

HOW DO CRIMINOLOGISTS ANALYSE QUALITATIVE DATA?

While there is no single correct way of analysing data, as it is a quite subjective process, there are a number of conventions that are normally followed in criminological ethnography, and in all good qualitative research analysis. As I suggest in the introductory chapters, research tends to follow rules and laws, even if on occasion these can be ignored or broken. Despite the multiple variations in perspectives concerning how data is conceived and analysed in ethno-graphy (which are premised on individuals' ontological and epistemological viewpoints) all ethnographers tend to seek to share the intent to bring order to the data that they have gathered (Brewer, 2000). To this end, in terms of practicalities, the data analysis process generally follows a relatively conventional path:

- the original research question is reiterated and comes to the fore
- the insights concerning the data, and their subsequent analysis that will have been formed in fieldwork.

From that point, further analytical insights come often in a process of data analysis that occurs fully once the researcher has left or exited the field, thereby creating a degree of space between the physical process of data gathering and fieldwork, and data analysis. This data analysis is a series of steps that are followed, sequentially, and given the extensive nature of ethnographic data, they are often time consuming and laborious (another reason that they are best undertaken when the researcher has disengaged from fieldwork). The steps followed as a general rule are:

- data management (the data are organised into manageable units)
- coding (indexing the data into categories or themes)
- content analysis (re-reading the data and analysing the content)
- qualitative description (identifying key events, people, behaviours, activities, providing vignettes)

- establishing 'patterns' in the data (looking for recurring themes)
- developing a systematic way of classifying and generating ideas/theories.

Different academics give different prominence and different terminologies to these constituent elements, but in essence, the process is relatively straight-forward. The process largely begins with index coding, that is, the data is read and re-read and the material is assigned to codes, where data begin to be ordered into topics which are then categorised. Say, for example, one has material generated from an ethnography of a youth gang. Index codes might be terms such as relationships, violence, crime, drugs, victimisation, margin-alisation, terms which essentially allow data to be grouped together and later revisited as one, and the ethnographer will know where each reference to that topic appears in the broad body of data. However, given that the aim of ethno-graphic research in particular is a desire not simply to describe, but to describe the prevailing structures, attitudes, behaviours and practices in a group in light of the prevailing socio-economic, political and cultural context, analysis requires more than simply coding the data and putting it out there under themes. The researcher searches for patterns in the data. Some ethnographers then move to create either typologies or taxonomies, for example as is encountered in Elijah Anderson's *Code of the Street* (1999) where he describes how the culture of the street thrives and often defeats decency because it controls public spaces, so that individuals with higher, better aspirations are often entangled in the code and its self-destructive behaviours, and separates out street culture from that of normal, decent behaviour. That tendency is also seen in texts such as Ken Pryce's *Endless Pressure* (1979) where he con-trasts 'stable-law abiding' orientations of some people with the expressive-disreputable character of others and separates off his black, West Indian heritage subjects into various groups: 'hustlers', 'teenyboppers' 'proletarian respectable' 'saints' and 'mainliners'. Groups such as police officers and pris-ons staff may already be separated into taxonomies even by those working with them, and hence it is possible for these existing types and roles to be employed as part of the process.

While there are various ways that data can be coded, there are also prefer-ences in terms of how the process is done. Some ethnographers now use com-puter packages such as NVivo, which is a qualitative data analysis (QDA) computer software package produced by QSR International. It has been designed for qualitative researchers working with very rich text-based and/or multimedia information, where deep levels of analysis on small or large vol-umes of data are required. It is common to see projects coded using the 'Node' functions in the QSR NVivo 11 Software, and such skills can be relatively easily learned as part of methods training.

Again, whether this is used depends upon the project and the researcher who can use the package to test theories, identify trends and cross-examine information in a multitude of ways using its search engine and query functions. They can make observations in the software and build a body of evidence. However, while it allows for an array of research methodologies and can be useful in coding and analysing data, many good contemporary ethnographers still prefer less advanced methods such as printed transcripts, highlighter pens, and their own unique systems of coding. Much like tape recording, opinions vary, but it is certain that for large scale projects and substantial data sets, such programmes can be very useful.

While there is a range of research methods with different means of analysing data, it seems uncontroversial to suggest that the dominant one in ethnography tends to be grounded theory, which is now so heavily identified with ethnographic data analysis and research that it strikes as relatively unusual when an ethnographer does not mention the term. Indeed, the external observer could quite easily get the impression that the two are synonymous, and an array of criminological researchers claim to use 'grounded theory' as the epistemological framework for analysing data. Indeed it is probably one of the most common terms to see deployed in discussions of analysis in criminological ethnographies.

GROUNDED THEORY

Grounded theory is a systematic methodology involving the construction of theories through methodical gathering and analysis of data. Associated with Barney Glaser and Anselm Strauss and their book *The Discovery of Grounded Theory*, first published in 1967, and underpinned by several participant observation studies, the term 'grounded theory' essentially describes a research methodology and approach to data analysis that operates inductively, in contrast to the hypothetico-deductive approach. A study using grounded theory is likely to begin with a question, or even just with the collection of qualitative data. As researchers review the data collected, repeated ideas, concepts or elements become apparent and are tagged with codes (researchers call this process coding), which have been extracted from the data. As more data are collected, and re-reviewed, these codes can be grouped into concepts, and then into categories. These categories may become the basis for new theory which is crafted from bottom upward. Thus, grounded theory is quite different from the traditional model of research, where the researcher chooses an existing theoretical framework, and only then collects data to show how the theory does or does not apply to the phenomenon under study. Hence, from an ethnographic perspective, the most important component of grounded theory would probably be 'theoretical sampling' where you use fieldnotes and memos to keep track of your emerging theoretical insights, and then select further additional types of observations (or interviews), based on what would do the most to advance your current insights.

However, there is a range of ways that ethnographic and participant observational and qualitative interview data can be coded. The grounded theory method does not aim for the 'truth' but rather to conceptualise what is going on by using empirical research. In a way, the grounded theory method resembles what many researchers do when retrospectively formulating new hypotheses to fit data. However, when applying the grounded theory method, the researcher does not formulate the hypotheses in advance. Yet there are problems with grounded theory for some academics. For example, some have argued that the grounded theory method offers nothing more than a procedure for inventing ideas. It is, quite simply put, a justification for a way or style of generating theory, related to some topic currently under observation, which is then prioritised and made more valid than others. In part this criticism holds that ideas can be invented in a multitude of ways and there is nothing in grounded theory that gives any logical reason to prefer its procedures as a basis for inventing, and more significantly for preference between competing theories. It therefore offers only one method for devising patterns in data. Furthermore, critics of grounded theory suggest that what makes theory of value is not the method used to generate it, but a subsequent stage, that theories developed are then re-tested, but often this is the opposite of what many adherents and users of grounded theory actually do. Critics also note that researchers should search vigorously for disconfirming evidence to the emerging ideas.

What is certain is that many of the debates around how to analyse ethnography are conducted in a manner that is not necessarily welcoming, comprising of highly technical and jargonistic language and terminology that can simply be impenetrable, even to some of the most practised field researchers. What is important is that those undertaking ethnography remember that the task is not simple description of phenomena under study or the events in the field site, but that ethnography as a an academic exercise must engage with theory, and it must always remain alert to the social, economic, political, cultural and technological contexts that give rise to and shape the activities and practices that are witnessed. The ethnographer is crafting a critical piece of inquiry that is seeking to illuminate and shed light on far more than behaviour and inter-group dynamics and interactions.

REFLEXIVITY

Impactful ethnography is not only that which is academic, theoretical and convincing, it is also work that recognises the author's role within it, as part of the process of production and as impactful on the findings generated. As Hobbs notes, the production of the ethnographer's criminological text may change the way that the world considers the subject, but it will also unarguably impact on the way the academic world looks at the author (Hobbs, 1993: 63).

In epistemology, and more specifically the sociology of knowledge, reflexivity refers to circular relationships between cause and effect, especially as it is embedded in human belief structures. A reflexive relationship is bidirectional, and one where both the cause and the effect affect one another in a reciprocal relationship in which neither can be assigned as causes or effects. In sociology generally, reflexivity refers to an act of self-reference where examination or action affects the entity instigating the action (or examination). It commonly refers to the capacity of an individual to recognise and alter their place in the social structure. In social science research methodology, it has a similar meaning, but is simplified to essentially describe the process of thinking carefully about who has done the research and how, under what conditions, how it was written, by whom, and what impact these might have on the value of the ethnography produced. Commonly, ethnographers perform and promote reflexivity by discussing how their research may reflect interests or biases that accompany their positions in hierarchies of domination.

Reflexivity in ethnography is a popular, yet complex process, which attempts to analyse personal, intersubjective and social processes that influence the research project at all stages (but particularly and expressly those using a qualitative approach). With the rising popularity of qualitative methods being used to examine crime and crime control practice, as well as the increased public and professional scrutiny of research, reflexivity provides a means of strengthening transparency about the positionality of the researcher in light of the research process. It was also used and largely promoted as a response to 'the reflexive turn', which refers to a dramatic change of perspective that occurred during the 1980s affecting many social sciences, especially ethnography. The ideas behind it came from philosophy and politics (including critical theory and feminism) and were also being debated and having their effect in other areas like textual criticism, cultural theory and literary theory. To put it very simply (and crudely), postmodernity was a term coined to describe the economic or cultural state or condition of society which is said to exist after modernity. Some schools of thought hold that modernity ended in the late twentieth century, in the 1980s or 1990s, to be replaced by postmodernity, while others would extend modernity to cover the developments denoted by some as postmodernity and talk about 'late' or 'accelerated modernity'. The idea of the postmodern condition is sometimes characterised as a culture stripped of its capacity to function in any linear or autonomous state as opposed to the progressive, rational and structured phase of modernism.

However, one particularly influential aspect of postmodern thinking is the death of metanarratives or grand narratives, and notions of a universal truth. With that as a backdrop, the very nature of reality and how we can understand it as social scientists came into question. Scholars were asking how we can know anything for sure when different social scientists come up with different ideas. Many things we think we understand are not ever really seen, like atoms and gravity, so they rely on trust. Science is subject to fashions and fads. It relies heavily on the ability to predict the future based on the past, but that is nothing more than a mind game. Science and rationality were said to have failed in their promise to find answers to society's problems, indeed, in the wake of the atom bomb and nuclear power, science had created things that might destroy the world as readily as they might improve it.

The problem was seen to be even more pronounced in the social sciences that are considered more subjective (as in the interpretivist epistemology) and because, some would suggest, the social world we study can never truly be objectively understood. The issue then was why should these subjective judgements or claims to truth be privileged with a scientific status or position of power above or beyond any other claim? If everything social scientists and ethnographers try to understand is filtered through personal experience and our own way of seeing the world, and hence what people mean when they tell us things is interpreted, there is the capacity for the researcher to get meanings entirely wrong. We are always in danger of being ethnocentric, of making sense of the world by relating it to what we already know and believe, by subjectively interpreting.

As a result of the reflexive turn, and challenges to ethnography and qualitative methods that suggested that social scientists could claim no greater claims to authority than others, ethnographers began to look more critically at the ways in which their fieldwork had been (and was being) produced. They revealed that ethnographers were often privileged, and in many cases the researcher and researched population had an unequal relationship.

One response to the reflexive turn was the postmodern ethnography. This claimed to not privilege the ethnographer, but instead to accept and celebrate the complex, ambiguous, messy nature of the social world and of ethnographic research. However, for many, such accounts can simply come across as rather self-referential, narcissistic, self-indulgent and pointless. While postmodern ethnography self-consciously abandons the attempt to provide a neat, linear and ordered narrative account structured with a single authoritative voice, the view that there is a reality that exists external to the way we think about and experience it is far from endorsed by all ethnographers, and several important figures in ethnography were critical of some of the more extreme elements of postmodern thinking, while accepting that some of the criticisms that the movement had made did need addressing.

Several academics suggested that the proper response to the challenge of postmodernity was not the wholesale abandoning of any sense that there is a real world we wish to learn about, and which our research participants live in, experience, feel constrained by, and help create. This was especially true perhaps in criminology, where academics close to their subject were alert to the very real nature and harms of crime that occurred in some communities. Some academic criminologists simply ignored much of what were quite abstract philosophical and methodological debates (there were certainly good ethnographies of crime and its control being produced while many social scientists became obsessed with rather jargon filled and largely irrelevant debates). Additionally, it ought to be remembered that this epoch in social science witnessed its falling popularity as an academic subject, and the start of the growth of more practical and focused social sciences such as criminology. In methodological texts penned by the likes of Hammersley and Atkinson (2007), Brewer (2000) and Willis (2000) a less defeatist response to the challenges presented by postmodernism and as part of the reflexive turn was to continue to claim some authority for the academic ethnographer, but to methodologically re-orientate and promote new approaches to ethnographic studies, which recognise that they were crafted by human beings who make subjective judgements about what to and how to research, interpret what they see and hear, decide what to write and how, and that they do all this in the context of their own personal biographies and backgrounds that are entrenched in scientific and disciplinary environments. Reflexive ethnographers therefore sought to meet the challenges to their authority and value by suggesting that reflexivity that includes analysis of wider structures of power and control but recognises the role of the researcher is core to crafting good qualitative and ethnographic research. Hence, they attempt to suggest that the way to meet the challenge of postmodernism is a more transparent research that is honest about who has what influence over their work. Therefore, reflexive ethnographers, in the words of Altheide and Johnson:

> illustrate that each and every setting, without exception, is socially stratified. The stratified hierarchies vary from one setting to another, and the stratification has different consequences in one setting compared to others, but all settings are stratified in some manner, and commonly on the basis of gender, age, race, and/or ethnicity, or social class/education/occupation. The personal qualities of a given ethnographer will 'fit' or 'not fit' somewhere in this schema. The quality and validity of the information thus obtained will be related to how a given observer met and resolved these issues for the particular setting studies. (Altheide and Johnson, 1998: 295)

Hence the reflexive ethnographer should seek to describe the context of the research and their place in that context, and perhaps provide some autobiographical details to help the reader understand their perspective better.

They engage in conversations with research participants, rather than subjecting respondents to interviews. They seek to make research more transparent, and locate themselves within it, showing where the voice is theirs and when it belongs to the participants.

Brewer, for example, suggests several questions for ethnographers:

- In what manner do you keep fieldnotes?
- What was the rate of data accumulation or waves of data accumulation?
- How did you record the data?
- How did you file, code or otherwise sort or order the material?
- How did the leading ideas or concepts or frame of focus evolve?
- What kind of models are you aware of employing in order to organise the materials?
- To what extent did you organise or craft your analysis before writing it out in text?
- What were any difficulties or stumbling blocks experienced in analysis and writing up?
- How would you/could you have modified your practices? (Adapted from Brewer, 2000: 131)

The core issue for now is that few who work in the field of criminological ethnography can report being pure neutral conduits who report 'the facts' of the field, and where this happens, such accounts should be met with a degree of scepticism. Reflexivity in many ways makes for impactful ethnography precisely because it makes for a more transparent form of ethnography, and therefore, in so doing meets with some of the recent challenges to the veracity and accuracy of urban (and criminological) ethnography (Lubet, 2018). However, reflexivity alone does not ensure this, and therefore it is only one element of judging what constitutes good quality ethnography.

LONGITUDINAL ETHNOGRAPHY AND TIME IN THE FIELD

While most ethnography tends to stress the importance of the contact with the field and the way that this contact and engagement shapes authoritative knowledge, it is fair to suggest, in keeping with Lubet's criticisms of criminological ethnography, that criminological fieldwork is often more opaque about how much data was generated and in which ways than other forms of qualitative social science (Lubet, 2018). Perhaps there is a case to be made that ethnographers should more clearly document the overall level of their engagement in and familiarity with the field (how many days, weeks and hours were spent, with whom?). Often ethnographers will make some time claims, such as 'twelve months fieldwork', but that does not tell us all that much and can be used to obscure what is very limited engagement (only three site visits were made in the course of twelve months fieldwork would clearly change the previous claim). Some researchers will make numerical claims about the number of interviews, but that does not tell us how long the interviews lasted. Indeed often, it can be difficult to determine just how long-standing their contact with the field is. Certainly, as Ancrum (2013) has noted, much ethnographic research is based on short- rather than long-term immersion in fieldwork.

As most ethnography is relatively limited in terms of time spent in the field, and for the most part criminological researchers enter into the field for a limited period, the term longitudinal ethnography is not one that is commonly used or has a currency, but given that quality is often (although never exclusively) linked to time and familiarity with the subject being studied, would longer term, longitudinal forms of ethnographic work merit some additional appreciation? Certainly, some of the most notable criminological ethnographers confound the notion that fieldwork is time limited. For example, Dick Hobbs' work, spanning an ethnographic trilogy between *Doing the Business* (1988) and his final ethnography of crime, *Lush Life* (2013), considers the world of crime and London-based professional crime in flux and truly spans over thirty years in the field. Other researchers might visit the field, exit and yet revisit. Howard Williamson wrote *Five Years*, an ethnography of teenage offenders, with his partner Pip Williamson in 1985, but the more accessible book now is *The Milltown Boys Revisited* (Williamson, 2004). In *Five Years* the authors undertook a ground-breaking study of youth, poverty and crime in the 1970s. At its close, the boys they interviewed were left with few prospects and bleak futures. Twenty-five years later, Williamson returns to find out the sort of men these boys have become and narrates their stories. He finds that of the original 67 boys he interviewed, seven have passed away (not one from natural causes) but tracking the others down he presents a staggeringly diverse range of lives, and as a longitudinal picture of those involved in drug use, crime and poverty growing up (and in some cases moving on) it is fascinating and yet it gets little traction in debates about crime, rehabilitation and desistence. Other academics such as Ancrum (2011) have questioned whether, if the field of study is connected with one's own biography, there can ever be a point of exit, although as Winlow notes towards the end of his study of professional crime in the north east of England, exit is precisely one of the advantages that the academic ethnographer does have compared to one's participants (Winlow, 2001). An additional take on the longitudinal ethnography is that of Wilson, whose involvement in the Northern Soul scene spanned 1973 to 1981. Yet Wilson (2007) also returned to participants and continues to excavate the biography of himself and others as part of his study, making it a work that blurs the lines between ethnography, history and autobiography in interesting ways.

CHAPTER SUMMARY

This chapter has considered how ethnographic data are analysed, and asserts that good analysis is as instrumental as fieldwork and gathering data in making a successful criminological ethnography. It can be argued that what is vital is not so much the manner in which analysis is undertaken, but that some things are self-evident in the making of good criminological ethnographies, such as the transparency and reflexivity of the ethnographer as researcher. By this, I do not mean gratuitous, confessional or sensationalist reflexivity, but rather a clear and communicated sense of how knowledge is accumulated, of what the scholar's relationships with the community is, of the presence of people in the text as characters who appear as themselves, as real people who are complex. Also important is a clear demonstration of the topic being studied as impact- ful and 'mattering', by this I mean mattering not only in an criminological sense, but that the work is relevant to the people in the community under study as well as to the scholarly community. To me these also stand as hall- marks of ethnographic realism.

FURTHER READING

A fantastic introduction to auto-ethnography and reflexivity is Stephen Wakeman (2014) 'Fieldwork, biography and emotion', as well as Craig Ancrum (2011) '"Knowing the dance"' and Ancrum (2013) 'Stalking the margins of legality'. A good overview text is John Martin Chamberlen (2018) *Understanding Criminological Research*, but there is no substitute for reading a range of research studies and reports and gaining a sense and insight into how various criminological ethnographers differently make sense of and analyse their data, as there is a multiplicity of approaches and techniques.

9

EMERGING PERSPECTIVES AND FUTURE CHALLENGES

LEARNING OBJECTIVES

An aim of this text has been to attempt to give the reader a better understanding of some core aspects of criminological ethnography. This final chapter seeks to consider the changing landscape for criminological ethnography, considering in specific how changes in the social sciences, and society more generally, may impact on ethnography. By the end of this chapter you should have a better understanding of:

- the importance of the global for ethnography
- the rise of visual and new methods of ethnographic working
- the contemporary socio-economic, political, cultural and technological context of ethnography
- debates concerning the role and place of criminological ethnography in the twenty-first century and the challenges the method faces.

The final chapter of the book will look at new directions for criminological ethnography. It will look towards the future and consider how technological advances and new forms of social media, recording technologies and criminological perspectives challenge fundamental ideas about ethnography. This includes how digital and visual ethnography as well as instant immersion, such as that employed to study riots (Treadwell et al., 2013; Winlow et al., 2015) or 'Black Friday' shopping (Smith and Raymen, 2015), which challenge traditional notions of ethnography and deeper understandings of contemporary culture. It will consider the role of images in ethnography, as images encode data about values, norms and practices that are often inaccessible to other forms of collecting and reporting information. It will look at how some researchers construct images with the research participants as a research method, and how others are bringing participants to the fore through this new method. This will allow me to close the text by raising more questions about what the role, function and purpose of a specific criminological ethnography might look like.

As this book moves towards its conclusion I am aware that a great deal of what has been written and produced here is retrospective, it looks backward, and this in many ways is the antithesis of what much ethnography seeks to do. Understanding culture is about understanding traditions, emergence, evolution, and while history is necessarily a part of that process, it is always as vital that ethnography can look forwards .

Criminological ethnographers deal with criminals and those who exert control over them (or attempt to). It deals with the everyday stuff of crime, harm, victimisation and power. At its best, ethnography reveals that crime is a complex process, which is connected to a wider range of issues and forces, be they social, cultural, political, economic, technological, geographical or historical.

OLD LEGACIES – NEW AGENDAS

Being a criminal does not make the individual a terrible person all the time, just as criminal is not really a permanent state of being. But being a criminal probably makes an individual able and willing to press pause on their morals for a minute and do what needs to be done ... be that selling a car with dodgy parts to a single mum who's going to put her kids in the back seat; to beating the shit out of someone because they were 'taking liberties' by not paying their debts. Criminological ethnographers who have studied active criminals are perfectly placed to know the experience of feeling at once repulsed by and drawn to certain people in those settings, and also to know the maxim that good people do bad things, just as bad people can do good things. People who can be vicious, violent and nasty can also be gregarious, generous and alluring. It is exactly that message which makes for the best drama (and if you were in any doubt, *The Sopranos* is the best drama ever, probably closely followed by *The Wire*) and criminological ethnographers who take crime as their subject see just such complexity and nuance play out in real life as we see in James Gandolfini's phenomenal portrayal of the character of mob boss Tony Soprano in the HBO television show *The Sopranos*. Gandolfini portrayed the Italian American mob boss and central character as loving, gregarious, funny, vicious, narcissistic, egotistical, insecure, anxious, callous and considered, an often walking paradox. Tony Soprano was complex, and that complexity was likely the root of why *The Sopranos* was so widely liked and critically well received as a gangster drama. It became widely regarded by many critics and members of the public alike as the best television show of all time because it was both action-filled and mundane, and its characters were contradictory and complex, and often flawed. *The Sopranos* showed that crime is complicated. Ethnography often does the same, it shows that when it comes to crime much is not common sense, often things are counter intuitive. Ethnography paints the portrait warts and all.

Criminology as a discipline and some of the people who practise it do not always emphasise such complexity and nuance. Arguably too often qualitative researchers have placed too much emphasis on concepts such as 'stigmatisation', 'labelling' and 'resistance'. What's more, a lot of criminologists in the past have self-identified as the champions of the poor and the oppressed. They have used their privileged position in society to tell the stories of those poor souls who are denied agency or a voice that is heard by wider society. Yet some would aver that they may have mistaken the nuances and complexities for the unchallengeable and unassailable validity of social constructionism and its epistemological and ontological assumptions. They have been keen to stick with an interpretivist ethnography developed in the 1920s and stick with it as if it was ever right, barely acknowledging that critical realist epistemology has emerged or that the world as it was has changed.

This is ironic because during their research, some ethnographers zealously believe in social constructionism and will likely witness those same individuals they were researching often exert an awful lot of agency and a very well-heard presence within the communities that criminological researchers enter, but largely as temporary visitors. Perhaps this trend is slowly being reversed with the influence of ethnographers such as Hobbs, Ditton and Winlow. I am struck by how few people there are who can claim to have consistently undertaken ethnography (or at least participant observation) throughout their careers. It seems more common, perhaps understandably, so that most academic researchers have undertaken a single ethnographic project which is quite fleeting and then stepped away from the field. Yet perhaps the best ethnographers must stick at it, to stay somewhat connected to the field, which is the only way you can see the social shifts and how society changes over time.

When the world enters a period of rapid change, the orthodox theoretical ways of seeing it which have dominated an era often become exhausted and begin to lose their credibility. It is precisely at those moments that an opportunity emerges for fresh thinking, new ideas, new ways of seeing, looking and doing research. That is arguably the most important lesson from the legacy of urban Chicagoan ethnography and social science of the 1920s that inspired the first ethnographic works in social science. However, it is not often that story which is told when that legacy is reduced to bad textbook descriptions of 'zones of transition' or 'concentric circles'. The ethnography of the Chicago School proved so powerful, and gained such a legacy, I would suggest, because it was the only method to capture the world in such a state of flux as it was then. The way that social science (and criminology for that matter) is taught often places a great deal of attention on less relevant detail than the crux of the matter. In criminology degrees and courses, the Chicagoan School often becomes mere symbolic interactionism, social constructionism rather than methodological and theoretical innovation. Indeed, one only need to glimpse almost any basic criminology textbooks to see this happen.

Now the world faces up to new transformations. The work of the Chicago School (or some of it at least) stands out now largely only as a historical record. The once detailed ethnographic work that was a bedrock of criminology might soon become more a part of history than a methodological instruction relevant for today. Now if one reads Chicagoan research, it seems oddly twee and dated. The connections that once existed between crime, political economy, technology and urbanised (working-class) culture, and the relationships between people are both similar and different. The world today is changed and changing. That is a reason we must not simply cling to past methods and ideas.

For most ethnographers now, the method is something that is used and then cast aside in favour of greater engagement with the theoretical rather than the empirical. It is not unfair to suggest that few ethnographers (such as Dick Hobbs for example) have made a career from retaining contact with the field that has lasted more than a few years. When they have, they can show longer processes of social change all too well. In hearing the stories, we are helped in working things out. That is why, whatever direction criminology as a master discipline decides to follow, whatever the theoretical trajectory, good qualitative research and ethnography, and thick description need to remain.

Classis historical ethnographic criminological works will continue to act as sources of inspiration for the new theoretical programmes and perspectives in criminological research and theory. However, that does not mean that future criminological ethnography is inexorably wed to the social constructionism and symbolic interactionist traditions. Indeed, the very continued relevance of ethnography arguably requires a revisiting of some of the foundational ideas and a reformation to take us into a new epoch. When William Foote Whyte and Fredrick Thrasher walked the streets of Chicago, they did so in a world very different from that of today. Would their methods be the same today, I wonder? What would change, what should contemporary criminological ethnography look like? It is with such a provocation and call to action I intend to conclude this book.

WELCOME TO THE CRISIS, WELCOME BACK ETHNOGRAPHY

As criminologists, we face two contemporary crises. The first is the unfolding crisis of global capitalism and state governance, and with it the spiralling social harms of dislocation, incarceration, impoverishment, and environmental degradation. Amidst these spiralling harms will surely emerge, sadly, a further host of phenomena demanding the critical attention of criminologists: new forms of acquisitive violence, new crimes attuned to economic and existential uncertainty, new moments of down-market corporate malfeasance, new strains on social and environmental sustainability, and new patterns of state surveillance and control … The second crisis is the crisis of criminology. Criminology is today crippled by its own methodology, its potential for analysis and critique lost within a welter of survey forms, data sets, and statistical manipulations. (Ferrell, 2009: 1)

Ethnography has a long and protracted history within sociology and other social science disciplines. It has now been widely suggested across disciplinary subject areas that ethnographic fieldwork is in a place where it faces competing pressures, and many laments the health of the approach. It is not uncommon to see or hear scholars lament that the place of ethnography more broadly is not what it used to be, and that it is not always desirable or feasible to reproduce 'older' or traditional forms or ways of doing ethnographic research, whether the focus is on crime and control or on broader social issues. Such a break-away from the classical anthropological design of ethnography has been facilitated by imperatives of time and funding, or risk and the very state and nature of contemporary academe, as well as by the fact that certain aspects of contemporary social (and particularly criminal) life may not be susceptible to be harnessed through those traditional methods of ethnography. A plethora of innovative, experimental and adaptive ethnographies have emerged in direct response to those changes, and I have described and covered some of those in the previous chapters, such as auto-ethnography, ultra-realist ethnography, sensory ethnography, performative ethnography, netnography, visual ethnography and instant ethnography among others.

Criminological ethnographers have long sought explanations of cultures, emotions and subjectivities in the socio-economic and geographical contexts in which people spend the bulk of their everyday lives, because crime in many ways is a very human phenomena, and that is something that criminological ethnographers of all persuasions would be certain to agree on. That does not mean that we should slavishly adhere to the legacy and traditional ideas underpinning ethnographic enterprise. Like crime, ethnography and social research must move with the times. To simply stand still presents a huge risk, the risk of redundancy and irrelevancy.

At the very moment that many criminologists and social researchers of a cultural persuasion instructing legions of eager graduate students to regard all representations of reality as mere social constructs, outcomes of the ability of powerful groups to utilise language in order to construct a narrative that can pass for truth, others have presented to the pious liberal philanthropists of the university mainstream an image of reality that was authentic and born of an intimate relationship with the research field. Descriptive ethnographic work produced by the inspiring fieldworkers that is well written and impactful immediately grabs us and demands we pay attention. It does so not only because of its 'thick description', its humour, its energy, but it does so because it connects the stuff of theory to those believable accounts of reality. It tells stories that people want to hear, and it makes phenomena come alive.

Here I should say that for me, the very value of criminological ethnography when done well is its ability to present a world of crime that is convincing to those familiar with it, and to those who are not, that reflects the often complex, contradictory and counter intuitive messy realities. Crime is, at best, a messy business, and one where one-dimensional portraits and simplistic portrayals often abound unchallenged. While appeals to common sense or sentiments such as 'everyone knows that' often have an immediate purchase, often these fall when subject to more critical scrutiny. Crime is not simply bad people doing bad things as if there is an easy consensus morality. Often crime is a comedy, a tragedy and a farce all rolled into one. It is a world of selfishness and generosity, of good people doing bad things, and bad people doing good things and everything in between. It is not always about rational actions, but emotive irrational responses.

Criminological ethnography is the method that gets us closest to the lived reality of crime, and it ought never to be forgotten by criminologists of any persuasion that while the maxim that crime has no ontological reality and that crime is a construct and is based on social judgements is one heavily relied upon in cultivating critical thought, it would not be a means of entering into a discussion with someone in a rape crisis centre or a topic of conversation from a paramedic to comfort a young man who has just had a pint glass pushed into his face. The physical and emotional impact of crime can be devastating, for victims and communities. We should not lose sight of the fact that crime, like ethnography, is concerned with humans. The intention of those who seek to show the greater complexity is perfectly good, and yet the path to hell might be paved with good intentions. Much crime, as it is conventionally understood, is a power process, but traditionally we should not lose sight of the way in which some emic understandings have cultivated deeply romantic images of that which should not be celebrated. That is not to deny that criminal law disproportionately targets those as the lower strata of society, or to ignore the fact that powerful actors have far greater capacity to do excessive harms to people than those conventionally held up as criminal.

However, we should be realistic about the fact that, as typically understood, most crime is both perpetrated by those, and against those at the bottom of the social order, and it is no form of proto rebellion. The everyday world of crime where criminologists such as Felson would send students to count syringes (Felson, 2002) is a world of people. A world in which working-class conservativism exists in abundance, a world of shady business and occasional violence, a world of proletarian entrepreneurs on the look-out for a deal, a quick trade, a world of laughs, jibes, stories, hangovers and short-termism, but also of a world of danger, sadness, trauma and loss. The best ethnographers have been showing that for years. It is very human. It is a world that is not necessarily all that familiar to many people, from the policy-makers in the Home Office or the politicians to the students in universities studying criminology. It is also one that too frequently is alien to a criminology dominated by quasi-scientific empiricism, quantitative data and quite aloof and abstract theoretical discourses. Criminology whether as an academic discipline, or as criminal justice (as a governmental practice) or as an individual pursuit (done by police, prison and probation officers, for example) is often ultimately dominated by a view that is informed by and formulated by the more privileged in society. There is always a danger in any criminology and criminal justice that is disconnected from its subject (the offender, criminal, prisoner, suspect) as the reality experienced in the everyday world of criminal justice and crime. Criminological ethnography is a bridge between those perspectives and views. If used properly.

AUTO-ETHNOGRAPHY AND THE ROLE OF THE RESEARCHER

While relatively new to criminology, the term auto-ethnography is likely to see significant rise in stock and currency in coming years. While it might be fair to suggest that there has long been a biographical element to criminological ethnographic research, it is only recently that academics have really begun to consider the place and function of the autobiographical as part of criminology (Wakeman, 2014). While the use of offender biographies has a long history, a similar use of biographical reflection is rarer (though not unknown) in criminological circles (for example, Sir Leon Radzinowicz *Adventures in Criminology* is perhaps the best known example). While the term 'auto-ethnography' could be criticised as an unnecessary neologism, it is undoubtable that there is now a greater focus on the researcher's part on the production of knowledge, which may also be regarded as an important demonstration of reflexivity in praxis.

Recent examples of criminological auto-ethnography include a focus on biography as part of the emergence of cultural criminology. For example, the late Mike Presdee mounted calls for greater focus on personal biography in the embryonic stages of cultural criminology. That call seems to have now been heeded, for example, Simon Hallsworth's (2013) use of auto-ethnographic recollections of his personal experience of life on the streets in the 1970s and 1980s to question the ontological claim behind the 'gangland' thesis. Do 'gangs', he asked, actually exist as positivists and realists describe them? He argued that we see arboreal (fixed) gangs rather than transient and nomadic networks because of our historical tendency to think like that.

On the other hand, most ethnographies contain an autobiographical (or reflexive) element, and others are extremely sceptical about the value of placing the researcher too centrally, regarding this as verging on the narcissistic and self-indulgent. Yvonne Jewkes, for example, has reflected on how for much of her early career she was cautioned away from writing about emotion or autobiographically when undertaking prison research (Jewkes, 2011). Therefore some argue that auto-ethnography is self-indulgent and inappropriate in its over-generalisation of limited singular experience, and memories are not reliable representations of original experiences but come into operation after those experiences. There is no way to verify data that exists exclusively in the memory of the researcher, and some argue that a third party would be able to evaluate data and theoretical concepts in a more balanced way. Yet Wakeman contends that 'prior involvement with criminality, criminal/deviant cultures and/or the various processes of criminal justice can provide an enhanced heuristic perspective on such phenomena that criminologists should take heed of' (Wakeman, 2014: 706). Similarly Ancrum has argued persuasively that any stated ambitions of pursuing complete academic objectivity, generalisability and ethical purity are both naïve and unattainable, and that an established biography where one knows the experiences of crime from outside of the protected towers of academe can be of great assistance in unpredictable environments where the researcher has no choice but to proceed under the existential guidance of his or her own good sense and personal ethical code (Ancrum, 2011; 2013). The core it seems is to be honest and transparent about identity and to harness its heuristic potential when practical. Ethnography is, after all, a way of studying others and studying ourselves as we attempt to work it out.

VISUAL ETHNOGRAPHIES OF CRIME

Visual ethnographic approaches are becoming more common in anthropology and sociology and are more frequently being used as an aid to participant observation in realist or interpretivist frameworks. Simply speaking, visual ethnography is the term that is employed when ethnographic research is conducted using photography, video or film.

Hal Foster argued that visual ethnography emerged as a debate in art in the 1960s, thanks to the rise of performance art and social movements like feminism. With the onset of postmodernism, many commentators believed that it was no longer possible to describe audiences as simply observers, and hence, in some ways visual ethnography may shift from traditional written detail alone to visual representations. For example, Janet Mendelsohn's work as part of BCCCS in the 1960s photographs of Birmingham's red light district, Varna Road, with extensive photographs of street children, prostitutes and pimps. Additionally 'visual ethnography' would seem an appropriate term to describe the TATE gallery Artangle exhibit *The Battle of Orgreave Archive (An Injury to One Is an Injury to All)* (2001), an installation comprising texts, documents, objects, videos and other archival material, which provides a context for examining intertwined narratives the 1984 strike by the National Union of Mineworkers (in particular the specific confrontation between striking miners and the police that occurred at the Orgreave Coking Plant in Yorkshire on 18 June 1984). The installation draws heavily on artist Jeremy Deller's 2001 re-enactment of the same conflict. Deller staged *The Battle of Orgreave* in 2001, bringing together almost 1,000 people in a public re-enactment of a violent confrontation from the 1984 miners' strike. Phillipe Bourgois' *In Search of Respect* contained a number of photographs and makes no mention of visual ethnography. Therefore, perhaps an appropriate question is what actually constitutes visual for the purpose of ethnography? Traditionally in the social sciences there was some scepticism about the extent to which, as a data collection method, visual recording might aid empirical research. For some, the visual was too subjective, unrepresentative and unsystematic, but for others it is a new subject and tool that needs to be considered in criminology.

Maggie O'Neill and colleagues have suggested that by reconsidering how ethnographic data is represented and presenting it in more novel ways such as in a dramatic and artistic manner, researchers can 'access a richer understanding of the complexities of lived experience which can throw light on broader social structures and processes' (O'Neill et al., 2002: 70) and engage audiences more. Yet the most innovative approaches arguably exist beyond criminology. For example, Professor Nick (Nicola) Mai is a sociologist, an ethnographer and a filmmaker whose writing and films focus on the experiences and representations of migrants working in the sex industry. Through participative ethnographic films and original research findings, he seeks to challenge prevailing representation of sex work in terms of trafficking. Mai is involved not only in writing but creates and directs films focused on the experiences of migrants selling sex in the globalised sex industry in order to live their lives. Through what he terms experimental ethnofictions and research findings he challenges the humanitarian representations and borders framing the nexus between migration and sex work and seeks to present a more complex narrative than that which emerges concerning how people are trafficked for sexual exploitation. Arguing that the actual lives of the individuals involved – and, more importantly, the decisions that led them to sex work – are too often overlooked, Mai brings those back into focus in a manner that is novel, innovative and impactful. Such new ideas may bridge the gap between ethnographic data and audiences and broaden the appeal for a wider audience.

A core proponent of visual ethnography, Sarah Pink, has argued a shift from ethnography's roots in anthropology, sociology and cultural studies to a 'visual ethnography that is informed by recent theoretical turns to theories of place and space, practice, movement and the senses', and hence senses of feeling and emotion. She argues for a multisensory ethnography that incorporates input from all the other senses, which might compensate for the inadequacy of linguistic accounts and descriptive writing alone.

It is certain that there are both benefits and drawbacks to using the visual approach in ethnographies of crime and control. While images can be supplied by research participants or produced in partnership with researchers (allowing self-representation to become part of the research). It is not always easy to access visual material on crime, and there can be real ethical complexity. While films and photographs are useful for eventual theory construction because they are permanently available for re-analysis, and visual ethnography can be enhanced by technological innovations in multimedia, such as small, portable video cameras and sensitive recording equipment, much of that which criminologists might want to use (for example, body worn camera footage from police or prison staff) is not readily available to researchers, and there are still many areas where the camera may be a no-go or may prevent people from talking or heighten the risks to the researcher.

ONLINE (OR VIRTUAL) CRIMINOLOGICAL ETHNOGRAPHY

This is a new and useful addition to criminology. Essentially it is participant observation adapted to operate effectively in cyberspace. Now that the overly optimistic 'crime decline' narrative has been put into question after the statistical decline was almost cancelled out in the UK in 2016 after the addition of various types of cyber-crime to the survey data, some criminologists have realised crime has mutated rather than declined (Treadwell, 2012). Most new crimes or advanced means of committing traditional crimes and operating criminal markets are now associated with the internet and are crying out for research. The internet is a place where virtual forms of economic, social and cultural interchange take place, therefore the ethnographer, far less hampered by initial access, must learn the virtual community's protocols to be accepted as a member. The internet hosts many different and specific forms of disembodied 'community' – markets, hobbies, identities, political groups, sexual preferences and so on – that are in constant flux. As they attempt to join these communities, online ethnographers can use avatars to circumvent the ethical problems of deception, risk of harm, anonymity and confidentiality because in most cases members have already agreed that identities should be hidden in a 'covert community'. Webber and Yip's (2013) research into the online trade in fake credit cards or Antonopoulos et al. (2018) on fake goods are developing innovative methods for online research on the web, yet the 'dark net' will continue to provide opportunities and topics where the ethics, including even non-participant observation, are hugely complex. It would not be possible to 'lurk' and observe the behaviour of the likes of extreme paedophile Matthew Falder without risking a substantial spell in custody, and the collection of screenshots that can be added as part of a visual methodology is possible only in some contexts. So too new forms of crime and control that arise out of the net and the online world will likely keep criminologists busy theorising and documenting, but so too, we must remember these are ultimately still human processes involving human interactions.

While the sociological study of behaviour on the web often involves juxtaposing the words 'virtual' or 'digital' to 'ethnography' (or blending 'ethnography' with 'internet', giving 'netnography') some regard this as problematic, not least because 'being there' online can still be still quite a detached position, and does not neccessarily equate to the way ethnographers work in offline settings. In his ethnography of crime on the auction website eBay (and in an early argument that conventional patterns of crime were mutating online) Treadwell (2012) was one of the first to question the established narrative of the acquisitive 'crime drop' when he used ethnographic criminological approaches to talk to web criminals using auction websites to sell counterfeits in pubs and bars. Indeed, it is worth remembering that 'being online' also now happens in real space, and while crime might mutate and occur more frequently online, it is not necessary to study it solely through a computer. For that reason, it remains one of the few studies of cybercrime that is based on a more ethnographic sensibility. Perhaps the gold standard in criminological ethnography thus far is Hall and Antonopoulos's (2016) research into legal and illegal online pharmacies, which used advanced online methods to research the supply side of the global market in counterfeit pharmaceuticals, while simultaneously using traditional participant observation and interviews with consumers to research the demand side. However, the use of 'honeypot websites' and covert research among users of pharmaceuticals bought online did involve some deception.

The ubiquitous use of the internet has the potential to open criminal practices hitherto closed off to researchers, such as paedophile networks, fraud, corruption, state crime, tax evasion and far-right extremism. However, it similarly can come with risks, as the online world is not the anonymous space that some people initially assume it to be.

A CRIMINOLOGICAL ETHNOGRAPHY FOR THE CRIMES OF THE CONTEMPORARY

For me, impact in the social sciences (and impact in and through ethnography) often is not going to be about being able to point to a single outcome. We are not physical scientists, we are not sitting together in a laboratory producing a cure. But what we are doing is having impact in a cultural context, and by that, I mean making ideas seem normal, from which change flows, by garnering a better picture that shows the counter intuitive, that which often is not simple common sense, but which asks questions and takes us towards a better social understanding. Systems and algorithms that come out of positivism still exist, and have significant ethical problems associated with them, take for example Artificial Intelligence (AI). Many of us are familiar with the idea that artificial intelligence systems are regularly making benign decisions, like recommendations on purchases made via Facebook or viewing recommendations on Netflix. But what about decisions that have a significant impact on someone's life? Should AI systems be used in life-changing situations, like criminal sentencing? Or in judicial decisions, from setting or denying bail, is 'risk of recidivism' – the likelihood of reoffending – the sort of place where we will always need human judgement? Prior to using algorithms to make these decisions – something which has grown over the last 30 years – the suggested risk of an offender's likelihood of recidivism was a subjective judgement made by an individual, often on subjective personal opinion. Mechanistic approaches are also increasingly being used to target criminal justice at places and crime types, be they hotspots for particular crimes, or particular recurrent types of offending (such as assaults). And yet, with the use of AI in decision making, there is the potential to stigmatise, to re-enforce inequalities and inequity. The AI system may well have eliminated some of the justice system's implicit biases, yet it may have also incorporated the aggregate biases of all the decisions it is premised on. Sometimes value neutral actuarial and artificial intelligence based 'crime science' might be hardly that. Might it be that criminological ethnographers working at the fore in disadvantaged communities will have a role to play in challenging any inbuilt biases that such systems have?

Contemporary criminology must be able to offer convincing, cogent and compelling explanations of mutating forms of crime and harm in today's rapidly changing and accelerated world. To do this, the discipline of criminology must broaden its horizon beyond that which normally frames it – sociology and law – and look to embrace new conceptual developments in other important cognate disciplines, and to import and use those. Criminology is at its best as a rendezvous discipline, that draws on associated subjects such as anthropology, economics, politics, philosophy, psychology and psychoanalysis. It must also recognise the flaws in the quantitative methods and again create an environment conducive to methodologically innovative research, including ethnography. Criminology for a global world needs ethnographic networks that can produce deeper and more sophisticated understandings of crime and its control. Ethnographic networking is important as a method of improving the generalisability of ethnographic findings and connecting them to broad socio-economic structures and the new theoretical ideas. Without this form of networking, ethnographic findings in criminology tend to be restricted to specific locales and criticisms of its validity when judged against other methods. It has long been accepted that ethnography can show changes at the micro level, but ethnography can support generalisations, and help us understand human activities in a world in flux. So too, the emergence of team-based ethnography, as a departure from the traditional lone researcher working 'in the field', is in part a response to the globalisation of societies, economies and organisations, and that is another development that ought to be grasped. As Fader notes, such strategies might be necessary in the accelerated and demanding world of the modern, neoliberal university (Fader, 2018).

Ethnographic work produced by once great 'sole' ethnographers who went out into the field alone for extended periods has always been valuable, particularly those previously mentioned in this text who jettisoned the naïve romanticism of timeless dissent, resistance and political agency. The best ethnographers did not paint criminals as either romantic rebels or hopeless dupes, but recognised that they were complicated people in complicated circumstances who did things that were socially harmful for themselves and those around them. Against a myth that is prevalent – one might say dominant – on the radical side of criminology's fence that criminals were rebellious souls, the more complex realities presented by academics across the world was to show things warts and all. While some ethnographers in this vein might be praised for the brutal honesty that might make some of us flinch, or make others despair, the best ethnographers were able to walk a tightrope that avoided both romanticism and stigmatisation. Following the legacy of the original Chicago School ethnographers, whatever condemnation or questioning might be necessary, truly excellent ethnographers craft work that is alert to nuances and complexities, and work which is balanced by an empathy and appreciation.

Criminological ethnographers deal with human beings, and the settings of crime will doubtlessly feature some of the most damaged and difficult people. Yet these are people whose practices do not always reflect their ethical being, people who might have been very different human beings in different circumstances, or had their lives been different. Those great criminological ethnographers of the past had a sociological awareness of fluidity, mutation and the fleeting and often volatile collaborations that melt away as quickly as they come into being, often quicker than can be observed by a wider context framed by IRBS and funding bodies that too often seem reluctant to support vital qualitative forays into the reality of our times (well certainly outside and away from several elite establishments built around ethnographers empowered by their privileged access and contacts). It is undoubtedly the case that ethnography is hard to do, time intensive, and it can be very costly (although that cost is frequently borne most heavily by those who enjoy the least support and reward in an academic social science and in this regard the university system that is not too dissimilar to the world inhabited by criminals, see Hobbs, 2013) and so the fact that now, most money funds a small number of established academics who simply re-enforce their own fiefdoms is problematic. Ethnography often thrives not because of nepotism, but because of a self-started determination and a desire to get on. Ethnographers tend to be maverick, but we might ask, does the current structuring of the university support the maverick enough?

I have written this book in part in recognition of that, not because I am a committed ethnographer, but rather precisely because I am keen to keep the methods others have helped to school me in evolving, vibrant, useful and alive. I have been lucky to meet and learn from ethnographers and social researchers who have kept the best inquiring spirit of Robert Park alive, who inspired me, sometimes with a brief word of encouragement, sometimes by extending the hand down and recognising that academic progress comes from offering the hand up rather than kicking the ladder away from behind them. Unfortunately, not all ethnographers or criminologists are made in that way. The neoliberal university arguably prioritises a selfishness and instrumentalism that is not conducive to sustaining ethnography as a method, and yet, I am proud to see friends and colleagues keeping ethnography alive by working with others on ethnographic projects in a truly collaborative and encouraging manner, seeking to empower and assist new scholars, generate new knowledge and look again.

These are also scholars who have produced work that will undeniably remain of considerable utility for generations of scholars keen to understand the reality of crime, even if it is only now as a historical portrait. The sentiment at the very heart of criminological ethnography, I would argue, must be an enduring commitment to depicting the world as it really is. There are some things you cannot measure with a chi-square test.

That is a view that is frequently shared among qualitative researchers generally, and among criminological ethnographers generally. There are of course differences between criminological ethnographers, between those whose perspective is influenced by phenomenology, or social constructionism and symbolic interactionism, or say ultra-realism. Critical criminologists may have different concerns from ethnographers of the police or prisons. Yet while there can be some significant differences and disagreements between the different approaches and criminological perspectives that criminological ethnographers ascribe to, there is also a lot in common. They share a recognition that the world takes place out there in the field, and that it cannot all be captured or shown objectively in the measurements and findings and modelling of statistical, mathematical or numerical analysis of data collected through polls, questionnaires and surveys.

Yet criminological research in recent years has largely and quite rightly moved beyond a narrow and silly qualitative–quantitative dichotomy or binary, and it seems to me that at least in part, criminological ethnography is less about the death of participant observation, and more about the interwoven way in which qualitative methods are now combined in a great many studies where academics are showing a far greater willingness to depart the ivory towers and look at crime on the streets and in situ. Yet for all that I could sound progressive and optimistic, it remains the case that overall, both in the US and in the UK (although it is perhaps more pronounced in the former) the dominant methodological preference remains unwaveringly committed to positivism and measuring the empirical dimension and remains all to wed to positivistic notions.

Past works of criminological ethnography leave us with a truly important legacy. While some of our colleagues in sociology and criminology departments across the country might consider ethnographers rough and ready, unscientific (perhaps slightly risky), among this number have long been the real mavericks who do much to keep pushing the boundaries and to keep a future generation of students and scholars engaged and interested. Criminological ethnography is or certainly can be 'colourful' and ethically complex, characteristics that represent the background and real world experiences of both the researchers and ethnographers who produce ethnographic work and the subjects and participants who live in the places that they study every day, but it is more than that. It is a real method and a real approach that can give real, useful and impactful knowledge.

Criminological ethnography does so much more than is often recognised. Ethnographers were sceptical of the crime drop narrative while other criminologists seemed convinced, precisely because they were on the streets and in the places that criminality takes place and they could see the shifts and mutations. If crime is not static and changes over time, then good ethnographers who are ready to say what is happening out there in the everyday are essential. It is why in 2025 we will need good ethnography as much as when a maverick Fredrick Thrasher was out on Chicago's streets looking at 'the gang'. Qualitative research as a whole and criminological ethnography generally have been constantly critiqued, if not disparaged, by the lack of consensus for assessing their quality and robustness, but they have also led to huge advances in practice. Conversely while conceptual and practical advances can be made through the systematic application of particular modes of enquiry, such as meta-analysis and randomised control trials, it can also come as a result of ethnography, and there are countless examples of this happening.

We should never assume that statistics alone are an accurate reflection of reality. The correct approach is to remain sceptical, mindful of the limitations of statistical methods, alert to the complexity of everyday life, and aware that the results of even the most robust and expansive crime surveys are there to be interpreted, contextualised and explained rather than simply accepted as social facts. Some crime forms are clearly amenable to statistical measurement, while many others are not. For example, homicide statistics are quite reliable. It is very difficult to dispose of a dead body, and medical science can now quite accurately identify the cause of death. But how can we, in an age in which internet connected handheld devices are ubiquitous, produce a reasonably reliable statistical measure of hate crime, or bullying and harassment? If we accept that the counter stance to ethnography is almost as ridiculous, then we at least understand that ethnography still has the advantage of showing us human life as it is practised every day.

How can we accurately measure insider share dealing, violent assault, stock manipulation, illegal drug transactions, soliciting, domestic violence or curb-crawling? How can we truly come to know the reality of the low-level crime that afflicts so many low-income neighbourhoods? How can we capture the reality of what appears to be routine illegality in the city of London's financial district? The answer is perfectly straightforward: we must dispense with surveys and head out into the real world to observe and speak to the perpetrators and victims of such crimes and dispense with the notional nonsense that this is easily done, but in doing this we need also to be aware that our ethnographic engagements can also sit happily alongside quantitative methods. But we must not lose sight of crime being a human process. To understand it we must ask victims and offenders, as well as those charged with dealing with crime and control, about their lives, ambitions, motivations and feelings. We must ask them about the pressures they face, their interactions with the criminal justice system, and the emotions that grip them when they find themselves embroiled in a criminal event. We must look at the world with unflinching honesty and boundless curiosity and ask ourselves, what's really going on here? And when all of that is done, we must interpret our data and use it to produce new and insightful accounts of human beings and the complex world we live in.

Ethnography is intimate. Hanging around, chatting, participating in every day and daily activities and trying to understand, require the development of relationships of trust. In the kinds of sites where crime is prominent, criminologists strive hard to forge relationships, but now as the world changes, where is the place for the criminological ethnographer? The world is increasingly global. Criminals and the powerful are wary of outsiders. Add in the linguistic, cultural, ethnic and gender differences crafted by a more global world and the possibility arises that connections seem, or indeed are, more difficult to make. Yet the global nature of the world today creates an abundance of opportunities, and opportunities for networked and collaborative work. We know the value of ethnography in giving us quality data, but the mechanisms that are set up for funding and promoting research unavoidably stand in the way of good ethnography. It is the least well-funded, least administratively supported form of research.

Research councils and funding bodies have tended to prioritise simpler and short-term interviews, case studies, mixed methods. It is beholden on good social scientists to challenge this. Perhaps a first step is a greater transparency for ethnography. Criminologists rarely discuss the challenges they encounter in their fieldwork, their misgivings or their mistakes. There are exceptions (for example, in the literature on the prison, scholars often admit they found their work emotionally taxing) but is there a real honesty about motivations, what draws researchers to subjects, that amounts to true, honest reflexivity? There are emergent examples of this (Wakeman, 2014) but should such honesty be a norm? Is it?

Qualitative scholarly evidence and argument in criminology are presented as though they emerged effortlessly from well thought out questions and diligent labour, and yet the context today is very different from that in which many of the more established ethnographers cut their teeth. The research environment in universities in the UK and the US has become ever more prohibitive and set against ethnographers, and while many are aware of this, they are unwilling to articulate it because of their own self-interest. In the UK a narrow club of elite universities benefit most from the current system, with an array of too many experts who are way too detached from the topic they claim authority on. Yet if one is a career criminologist who has never set foot in a prison or onto a high crime estate, do you deserve to be acclaimed as an expert? Yet classic ethnographic studies such as many of those discussed in this book were years in the making. The modern university has ramped up expectations, especially for early career members, in terms of publishing outputs. The requirements of probation, promotion, tenure and job security mean that ethnography, while increasingly popular, is also in many ways far from appealing.

Criminological ethnographers are people experts, and crime is at heart a human phenomenon. The greatest quality that those who have undertaken ethnographic fieldwork have is that they are better placed to appreciate the complex and often contradictory reality that is the backdrop to crime. They also know well that fieldwork (and life generally) will rarely feel or be straightforward. It is often messy. In the field, looking at crime and control, days can go by without much engagement, leaving the researcher at a loose end. For a long time, environments can be confusing, sometimes they can feel quite stressful, occasionally dull. Participants are not always willing, nor are they always friendly, or helpful. They may be threatening, hostile, angry and emotional. They may be simply indifferent. Such matters are inherent to applied qualitative research of any kind. Whether we have a clipboard in hand with a survey, or if we are asking about people's life stories, we must, as outsiders, persuade people we barely know to talk to us. We must do the best we can to work across and through differences and communalities – gender, ethnic, cultural, national, linguistic, religious – to forge ethical relations of trust with participants.

In thinking through ethnography as embodied research, our identities and experiences are especially salient to how we negotiate the research environment and engage with participants and are received by those we seek to study. The intimacy of ethnographic methods means that our bodies and biographies, our voices, thoughts, movements and actions are implicated in the research process. Conducting research may involve 'presentations of self', both conscious and unconscious. In doing ethnographic research, in working to develop relationships of trust with participants, researchers navigate the complexities of identity, of difference, of power and privilege, and I have sought thus far to consider and reflect on what are some of the central issues of ethnography as it relates to crime. But crime is changing and mutating, and we might need to ask whether, and to what extent, the past practices necessarily equip us for the future, and hence, in this conclusion I seek finally to consider what ethnography needs to be, rather than what it has been. What does the future of criminological ethnography look like for a criminology of the twenty-first century?

CRIMINOLOGICAL ETHNOGRAPHY FOR THE TWENTY-FIRST CENTURY

For the most part, the early adoption and promotion of qualitative social research and ethnography came about in a period of uncertainty surrounding the conclusion of the First World War. The first Chicago School, and its core figures such as Nels Anderson, Edward Franklin Frazier, George Herbert Mead, Robert E. Park, Walter Reckless, Edwin Sutherland and Frederic Thrasher, forged a distinctly urban sociology underpinned by commitment to human methods in a period of industrialisation, urbanisation, technological change and mass movement. The parallels with today should be all too apparent. However, the world has moved on considerably from the point where the first and second wave of Chicagoan researchers went into the city to map it and began to stumble across crime and criminality. Particularly, I suggest that criminological ethnography is well placed to consider the following questions:

- Is it the case that crime is rising and falling or changing or shifting in significant ways?
- Have modern technology and globalisation made criminal activity more common, more lucrative, easier to commit or harder to detect? How does new technology present new crime opportunities?
- Is the old distinction between 'organised' and 'white collar' crime being erased as traditional crime groups become more sophisticated, and bring their capital and skills to bear on the task of infiltrating and corrupting the legal economy?
- What are the main factors today that create and drive new criminal opportunities? What are the new crimes that are emerging and what do these look like? How are they understood for those who participate and offenders and victims?
- How can the impact of the crimes that are prevalent today be policed, controlled, assessed and prevented?
- What are the primary challenges likely to face the criminal justice system in the new century? How are these challenges met by statutory law enforcement and justice agencies, both national and international?

The crimes of today are framed by both changes and continuities. It could be argued, for example, that the nature of profit-driven crimes can be expected to remain the same, largely theft, extortion, commercial and financial fraud, trafficking in contraband goods and services and violence. There may be differences between the forms of crime experienced today and those of the past, for example, you may now be more likely to be robbed on the information superhighway than by a highway robber, but the essential elements of criminal conduct and the control of it remain largely unchanged.

However, though the underlying crimes may be the same, there will be three kinds of substantial differences. The first difference, in the case of market-based crime, is precisely which goods and services are trafficked. That is a function, in part, of what governments choose to ban. It is right that we do not accept legality as a given, slavery was legal, apartheid systems claimed legality, crime is of course a process of the excise of power underpinned by claims of rightfulness and morality, but who benefits?

This propensity of governments to use criminal law to control private behaviour is a commonplace and seemingly intractable instinct – but at the same time an inconsistently applied one. New psychotropic substances are invented, governments will create new forms of crime to ban them, and yet at the same time, there is wider recognition now of the failure of the war on drugs than in any other epoch. It should be pointed out that governments, facing such new narcotics, often seem to apply old logic, itself often based on myth and misunderstanding, that the importation is the preserve of criminal cartels and perpetrated by evil alien organised crime actors, while ignoring the deep functionality of the drug money generated (money that arguably that kept the global financial system afloat in the wake of the 2008 financial crisis).

Criminologists often attempt to embrace the role of problem solver while being aware of the broader socio-economic structures and power differentials that inhibit the life chances of some of our most vulnerable people. But they see how those vulnerable people and populations are impacted by, for example, new narcotic substances susceptible to abuse that are purely synthetic, home-made and often produced on a strictly entrepreneurial basis – and we ought to be asking does the rendering of this problem via the logic of 'organised crime' and prohibition over, say, regulated health-based approaches hold up? It is also unlikely that a picture of what is happening on the ground will emerge first from large scale statistical studies, rather, what is happening is far more likely to be shown in the first instance at a small scale by ethnographers and qualitative researchers. Ethnographers have long highlighted social shifts and changes like the ripples and the changes in the tide that come before the tsunami hits.

Criminological ethnographers will be at the forefront of understanding how illegal profits can be driven equally well by prohibition, regulation and taxation and governmental attempts to control a populace. They also sometimes are very apt at warning governments about the potential politics of unintended consequences that can come from a desire to legislate and do good. This has arguably happened in the past, it was the prohibition of alcohol that formed the backdrop to Thrasher's work in Chicago, but too few academics go back and read the original works as history to see that play out. What will emerge in the way of new crimes or at least new opportunities to commit old crimes will obviously depend on structural shifts in the patterns of trade and the resulting international price differentials. Trade liberalisation, when it leads to equalisation of costs across borders, has the potential to reduce those opportunities, but today, with rising nationalism and protectionism in the political realm, will we see the decline or the emergence of new opportunities for crime and corruption of power? I would suggest the latter is more likely.

The second difference concerns a change in the character of offenders. What do 'crime' and 'criminals' look like today? Certainly, with the likes of Mai (2018) and Parenti (2004; 2011), the way in which processes of crime are understood transcends the normal focus on the lower order offences and considers how the world today creates criminality among the most marginalised and excluded populace. Yet few criminological ethnographers look at the world in such a manner, and when they do, as in the case of Jacques and Wright (2015) in their examination of middle-class drug dealers or Salinas Edwards (2014) in a PhD study of youth transitions, they show that crime is far more ubiquitous than much criminology might have us believe. Yet shifting worlds and criminology need not wholly move away from a focus on the crimes that occur in precarious, post-industrial disadvantaged hubs all too often forgotten by political elites (Hall and Winlow, 2015). Are the crimes of today encountered in such places simply business as usual, or do things change, perhaps due to a 'democratisation' of criminal opportunities that accompany a more networked and global world? Ethnographers like Hobbs predicted that crime and criminal markets would be subject to change as much as continuities (Hobbs, 2013). Might I suggest that there may be greater temptations for employee fraud if workers feel less committed to a corporation as a result of cost cutting, globalisation and greater mobility? Might I reasonably suggest that the next great crime wave will more likely be predicated on behaviour encountered at the highest strands of the social strata? (Ho, 2009).

The third difference concerns the current trends towards greater disparities in the distribution of income while simultaneously life expectations keep rising might be extremely conducive to criminality (Hobbs, 2013). In many countries the frontiers between criminal and legitimate economic behaviour have become increasingly blurred as capitalist ideology extends ever greater sway. Could it be that how crimes are organised and conducted has shifted as opposed to dropped? While some liberal progressives suggest that we live in the least violent epoch ever, does that hold true when we look at the fact that human destruction of nature is rapidly eroding the world's capacity to provide food, water and security to billions of people, and human-made climate change and species extinction accelerate at an ever-greater rate?

To this end, ethnography is particularly useful, looking as it does at the everyday practices on the shop floor. Most crime is not 'organised crime' as that is broadly and conventionally understood, but much crime is driven by economic imperatives. Criminologists have provided far more ethnographies of thieves and shoplifters than they have of fly tippers, animal poachers, waste dumpers or commodity traders. Many criminologists prefer conventional forms of organised crime, and yet, numerous ethnographers have questioned the extent to which this concept is useful in any meaningful sense. Offenders who work in groups are often not very thoroughly organised at all, rather, they are loose networks of associates, and the democratising potential of new technology and new social media may reduce the emphasis on the importance of place on one hand and make such networks ever more widespread and looser (Hall and Antonopoulos, 2016). Conversely, as so much crime is tied to consumption practices, then the necessity for human interaction (the handover of the goods) may mean that such interaction does not disappear at all, but it may alter. An additional complication is that what should be discussed most of the time is not organised crime but organised crimes in the plural. Should the current focus of research and discussion be on acts, not on actors? If so, what is the implications for ethnography that has often taken the actor as its starting point? How might we ethnographers investigate the crimes of today? In 1978, to look at organised crime, William (Bill) Chambliss was able to commence his phenomenal and often overlooked ethnography *On the Take* by walking into a Seattle bar with no more than 'two days growth of beard, a pair of khaki pants and an old shirt' (1978: 14). He went on to provide a fantastic analysis of systemic police (and wider practices of criminal) corruption. How would we do the same today? Should our focus be corruption? Would we go looking in the same bars or start at the lower levels. What does the aspirant criminological ethnographer need today? A degree in computer science? An understanding of global finance? Friends in high places? A private education?

Traditionally criminological ethnography was borne of investigative reporters and journalists. Ironically, one element so frequently overlooked in much of both the first and second wave of Chicagoan sociology was the very media that had made Robert Park and Ernest Burgess. The role of the media in the construction of crime only became a focus once the spirit of interactionist sociology crossed the Atlantic to become part of the National Deviancy Symposium, and then, it was quickly subsumed into a rather simplistic and too often repeated claim of crafting 'moral panics'. Yet ethnographers at least have been far less useful in considering issues related to public perceptions on crime, and the extent to which these are mass-media derived. And the mass-media get their information partly through acts of pure imagination, and partly from the police, who in turn cite the mass-media as proof. Yet on the media, we might also want more generally to consider technology as tied to criminality today.

On one hand, in the early to mid-nineteenth century the impact of the railway, steamship and telegraph was far more revolutionary than the internet or mass air travel today. Indeed, virtually every kind of crime now conducted through modern electronic communications technology had some equivalent in the telegraph age – which saw everything from insider trading to price fixing to financial fraud. Today we may have crypto currencies and bit coin, but are the real differences that pronounced? Certainly, technological change can facilitate crimes by making detection more difficult and enabling multiple iterations in a shorter period. Call-forwarding, for example, can be used in telephone-based fraud operations and boiler room scams and in everything from selling securities and commodities to credit card scams. Certain frauds are based on misinformation that can be conveyed faster and disseminated more broadly, but does that new technology 'democratise' crime or make it likely ever more people will do it? Certainly today people may have an easier time entering into illicit enterprise as technology facilitates the conduct of crimes, but it also facilitates surveillance and detection, and again, how this happens and plays out in practice is a topic that criminological ethnographers can tell us much about. Yet while there are ample and growing instances of international cooperation in criminal justice, rarely do researchers look closely enough at such issues in that way and co-operative ethnographic networks remain a rarity. Ethnographers studying law enforcement and crime control today may need to spend less time on the streets or on police 'ride alongs', and more time in front of screens and talking with highly proficient specialists whose knowledge is far more technical. Are we prepared for such a challenge?

A criminology attuned to the powerful, such as critical criminology, might encourage academics to look upwards towards the top of the social strata when it comes to issues of crime, but arguably, when it comes to ethnography, that often does not happen all that much. Much that is good work in criminology could result from people taking legitimate roles and seeing from the inside the harms of the contemporary late modern world in the West, and the rapidly emerging new market zones in BRIC countries and beyond, particularly in the global south. Yet that does not happen much. Academics do this work, including ethnographers (Christian Parenti's *Tropic of Chaos* and *The Freedom* spring to mind) but are these appropriately recognised internally in criminology? While criminology has recently turned its attention to the global south, most criminological research remains primarily concerned with northern and western liberal social democracies. There are of course massive challenges to employing ethnography in some contexts (Xu et al., 2013) and it would be a brave ethnographer that simply turned up and attempted to ply their trade by asking questions in Pyongyang, Dushanbe or Tashkent. Yet similarly, and increasingly, criminology broadly is turning its attention to the global and failing to recognise that the local (or glocal) remains important in understanding the foreground dynamics of crime.

Be it the result of long-term developments, technological changes or sudden and unprecedented events, each era is faced with societal challenges that cause public anxiety and form the basis of political discussion and action. Our twenty-first century is no exception. Globalisation, mobility and migration, the rapid extension of human habitats, or the destruction of habitats due to large scale economic activity, the use of natural resources, and not least the pressing political developments in some parts the world are complex issues that pose a challenge for local, national and international governmental bodies. But also, for ordinary people there are challenges. Behind these technical administrative challenges there is the much more fundamental question of who the real victims are and who benefits from crises. Ethnography has long put a face to the crime and victimisation realities, and needs to continue to do this, but does it also need a better grasp of the rationale and the purpose of such work? The core question must be, what is the point? What are we building knowledge for?

For me, criminological ethnography is an approach that has real value because it can improve society. Arguably today we have a political elite largely incapable of understanding the new demands of society and of establishing a dialogue with citizens, leaving a vacuum that is filled by populists and ideologues. These populists are not usually motivated by a desire to deal with complex issues or to point out alternatives that are for the greater good. Indeed, simplicity and common sense are often the order of the day. From this pessimistic perspective, it is very easy to fall into despair and hopelessness, but we need not be negative. Ethnographic work and criminological ethnography can help to shape a better discussion on the intricacies of crime and control, but it can also help us towards better ways of doing and securing justice, in order to build a more sustainable, fairer and equitable world.

Early criminological ethnography emerged at a time where the building of new social democracies and welfare states were in view. It is important not to forget that ethnography as social science emerged in the 1920s and 1930s, a critical moment that was full of opportunities. The Second World War was clearly a dark spell, yet social researchers can now play a small part in using the dissatisfaction, frustration and indignation in contemporary society to create new relationships and new social pacts. We must find ways to harness this vision and to make sure that the vacuum is not filled by those who seek personal gain and that this indignation does not result in social isolation, nihilism, cynicism or even violence. Ethnographers can and should build accurate pictures and show the complexities, through investigating, observing and revealing the political and providing not just an explanation of the present, but a positive map for the future. I hope that having read this book you might feel a little bit better informed and perhaps even empowered to get out into the field and try to do just that.

CHAPTER SUMMARY

This chapter, and indeed the book, has sought to give readers what can only be a brief introduction to what I have termed criminological ethnography, and in doing that and using that terminology, I am arguing that there is an ethnographic sentiment that can be found at the heart of qualitative criminology. I have looked at both current studies in criminological ethnography and the development of this sentiment. As I have averred, the sub-discipline is once again gaining ground and yielding an abundance of fascinating and real insights. Building on recent works the book has explored the ways crime and criminalisation are tied to power and politics. It has looked at drug trade, human trafficking, prostitution, violence, deviance and white-collar crime. More generally, it has investigated the ways that crime and criminology have developed – becoming increasingly transnational and multi-modal – and the way policing is seeking to keep up with and combat novel kinds of crime and deviance emerging today.

The book is keen to encourage readers to look critically at crime and criminalisation and control as well as to ponder novel developments and future possibilities within criminological ethnography. In this final chapter I have sought to look at how crime challenges shift and alter, and how these are influenced by formations of power, and to contemplate what this might tell us about larger social, political and global change. For over a century, the ethnographic method has been one of best tools in the criminologist's kit to find out exactly what criminals do, why (they think) they do it and what the local cultural and material contexts in which they operate look like and feel like. I do not want you to read any more, I want you to take the lessons out into the world and try them, because all criminology can be improved with a bit of the ethnographic criminological sentiment.

GLOSSARY

Access the term used to describe the initial process, and then the ongoing and continually re-establishment of admittance and acceptance into the field of study and to participants. Access essentially describes the process of gaining contact to field settings, participants and fieldwork sites, determining whether and to what extent the ethnographer will conform to overt and covert roles, and how they will explain, rationalise and justify their place in fieldwork, both at the commencement of the project, and as part of a continued and re-negotiated contact throughout and potentially beyond the fieldwork processes.

Aetiology the term aetiology denotes cause, and specifically in criminology relates to issues around the causes or generative features that drive crime and criminality. Much early criminology was concerned with aetiology and, specifically, in criminology Jock Young made much of criminological abandonment of concern with aetiology as part of its administrative turn during the late 1970s and 1980s as part of a rational choice inspired governmental perspective.

Analytic realism is a postmodern ethnographic methodology that seeks to challenge the postmodernist view that ethnography occupies no particular scientific or privileged position. In the late 1980s, claims to objectivity, accuracy and truth brought about by thick description were being challenged by scholars who argued that such accounts did not represent reality as it is. Analytic realism details the view that researchers need to substantiate their findings via a reflexive process – to investigate ourselves while we are investigating others – and through that process ethnography becomes research that is privileged and stands above everyday accepted wisdom and observation, 'allowing ethnography to rise above the morass and meaninglessness of post-modern relativism and scepticism' (Brewer, 2000: 50).

Analysis in ethnography, analysis is not a neatly defined period or phase of research, or a linear or simple process of considering data and making sense of data, but rather tends to be an iterative phase (O'Reilly 2009) where the process of sense making is one that is ongoing, and where the researcher seeks to make sense of and continually re-appraise data and research strategy. There are various approaches for analysis of ethnographic data, from analytic realism through discourse and narrative analysis and grounded theory, and occasionally methods of analysis are combined.

Anthropology the study of humans and human behaviour and societies in both the past and present. Social and cultural anthropology study the norms and values of societies. Linguistic anthropology studies how language affects social life. Biological or physical anthropology studies the biological development of humans. As a research approach, anthropology has tended to traditionally employ ethnography and ethnology and it was traditional early anthropology and its practitioners that developed ethnographic approaches incorporated into the social sciences.

Auto-ethnography a form of qualitative research in which an author uses self-reflection and writing to explore anecdotal and personal experience and connect this autobiographical story to wider cultural, political and social meanings and understandings. Auto-ethnography is a self-reflective form of writing used both to validate findings and a heuristic device, particularly in criminological ethnography.

BCCCS the Birmingham Centre for Contemporary Cultural Studies was a research centre at the University of Birmingham, England. It was founded in 1964 by Richard Hoggart, its first director, the Centre played a major role in developing the field of cultural studies, and advances in associated disciplines such as sociology and criminology. The Centre was led by Stuart Hall (1969–1979) and it pioneered a variety of approaches to the study of culture, including: ideological analysis, studies of working-class cultures (and specifically subcultures), the role of media in construction of news and media audiences, feminist cultural and ethnographic research, and struggles in state politics such as in regards to race, and often the link between race and crime and control. While it championed an array of research approaches, some notable ethnographies such as Paul Willis (1978) *Learning to Labour* emerged from academics working in the centre.

Coding in the social sciences, coding is an analytical process in which data, in both quantitative form (such as questionnaires results) or qualitative (such as interview transcripts) is categorised and sorted in order to facilitate analysis. In some forms of analysis, such as grounded theory, the coding process assists in theory building and selecting prominent themes.

Chicago(an) in the social sciences, the department of sociology at the University of Chicago has long held a special symbolic appeal, due as much to its association with the transformation and incorporation of qualitative methods as with the theoretical ideas or topics it studied. This Chicagoan sociology was framed in symbolic interactionism. The Chicago School (sometimes described as the ecological school) produced the first major body of work during the 1920s and 1930s specialising in urban sociology, and research into the urban environment combining theory and ethnographic fieldwork. A second wave Chicago School became more prominent in the years after the Second World War and proved to be influential on the development of British criminology and sociology through the National Deviancy Symposium.

Covert covert participant observation is a method in social science research. Participant observation involves a researcher joining the group he or she is studying, and in the case of covert observation, the researcher's status is not made known or disclosed to the group. While this creates an association with deception, Calvey notes, covert research linked to ethnography has a long and established tradition in the social sciences and has been employed to study a range of phenomena where traditional informal informed consent and overtly negotiated access would not be possible (Calvey, 2017).

Critical (criminology) a theoretical (criminological) perspective that focuses on challenging traditional understandings and uncovering false beliefs about crime and criminal justice, often but not exclusively by taking a conflict perspective, such as Marxism, feminism, political economy theory or critical theory. Critical criminology frequently takes a perspective of examining the genesis of crime and nature of 'justice' within the social structure of a class and status inequalities and power dynamics, with the functions of empirical criminological research being to unearth and expose such social processes.

Deductive (reasoning)   the process of reasoning from one or more statements (premises) to reach a logically certain conclusion. Deductive reasoning goes in as linear direction and follows a sequential process, and links premises with conclusions. If all premises are true, the terms are clear, and the rules of deductive logic are followed, then the conclusion reached is necessarily true. Deductive reasoning is a top-down logic and contrasts with inductive reasoning (bottom-up logic). In deductive reasoning, a conclusion is reached reductively by applying general rules which hold over the entirety of a closed domain of discourse, narrowing the range under consideration until only the conclusion(s) is left. Ethnography, as an inductive process, is often contrasted with more deductive styles of positivistic research.

Discourse   this simply means the written or spoken communication or debate, so criminological discourse is communication or debate as it applies to criminology. However, in social science research it also used in 'discourse analysis', which is an approach that essentially seeks to analyse that discourse.

Emic   as the OED notes, emic is traditionally an anthropological term relating to or denoting an approach to the study or description of a language or culture in terms of its internal elements and their functioning rather than in terms of any existing external scheme, hence in criminological ethnography it is the attempt to understand the research subject or participants' inner world view.

#Epistemology   means 'theories of knowledge' and describes beliefs about how knowledge can be generated. In general terms, in the social science epistemological standpoints are generally positivist or interpretivist, although some also suggest a critical epistemology.

Ethics   are moral principles that govern a person's behaviour or the conducting of an activity. In the social sciences, the focus on ethics in relation to subjects or participants is framed around the fact that the subject is human, and hence the presumptions in general are against doing harm through research. To that end, the social sciences are guided by general ethical principles, and research ethics laid down in codes or guides seek to limit the potential harms of unethical research conduct.

Etic   the counterpoint to the emic perspective. In anthropology an 'etic' account is a description of a behaviour or belief by an observer, in terms that can be applied across cultures. Etic accounts and understandings seek to be 'culturally neutral', hence they limit any ethnocentric, political and/or cultural bias or alienation by the observer. It is often suggested that etic is the outsider overview or the objective descriptor of events in contrast to the emic internal meanings.

Ethnography   a research approach drawn from anthropology and the study of people and groups in their natural settings. Typically it involves a researcher (or team of researchers) spending prolonged periods in the setting in which the participants or subjects are normally encountered, gathering data about the everyday activities, practices and associated meanings for the group of individuals or individual that they are studying.

Feminism while there is no single feminist perspective (and feminists may ascribe to different branches or variant schools of feminist thought), feminism more broadly is a term used to describe perspectives that share a concern with the inequality of women and the discrimination that they face in a society that is patriarchal, and which disempowers women by structures and attitudes that assume and presume or promote the dominance and prioritisation of men.

Fieldnotes qualitative notes and data records that are gathered and recorded by social scientists or researchers in the course of field research, during or after their observation of a specific phenomenon that they are studying. The notes are intended to be read as evidence that gives meaning and aids in the understanding of the phenomenon. Fieldnotes allow the researcher to access the subject and record what they observe in an unobtrusive manner.

Fieldwork the process that involves the collection of data outside a laboratory, library or normal setting. The approaches and methods used in field research vary across disciplines, but social scientists conducting field research may interview or observe people in their natural environments to learn their languages, folklore and social structures. In particular, fieldwork is often described as ethnographic if it is done over a sustained period of field research involving variable methods: informal interviews, direct observation, participation in the life of the group, collective discussions, analyses of personal documents produced within the group, self-analysis, results from activities undertaken off- or on-line, and life-histories. Although the method generally is characterised as qualitative research, it may (and often does) include quantitative dimensions. Qualitative fieldwork involving theories of law making, law breaking and law enforcement and issues of crime, crime control and deviant behaviour are the stuff of criminological ethnography.

Gakekeeper a key or core contact (sometimes, though not always a research participant themselves) who stands between the data collector and a potential respondent. Gatekeepers, by virtue of their personal or work relationship to a respondent, are able to control who has access, and when, to the respondent.

'Getting out' the term that ethnographers use to denote the formal leaving of the field research setting, a short hand for withdrawal from the fieldwork data collection stage of a qualitative project. However, while it denotes a simple process of entry, immersion, withdrawal, in contemporary criminological research, some academics are sceptical about the extent to which such notions of sequential and segmented research phases actually apply in reality to the complex and multifaceted forms of relationship that researcher and participants might establish (e.g. see Ancrum, 2014).

Heuristic a heuristic technique is any approach to problem solving, learning or discovery that employs a practical method that is not perfect but is sufficient for the immediate aims. Where finding an optimal solution is not possible, heuristic methods are utilised to speed up the process of finding a satisfactory explanations. Heuristics can be conceived of as the mental process of decision-making and coming to an understanding. Examples of this method include using a rule of thumb, an educated guess, an intuitive judgement.

Hypothetico-deductive method is a description of an approach to scientific method linked with positivistic perspectives that promotes scientific inquiry and empirical investigation whereby research proceeds by means by formulating hypotheses, which are then subject to testing, whereby they can be either proved (or disproved) through empirical experimentation and observation. The hypothetico-deductive method can never absolutely verify (prove the truth of a hypothesis) but commonly exists to falsify or disprove hypothesis. It is different and rooted more to the physical sciences from other research models such as the inductive approach or grounded theory which ethnography is more commonly traditionally associated with.

Inductive the opposite of deductive, inductive reasoning, also sometimes called induction or bottom-up (ground up) logic, constructs or evaluates general propositions that are derived from specific examples. Inductive reasoning, or induction, is reasoning from a specific case or cases and deriving a general rule, and hence, ethnography is a form of inductive research.

Interactionism (or symbolic) interactionism is a sociological theory that develops from practical considerations and alludes to people's utilisation of interactions and engagements with others. In other words, it is a frame of reference to better understand how individuals interact with one another to create symbolic worlds, and in return, how these worlds shape individual behaviours. It originates from a sociological perspective which developed around the middle of the twentieth century and that continues to be influential in some areas of the discipline, particularly associated with American philosophy of pragmatism and particularly from the work of George Herbert Mead and Herbert Blumer, and became a significant influence in the onset of the first and subsequent waves of Chicagoan sociology.

Interpretivism in the social sciences, interpretivism is a theoretical stance that proposes that the social realm cannot be studied with the scientific method of investigation applied to the natural world (as is claimed in positivism) and that investigation of the social realm requires a different epistemology. Fundamental to this epistemology is the belief that the concepts and language researchers bring to their research shape their perception of the social world under investigation where knowledge must be gained via interpretation.

Interviews or interviewing in qualitative social science are often the most popular form of gathering data for analysis. Ranging from structured and scripted through to semi-structured and unstructured (purely conversational), interviews have long been part of the underpinning method that informs the ethnographic approach alongside participant observation.

Life history a social research method first coined in anthropology for use with native American populations, but the method was latterly incorporated into Chicagoan sociology in its first phase as a means of documenting the lives of migrants, the homeless, criminals and prostitutes. Interviewers looked at social and police records, as well as the society in general, and asked subjects to talk about their lives. The resulting research sought to understand not simply the individual but their place in the social order, the subject's view of their own life (i.e. what it was like to be this particular person) and how society perceived the subject.

Narrative analysis   seeks to analyse the stories which occur when one or more speakers engage in sharing and recounting an experience or event. Typically, the telling of a story occupies multiple turns in the course of a conversation and stories or narratives may share common structural features, and irrespective of veracity or truth of such stories, lessons can be learned merely from the very construction of that narrative., In criminology in particular at present, narrative approaches are being popularised when combined with qualitative inquiry, particularly as part of what has been termed 'narrative criminology' (Presser and Sandberg, 2015).

Ontology   the philosophical study of being. More broadly, it studies and seeks to understand concepts that directly relate to being or the existence of reality. Ontology often deals with questions concerning what entities exist, can be known or may be said to exist and how such entities may be understood, for example whether there is a reality that can ever be known or understood.

Overt   (observations) are those which are undertaken with the knowledge of the group, or some members of the group under study where access has been negotiated through a process of gaining admission and participant consent. In contrast to covert research, which involves some degree of concealment or deception, overt research is presumed to be the default ethical standard to which ethnographers and qualitative researchers conform, with ethical norms expecting that most field research is undertaken with the participants' informed consent.

Participant observation   one type of data collection method typically used in qualitative research (and one of the two foundational methods employed in ethnography, alongside interviewing). It is a widely used approach and strategy in many disciplines, particularly employed in research in anthropology, sociology, communication studies, human geography and social psychology. Its aim is to gain a close and intimate understanding via watching and recording, and researchers tend to observe and, to various degrees of immersion, participate in the culture and practices with a given group of individuals in their natural and organic cultural environment, usually over an extended period. The method originated in the field research of social anthropologists, especially Bronisław Malinowski and his students in Britain, before its incorporation into the urban sociology of the Chicago School of Sociology in the United States from the 1920s.

Phenomenology   the philosophical study of the structures of experience and consciousness. As a philosophical movement it was founded in the early years of the twentieth century and incorporated into modern social science by Peter Berger and Thomas Luckmann in their seminal work *The Social Construction of Reality: A Treatise in the Sociology of Knowledge* (1966), where they positioned phenomenology as a perspective rather than as an alternative paradigm in sociology. In their rendering of a sociology of knowledge from a phenomenological perspective, they demonstrate how reality as such, not just social reality, is constructed and installed as objective reality, which in turn affects society's members subjectively through processes of internalisation and socialisation. The phenomenological perspective focuses on the subjective and everyday aspects of human existence, and hence has used ethnography as a means of attempting to understand this, for example in works such as that of Charlesworth (1999) on poverty and being working class in Rotherham, although phenomenology and ethnography are rarely connected in attempts to study crime or its control.

Positivism   a philosophical theory and standpoint in the social sciences that traditionally holds that the social sciences can mimic the natural sciences and arrive at understandings based on testing of hypotheses and experimentation with the ultimate goal to formulate abstract and universal laws on the operative causal dynamics. Hence society can be studied in a manner that is informed by the importation of general scientific principles where clarity, replicability, reliability and validity and the use of quantitative data tend to be hallmarks.

Postmodernism   a general and wide-ranging term which is applied to literature, art, philosophy, architecture, fiction and cultural and literary criticism, alongside the social sciences. Postmodernism is largely a reaction to the assumed certainty of modernist scientific, or objective, efforts to explain reality, progress or truth through meta narratives or grand theory, progressive rationalism or enlightenment. As a broad movement that developed in the mid- to late twentieth century it marked a departure from modernism, and is characterised by an attitude of scepticism, irony or rejection towards grand theory and universalist notions of objective reality, morality, truth, human nature, reason, language and social progress.

Qualitative research   essentially qualitative research is a scientific method of observation to gather non-numerical data. This type of research is orientated to meanings, concepts, definitions, characteristics, metaphors, symbols and description of things rather than numerical counts or measures. Hence qualitative research approaches are employed across many academic disciplines, focusing particularly on the human elements of the social sciences.

Quantitative research   quantitative research gathers data in a numerical form which can be put into categories, or in rank order, or measured in units of measurement. This type of data can be used to construct graphs and tables of raw data. Quantitative researchers aim to establish general laws of behaviour across different settings and contexts. Research is used to test a theory and ultimately support or reject it. Hence quantitative data tends to be traditionally associated with a positivist epistemological orientation.

Realism   in philosophy, realism accords with the view that things that are known or perceived have an existence or nature which is independent of individual cognition (i.e. they exist independent of whether or how individuals think about or perceive them). It has slightly different meanings in other contexts such as in the arts where it is associated with the attempt to depict subjects naturally, truthfully or with accuracy. In criminology, particularly during the 1970s onwards, it describes approaches that for the most part have tended to be affiliated with the political right and left, but which share a commonality in so far as they accept the general harmful nature of crime as it is commonly and conventionally understood as damaging for social cohesion and the social fabric.

Reflexivity   in ethnographic research reflexivity involves two things. First, it requires that researchers reflect upon the research process in order to assess the effect of their presence and their research techniques on the nature and extent of the data collected. Crudely put, researchers must consider to what extent respondents were telling the truth as opposed to what the subject perceived they wanted to hear, whether other factors may influence the data or the data collection process, whether the format of the data collection restricts the kind of data being collected, and any other factor that may have a bearing on the project and the data collection including the influence of their own presence in the field. Second (and probably more significantly), it is the term ethnographic researchers use to describe the process of critically reflecting upon the theoretical structures they have drawn out of their ethnographic analysis. Researchers are expected to reconceptualise their evidence using other possible models; rather than just fit details into a preformed schema they should try to reform the schema to see if the details have different meanings.

Schema   essentially a schema (plural schemata or schemas) describes a pattern of thought or behaviour that organises categories of information and the relationships among them. It can also be described as a mental structure of preconceived ideas, a framework representing some aspect of the world, or a system of organising and perceiving new information. Hence in ethnography it is the internalised system of organisation cognitively that the fieldworker uses to make sense of data.

Snowballing   or snowball sampling is a means of generating participants or interviewees. In sociology it is a non-probability sampling technique where existing study subjects recruit future subjects from among their acquaintances. Thus, the sample group is said to grow like a rolling giant snowball. As the sample builds up, enough data are gathered to be useful for research. This sampling technique is often used in hidden populations, such as criminals, drug users or sex workers, which are difficult for researchers to normally gain access to. As sample members are not selected from a sampling frame, snowball samples are subject to numerous biases. As a technique it has been employed and well documented as a strategy by a number of US criminologists including Richard Wright, Scott Decker and Bruce Jacobs.

Social constructionism   essentially an anti-realist, relativist stance which is rooted in both symbolic interactionism and phenomenology. It is a theory of knowledge in the social sciences that considers the development understandings of the world via human interactions where meanings are made and constructed rather than existing externally and independently. Constructionists and interpretivists in general tend to share that they focus on the process(es) by which meanings are created, negotiated, sustained and modified. It is particularly associated with British sociology from the 1960s onwards, and with second wave Chicagoan sociology.

Subjectivity   a central philosophical concept, related to consciousness, agency, personhood, reality and truth. These various definitions of subjectivity are sometimes joined together in philosophy. The term is most commonly used as an explanation for that which influences, informs and biases people's judgements about truth or reality. It is the collection of the perceptions, experiences, expectations, personal or cultural understanding and beliefs specific to a person into a specific category. Subjectivity is contrasted to the philosophy of objectivity, which is described as a view of truth or reality that is free of any individual's biases, interpretations, feelings and beliefs.

BIBLIOGRAPHY

Adler, P. (1985) *Wheeling and Dealing*. New York: Columbia University Press.

Adler, P. A and Adler, P. (1987) 'The past and the future of ethnography', *Journal of Contemporary Ethnography*, 16 (1): 4–24.

Adler, P. and Adler, P. (1998) 'Observational techniques', in N. Denzin and Y. Lincoln (eds) *Collecting and Interpreting Qualitative Materials*. London: Sage.

Agar, M. (2008) *The Professional Stranger: An Informal Introduction to Ethnography* (2nd edn). Bingley: Emerald.

Altheide, D. and Johnson, M. (1994) 'Criteria for accessing interpretive validity in qualitative research', in N. Dezin and Y. Lincoln (eds), *Collecting and Interpreting Qualitative Materials*. London: Sage.

Ancrum, C. (2011) '"Knowing the dance": the advantages and downfalls of a "criminal biography" in teaching criminology in higher education', *Enhancing Learning in the Social Sciences*, 3 (1): 1–21, doi: 10.11120/elss.2011.03030009.

Ancrum, C. (2013) 'Stalking the margins of legality: ethnography, participant observation and the late modern underworld', in S. Winlow and R. Atkinson (eds), *New Directions in Crime and Deviancy*. London: Routledge.

Ancrum, C. and Treadwell, J. (2016) 'Beyond ghosts, gangs and good sorts: commercial cannabis cultivation and illicit enterprise in England's disadvantaged inner cities', *Crime, Media, Culture*, 13 (1): 69–84.

Anderson, E. (1999) *Code of the Street: Decency, Violence, and the Moral Life of the Inner City*. New York: W. W. Norton.

Anderson, R. (2015) *Illegality, Inc.: Clandestine Migration and the Business of Bordering Europe*. Oakland. University of California Press.

Antonopoulos, G., Hall, A., Large, J., Shen, A., Crang, M. and Andrews, M. (2018) *Fake Goods, Real Money: The Counterfeiting Business and its Financial Management*. Bristol: Policy Press.

Archard, P. (1979) *Vagrancy, Alcoholism and Social Control*. London: Macmillan.

Armstrong, G. (1993) 'Like that Desmond Morris?', in D. Hobbs and T. May (eds), *Interpreting the Field: Accounts of Ethnography*. Oxford: Oxford University Press, pp. 3–43.

Armstrong, G. (1998) *Football Hooligans: Knowing the Score*. Oxford: Berg.

Atkinson, P. (1990) *The Ethnographic Imagination*. London: Routledge.

Atkinson, P. (2015) *For Ethnography*. London: Sage.

Atkinson, P., Coffey, A., Delamont, S., Lofland, J. and Lofland, L. (eds) (2001) *Handbook of Ethnography*. London: Sage.

Ayres, T. and Treadwell, J. (2012) 'Bars, drugs and football thugs: alcohol, cocaine use and violence in the night time economy among English football firms', *Criminology and Criminal Justice: An International Journal*, 12 (1): 83–100.

Baker, S. and Edwards, R. (2012) 'How many qualitative interviews is enough?', Review Paper, NCRM. Available at http://eprints.ncrm.ac.uk/2273/4/how_many_interviews.pdf (accessed 27 March 2019).

Bartels, L. and Richards, K. (eds) (2011) *Qualitative Criminology: Stories from the Field*. Sydney: Hawkins Press.

Becker, H. (1963) *Outsiders*. New York: Free Press.

Becker, H. S. (1967) 'Whose side are we on?', *Social Problems*, 14 (3): 239–247.

Bergmann, L. (2010) *Getting Ghost: Two Young Lives and the Struggle for the Soul of an American City*. Michigan: University of Michigan Press.

Bourgois, P. (2003) *In Search of Respect: Selling Crack in El Barrio*. Cambridge: Cambridge University Press.

Brewer, J. (2000) *Ethnography*. London: Sage.

Briggs, D. (2011) *Crack Cocaine Users: High Society and Low Life in South London*. London: Routledge.

Briggs, D. and Monge Gamero, R. (2017) *Dead End Lives: Drugs and Violence in the City Shadows*. Bristol: Policy.

Brougham, P. and Uttley, C. (2017) 'Risk for Researchers Studying Social Deviance or Criminal Behavior', *Social Sciences*, 6 (4): 130. https://doi.org/10.3390/socsci6040130.

Bryant, A. and Charmaz, K. (eds.) (2007) *The Sage Handbook of Grounded Theory*. London: Sage.

Bucerius, S. (2014) *Unwanted Muslim Immigrants, Dignity, and Drug Dealing*. Oxford: Oxford University Press.

Bulmer, M. (1984) *The Chicago School of Sociology*. Chicago: University of Chicago Press.

Burawoy, M., Blum, J. A., George, S., Gille, Z. and Thayer, M. (2000) *Global Ethnography*. Berkeley: University of California Press.

Burkitt, I. (2012) 'Emotional reflexivity: feeling, emotion and imagination in reflexive dialogues', *Sociology*, 46 (3): 458–472.

Calvey, D. (2008) 'The art and politics of covert research: doing "situated ethics" in the field', *Sociology*, 42 (5): 905–918.

Calvey, D. (2017) *Covert Research: The Art Politics and Ethics of Undercover Fieldwork*. London: Sage.

Campbell, A. (1986) *The Girls in the Gang*. Oxford: Blackwell.

Canning, V. (2017) *Gendered Harm and Structural Violence in the British Asylum System*. London: Routledge.

Carlen, P. (1976) *Magistrates Justice*. London: Martin Robertson Company.

Carlen, P. (1983) *Women's Imprisonment*. London: Routledge and Kegan Paul.

Chakravarti, L. (2016) *Made in Egypt: Gendered Identity and Aspiration on the Globalised Shop Floor*. New York. Berghahn.

Chamberlen, A. (2018) *Embodying Punishment: Emotions, Identities and Lived Experiences in Women's Prisons*, Clarendon Studies in Criminology Series. Oxford: Oxford University Press.

Chambliss, W. (1978) *On the Take: From Petty Crooks to Presidents*. Bloomington: Indiana University Press.

Charlesworth, S. (1999) *A Phenomenology of Working-Class Experience*. Cambridge: Cambridge University Press.

Charmaz, K. (2014) *Constructing Grounded Theory*. London: Sage.

Clemmer, D. (1940) *The Prison Community*. New York: Holt, Rinehart and Winston.

Clifford, J. and Marcus, G. (1986) (eds) *Writing Cultures*. Berkeley: University of California Press.

Clough, P. (1992) *The End(s) of Ethnography: From Social Realism to Social Criticism*. London: Sage.

Coffey, A. (1999) *The Ethnographic Self*. London: Sage.

Cohen, S. (1972) *Folk Devils and Moral Panics: The Creation of the Mods and Rockers*. London: Routledge.

Cohen, S. and Taylor, L. (1972) *Psychological Survival: The Experience of Long-Term Imprisonment*. Harmondsworth: Penguin.

Collison, M. (1995) *Police, Drugs and Community*. London: Free Association Books.

Colosi, R. (2010) *Dirty Dancing: An Ethnography of Lapdancing*, Abingdon: Willan/ Routledge.

Contreras, R. (2008) '"Damn, yo – who's that girl?" An ethnographic analysis of masculinity in drug robberies', *Journal of Contemporary Ethnography*, 38 (4): 465–492.

Contreras, R. (2013) *The Stickup Kids: Race, Drugs, Violence, and the American Dream*. Berkley: University of California Press.

Coomber, R. (2002) 'Signing away your life? Why research ethics committees (REC) shouldn't always require written confirmation that participants in research have been informed of the aims of the study and their rights — the case of criminal populations', *Sociological Research Online*, 7 (1): 1–4.

Cowburn, M., Gelsthorpe, L. and Wahidin, A. (eds) (2016) *Research Ethics in Criminology: Dilemmas, Issues and Solutions*. London: Routledge.

Creswell, J. and Plano Clark, V. (2007) *Designing and Conducting Mixed Methods Research*. London: Sage.

Crewe, B. (2009) *The Prisoner Society: Power, Adaptation and Social Life in an English Prison*. Oxford: Clarendon.

Deegan, M. J. (2001) 'The Chicago School of Ethnography', in P. Atkinson , A. Coffey, S. Delamont, J. Lofland and L. Lofland (eds). *Handbook of Ethnography*. London: Sage, pp. 11–25.

Densley, J. (2013) *How Gangs Work: An Ethnography of Youth Violence*. London: Palgrave Macmillan.

Denzin, N. (1998) 'The art and politics of interpretation', in N. Denzin and Y. Lincoln (eds.), *Collecting and Interpreting Qualitative Materials*. London: Sage, pp. 435–472.

Ditton, J. (1977) *Part-Time Crime: An Ethnography of Fiddling and Pilferage*. London: Macmillan.

Drake, D. H., Earle, R. and Sloan, J. (eds) (2015) *The Palgrave Handbook of Prison Ethnography*. Basingstoke: Palgrave.

Elliott, T. and Fleetwood, J. (2017) 'Law for ethnographers', *Methodological Innovations*, 10 (1): 1–13.

Ellis, A. (2016) *Men, Masculinities and Violence: An Ethnographic Study*. Abingdon: Routledge.

Ellis, A., Winlow, S. and Hall, S. (2017) '"Throughout my life I've had people walk all over me": trauma in the lives of violent men', *The Sociological Review*, 65: 699–713.

Fader, J. (2018) 'Keeping classic ethnographic traditions alive in the modern day academy', in S. Rice and M. Maltz (eds), *Doing Ethnography in Criminology: Discovery Through Fieldwork*. Cham, Switzerland: Springer, pp. 129–146.

Fassin, D. (2008) 'Beyond good and evil? Questioning the anthropological discomfort with morals', *Anthropological Theory*, 8 (4): 333–344.

Fassin, D. (2013) *Enforcing Order: An Ethnography of Urban Policing*. Cambridge: Polity.

Fassin, D. (2016) *Prison Worlds: An Ethnography of the Carceral Condition*. Cambridge: Polity.

Felson, M. (2002) *Crime and Everyday Life* (3rd edn). London: Sage.

Ferrell, J. (1997) 'Criminological verstehen: inside the immediacy of crime', *Justice Quarterly*, 14 (1): 3–23.

Ferrell, J. (2002) *Tearing Down the Streets*. London: Palgrave/Macmillan.

Ferrell, J. (2006) *Empire of Scrounge: Inside the Urban Underground of Dumpster Diving, Trash Picking, and Street Scavenging*. New York: New York University Press.

Ferrell, J. (2009) 'Kill method: a provocation', *Journal of Theoretical and Philosophical Criminology*, 1 (1): 1–22.

Ferrell, J. and Hamm, M. (eds) (1998) *Ethnography at the Edge: Crime, Deviance and Field Research*. Boston, MA: Northeastern University Press.

Ferrell, J., Hayward, K. and Young, J. (2015) *Cultural Criminology*. London: Sage.

Fine, M. (1994) 'Working the hyphens', in N. Denzin and Y. Lincoln (eds), *Handbook of Qualitative Research*. Thousand Oaks, CA: Sage, pp. 65–84.

Fleetwood, J. (2011) 'Five kilos: penalties and practice in the international cocaine trade', *British Journal of Criminology*, 51 (2): 375–393.

Fleetwood, J. (2014) *Drug Mules: Women in the International Cocaine Trade*. Basingstoke: Palgrave Macmillan.

Fleetwood, J. and Potter, G. R. (2017) 'Ethnographic research on crime and control: Editors' introduction', *Methodological Innovations*, 10 (1): 1–11. https://doi.org/10.1177/205 9799117728859.

Fleisher, M. (1998) 'Ethnographers, pimps, and the company store', in J. Ferrell and M. S. Hamm (eds), *Ethnography at the Edge: Crime, Deviance and Field Research*. Boston, MA: Northeastern University Press, pp. 44–64.

Flick, U. (2014) *An Introduction to Qualitative Research* (5th edn). London: Sage.

Foster, J. (1990) *Villains: Crime and Community in the Inner City*. London: Routledge.

Fraser, A. (2015) *Urban Legends: Gang Identity in the Post-Industrial City*. Oxford: Clarendon.

Gadd, D. and Jefferson, T. (2006) *Psychosocial Criminology*. London: Sage.

Gadd, D. and Jefferson, T. (2007) 'On the defensive: a psychoanalytically informed psychosocial reading of *The Jack-Roller*', *Theoretical Criminology*, 11 (4): 443–467.

Galliher, J. F. (1995) 'Chicago's two worlds of deviance research: whose side are they on?', in G. A. Fine (ed.), *A Second Chicago School? The Development of Postwar American Sociology*, Chicago, IL: University of Chicago Press, pp. 164–187.

Garrett, B. (2013) *Explore Everything: Place-Hacking the City*. London: Verso.

Garthwaite, K. (2016) *Hunger Pains: Life Inside Foodbank Britain*. Bristol. Policy Press.

Geertz, C. (1973) *The Interpretation of Cultures*. New York: Basic Books.

Glaser, B. and Strauss, A. (1967) *The Discovery of Grounded Theory*. Chicago: Aldine.

Gobo, G. and Mollie, A. (2017) *Doing Ethnography* (2nd edn). London: Sage.

Goffman, E. (1959) *The Presentation of Self in Everyday Life*. New York: Doubleday.

Goffman, E. (1961) *Asylums: Essays on the Social Situation of Mental Patients and Other Inmates*. New York: Anchor.

Goffman, A. (2014) *On the Run*. Chicago: Chicago University Press.

Gold, R. L. (1958) 'Roles in sociological field observations', *Social Forces*, 36 (3): 217–223.

Gonzalez Van Cleve, N. (2016) *Crook County: Racism and Injustice in America's Largest Criminal Court*. Stanford: Stanford Law Books

Goodey, J. (2000) 'Biographical lessons for criminology', *Theoretical Criminology*, 4 (4): 473–498.

Gouldner, A. (1968) 'The sociologist as partisan: sociology and the welfare state', *The American Sociologist*, 3 (2): 103–116.

Gouldner, A. (1975) *For Sociology*. Harmondsworth: Pelican.

Gov.UK (2016) User research. Available at www.gov.uk/service-manual/user-research (accessed 21 December 2016).

Gray, G. (2002) 'A socio-legal ethnography of the right to refuse dangerous work', *Studies in Law, Politics & Society*, 24: 133–169.

Gray, G. (2009) 'The responsibilization strategy of health and safety: neo-liberalism and the reconfiguration of individual responsibility for risk', *British Journal of Criminology*, 49 (3): 326–342.

Haggerty, K. (2004) 'Ethics creep: governing social science research in the name of ethics', *Qualitative Sociology*, 27 (4): 415–416.

Hall, S. (2012) *Theorising Crime and Deviance: A New Perspective*. London: Sage.

Hall, S. (2018) 'Doing ethnographic research in criminology', in P. Davies and P. Francis (eds), *Doing Criminological Research*. London: Sage, pp. 385–412.

Hall, A. and Antonopoulos, G. (2016) *Fake Meds Online: The Internet and the Transnational Market in Illicit Pharmaceuticals*. London: Palgrave Macmillan.

Hall, S. and Winlow, S. (2015) *Revitalizing Criminological Theory: Towards a New Ultra-Realism*. London: Routledge, Taylor and Francis.

Hall, S., Winlow, S. and Ancrum, C. (2005) 'Radgies, gangstas, and mugs: imaginary criminal identities in the twilight of the pseudo-pacification process', *Social Justice*, 32 (1): 100–112.

Hall, S., Winlow, S. and Ancrum, C. (2008) *Criminal Identities and Consumer Culture: Crime, Exclusion and the New Culture of Narcissism*. Cullompton: Willan Publishing.

Hallsworth, S. (2013) *The Gang and Beyond: Interpreting Violent Street Worlds*. Palgrave Macmillan: Basingstoke.

Hammersley, M. (2006) 'Ethnography: problems and prospects', *Ethnography and Education*, 1 (1): 3–14.

Hammersley, M. and Atkinson, P. (2007) *Ethnography: Principles in Practice* (3rd edn). London, Tavistock.

Hart, C. (ed.) (2010) *The Legacy of the Chicago School of Sociology*. Kingswinsford: Midrash Publishing.

Harvey, J. (2007) *Young Men in Prison: Surviving and Adapting to Life Inside*. Cullompton: Willan.

Harvey, J. (2015) 'The ethnographic practitioner', in D. Drake, R. Earle and J. Sloan (eds), *The Palgrave Handbook of Prison Ethnography*. Basingstoke: Palgrave, pp. 390–402.

Hasselberg, I. (2016) *Enduring Uncertainty: Deportation, Punishment and Everyday Life*. New York. Berghahn.

Heath, S. Brooks, R. Cleaver, E. and Ireland, E. (2009) (eds) *Researching Young People's Lives*. London: Sage.

Ho, K. (2009) *Liquidated: An Ethnography of Wall Street*. Durham, NC: Duke University Press.

Hobbs, R. (1988) *Doing the Business*. Oxford: Clarendon.

Hobbs, R. (1993) 'Peers, fears and academic careers: writing as fieldwork', in D. Hobbs and T. May (eds), *Interpreting the Field: Accounts of Ethnography*. Oxford: Oxford University Press, pp. 45–66.

Hobbs, R. (1995) *Bad Business*. Oxford: Oxford University Press.

Hobbs, R. (2001) 'Ethnography of deviance', in P. Atkinson, A. Coffey, S. Delamont, J., Lofland and L. Lofland (eds), *Handbook of Ethnography*. London: Sage , pp. 204–219.

Hobbs, R. (2013) *Lush Life: Constructing Organized Crime in the UK*. Oxford: Oxford University Press.

Hodkinson, P. (2005) 'Inside research in the study of youth culture', *Journal of Youth Studies*, 8 (2): 131–150.

Hoefinger, H. (2013) *Sex, Love and Money in Cambodia: Professional Girlfriends and Transactional Relationships*. London. Routledge.

Hoey, B. and Fricke, T. (2007) '"From sweet potatoes to God Almighty": Roy Rappaport on being a hedgehog', *American Ethnologist*, 34 (3): 581–599.

Holdaway, S. (1983) *Inside the British Police*. Oxford, Blackwell.

Holmes, M. (2010) 'The emotionalisation of reflexivity', *Sociology*, 44 (1): 139–154.

Honkatukia, P., Nyqvist, L. and Pösö, T. (2003) 'Sensitive issues in vulnerable conditions: studying violence in youth residential care', *Young: Nordic Journal of Youth Research*, 11 (4): 323–339.

Hopper, C. B. and Moore, J. (1990) 'Women in outlaw motorcycle gangs', *Journal of Contemporary Ethnography*, 18: 363–387.

Hoyle, C. (2000) 'Being a "nosy bloody cow": ethical and methodological issues in researching domestic violence', in R. King and R. Wincup (eds), *Doing Research on Crime and Justice*. Oxford: Oxford University Press, pp. 395–406.

Humphreys, L. (1970) *The Tearoom Trade: A Study of Homosexual Encounters in Public Places*. London: Duckworth Overlook.

Jacobs, B. (1998) 'Researching crack dealers: dilemmas and contradictions in ethnography at the edge: crime, deviance, and field research', in J. Ferrell and M. S. Hamm (eds), *Ethnography at the Edge: Crime, Deviance and Field Research*. Boston, MA: Northeastern University Press.

Jacobs, B. (2000) *Robbing Drug Dealers: Violence Beyond the Law*. New York: Aldine de Gruyter Publishing.

Jacobs, B. and Wright, R. (2006) *Street Justice: Retaliation in the Criminal Underworld*. Cambridge: Cambridge University Press.

Jacques, S. and Wright, R. (2015) *Code of the Suburb: Inside the World of Young Middle-Class Drug Dealers*. Chicago: University of Chicago Press.

Jewkes, Y. (2011) 'Autoethnography and emotion as intellectual resources: doing prison research differently', *Qualitative Inquiry*, 18 (1): 63–75 .

Juris, J. S. (2007) 'Practicing militant ethnography with the movement for global resistance in Barcelona', in S. Shukaitis, D. Graeber and E. Biddle (eds), *Constituent Imagination: Militant Investigations/Collective Theorization*. Oakland, CA: AK Press, pp. 164–178.

Kadir, N. (2016) *The Autonomous Life? Paradoxes of Hierarchy and Authority in the Squatters Movement in Amsterdam*. Manchester. Manchester University Press.

Katz, J. (1988) *Seductions of Crime: Moral and Sensual Attractions in Doing Evil*, New York: Basic Books.

Klockars, K. (1974) *The Professional Fence*, London: Tavistock.

Kulz, C. (2017) *Factories for Learning: Making Race, Class and Inequality in the Neoliberal Academy*. Manchester: Manchester University Press.

Lather, P. (2001) 'Postmodernism, post-structuralism and post (critical) ethnography: of ruins, aporias and angels', in P. Atkinson, A. Coffey, S. Delamont, J. Lofland and L. Lofland (eds), *Handbook of Ethnography*. London: Sage, pp. 477–492.

Lee-Treweek, G. and Linkogle, S. (2000) (eds) *Danger in the Field*. London: Routledge.

Letherby, G., Scott, J. and Williams, M. (2013) *Objectivity and Subjectivity in Social Research*. London: Sage.

Liazos, A. (1972) 'The poverty of the sociology of deviance: nuts, sluts, and perverts', *Social Problems*, 20 (1): 103–120.

Liebling, A. (1999) 'Doing research in prison: Breaking the silence?', *Theoretical Criminology*, 3: 147–73.

Liebling, A. (2001) 'Whose side are we on? Theory, practices and allegiances in prison research, *British Journal of Criminology*, 41: 472–484.

Lincoln, Y. S. and Guba, E. G. (1985) *Naturalistic Inquiry*. Newbury Park, CA: Sage.

Lloyd, A. (2018) *The Harms of Work: An Ultra-Realist Account of the Service Economy*. Bristol: Bristol University Press.

Loftus, B. (2012) *Police Culture in a Changing World*. Oxford: Clarendon.

Lubet, S. (2015) 'Did this acclaimed sociologist drive the getaway car in a murder plot?', *The New Republic*, 27 May. Available at https://newrepublic.com/article/121909/did-sociologist-alice-goffman-drive-getaway-car-murder-plot (accessed 17 June 2019).

Lubet, S. (2018) *Interrogating Ethnography: Why Evidence Matters*. Oxford: Oxford University Press.

Lumsden, K. (2009) '"Don't ask a woman to do another woman's job": Gendered interactions and the emotional ethnographer', *Sociology*, 43 (3): 497–513.

Lumsden, K. (2013) 'Survival of the fastest: ethical dilemmas in research with "Boy Racers"', *Youth*, 21 (3): 273–288.

Lumsden, K. and Black, A. (2018) 'Austerity policing, emotional labour and the boundaries of police work: an ethnography of a police force control room in England', *British Journal of Criminology*, 58 (3): 606–623.

Lumsden, K. and Winter, A. (eds) (2014) *Reflexivity in Criminological Research: Experiences with the Powerful and the Powerless*. Basingstoke: Palgrave Macmillan.

Lyng, S. (1990) 'Edgework: a social psychological analysis of voluntary risk taking', *American Journal of Sociology*, 95: 851–886.

Madden, R. (2010) *Being Ethnographic: A Guide to the Theory and Practice of Ethnography*. London: Sage.

Maeckelbergh, M. (2009) *The Will of the Many: How the Alter Globalisation Movement Is Changing the Face of Democracy*. London and New York: Pluto Press.

Mai, N. (2018) *Mobile Orientations: An Intimate Autoethnography of Migration, Sex Work and Humanitarian Borders*. Chicago: University of Chicago Press.

Malinowski, B. (1967) *A Diary in the Strict Sense of the Term*. Stanford: Stanford University Press.

Manning, P. (2014) 'Ethnographies of policing', in M. D. Reisig and R. J. Kane (eds), *The Oxford Handbook of Police and Policing*. Oxford: Oxford University Press, pp. 518–550.

Marcus, G. (1998) *Ethnography Through Thick and Thin*. Princeton, NJ: Princeton University Press.

Marcus, G. E. and Cushman, D. (1982) 'Ethnographies as texts', *Annual Review of Anthropology*, 11: 25–69.

Masters, A. (2005) *Stuart: A Life Backwards*. London: Harper Perennial.

McAuley, R. (2007) *Out of Sight: Crime, Youth and Exclusion in Modern Britain*. Cullompton: Willan.

McBarnet, D. (1981) *Conviction: Law, the State and the Construction of Justice*. London: Palgrave Macmillan.

McKenzie, L. (2015) *Getting By: Estates, Class and Culture in Austerity Britain*. Bristol: Policy Press.

McKinney, J. (1966) *Constructive Typology and Social Theory*. New York: Appleton-Century-Crofts.

McLeod, J. (2009) *Ain't No Makin' It: Aspirations and Attainment in a Low-Income Neighborhood*. London: Taylor and Francis.

Miller, J. (2001) *One of the Guys: Girls, Gangs, and Gender*. Oxford: Oxford University Press

Miller, J. (2008) *Getting Played: African American Girls, Urban Inequality, and Gendered Violence*. New York: New York University Press.

Mills, D. and Ratcliffe, R. (2012) 'After method? Ethnography in the knowledge economy', *Qualitative Research*, 12 (2): 147–164.

Morris, T. and Morris, P. (1963) *Pentonville: A Sociological Study of an English Prison*. London: Routledge.

Murphy, D. (1986) *Customers and Thieves: An Ethnography of Shoplifting*. Aldershot: Gower.

Naffine, N. (1997) *Feminism and Criminology*. Cambridge: Polity.

Newmahr, S. (2011) *Playing on the Edge: Sadomasochism, Risk and Intimacy*. Bloomington: Indiana University Press.

Oakley, A. (1981) 'Interviewing women,' in H. Roberts (ed.), *Doing Feminist Research*. London: Routledge, pp. 30–61.

O'Brien, K. (2009) 'Inside "Doorwork": gendering the security gaze', in R. Ryan-Flood and R. Gill (eds), *Silence and Secrecy in the Research Process: Feminist Reflections*. London: Routledge, pp. 117–132.

O'Brien, M. (2005) 'What is cultural about cultural criminology?', *The British Journal of Criminology*, 45 (5): 599–612.

Ocejo, R. E. (ed.) (2013) *Ethnography and the City: Readings on Doing Urban Fieldwork*. New York: Routledge.

O'Neill, M., Giddens, S., Breatnach, P., Bagley, C., Bourne, D. and Judge, T. (2002) 'Renewed methodologies for social research: ethno-mimesis as performative praxis', *The Sociological Review*, 50: 69–88.

O'Reilly, K. (2005) *Ethnographic Methods*. London: Routledge.

O'Reilly, K. (2009) *Key Concepts in Ethnography*. London: Sage.

Packard, J. (2008) '"I'm gonna show you what it's really like out here": the power and limitation of participatory visual methods', *Visual Studies*, 23 (1): 63–77.

Palmer, V. (1928) *Field Studies in Sociology: A Student's Manual*. Chicago: University of Chicago Press.

Parenti, C. (2004) *The Freedom: Shadows and Hallucinations in Occupied Iraq*. New York: The New Press.

Parenti, C. (2011) *Tropic of Chaos: Climate Change and the New Geography of Violence*. New York: Nation Books.

Park, R. E. (1915) 'The city: suggestions for the investigation of human behavior in the city environment', *American Journal of Sociology*, 20 (5): 577–612.

Parker, H. (1974) *A View from the Boys: A Sociology of Downtown Adolescents*. Devon: David and Charles.

Parker, T. (1963) *The Unknown Citizen*. London: Hutchinson.

Parker, T. (1969) *The Twisting Lane: Some Sex Offenders*. London: Hutchinson.

Parker, T. (1970) *The Frying Pan: A Prison and its Prisoners*. London: Hutchinson.

Parker, T. (1990) *Life After Life: Interviews with Twelve Murderers*. London: Secker and Warburg.

Parker, T. (1995) *The Violence of Our Lives: Interviews with Life-Sentence Prisoners in America*. London: HarperCollins.

Patrick, J. (1973) *A Glasgow Gang Observed*. London: Eyre Methuen.

Pastebin (2015) 'Accusations of Alice Goffman's dishonesty', 3 May. Available at https://pastebin.com/BzN4t0VU (accessed 17 June 2019).

Pearson, G. (1993) 'Foreword', in D. Hobbs and T. May (eds), *Interpreting the Field: Accounts of Ethnography*. Oxford: Oxford University Press, pp. vii–xx.

Pearson, G. (2009) 'The researcher as hooligan: where "participant" observation means breaking the law', *International Journal of Social Research Methodology*, 12 (3): 243–255.

Phillips, C. and Earle, R. (2010) 'Reading difference differently? Identity, epistemology and prison ethnography', *The British Journal of Criminology*, 50 (2): 360–378.

Pilkington, H. (2016) *Loud and Proud: Passion and Politics in the English Defence League*. Manchester: Manchester University Press.

Plows, A., Wall, D. and Doherty, B. (2004) 'Covert repertoires: Ecotage in the UK', *Social Movement Studies*, 3 (2): 199–219.

Pollard, A. (2009) 'Field of screams: difficulty and ethnographic fieldwork', *Anthropology Matters*, 11 (2).

Polletta, F. (2012) *Freedom Is an Endless Meeting: Democracy in American Social Movements*. Chicago, IL: University of Chicago Press.

Polsky, N. (1967) *Hustlers, Beats and Others*. London: Penguin.

Presdee, M. (2004) 'The Story of crime, Biography and the Excavation of Transgression', in J. Ferrell, K. Hayward, W. Morrisson and M. Presdee (eds), *Cultural Criminology Unleashed*, London: GlassHouse, pp. 41–48.

Presser, L. and Sandberg, S. (eds) (2015) *Narrative Criminology: Understanding Stories of Crime*. New York and London: New York University Press.

Pryce, K. (1979) *Endless Pressure: A Study of West Indian Life-Styles in Bristol*. London: Penguin.

Radzinowicz, L (1999) *Adventures in Criminology*. London: Routledge.

Raymen, T. (2019) *Parkour, Deviance and Leisure in the Late-Capitalist City: An Ethnography*. Bingley: Emerald.

Rhodes, R. (2000) *Why They Kill: The Discoveries of a Maverick Criminologist*. New York: Random House.

Rice, S. and Maltz, M. (eds) (2018) *Doing Ethnography in Criminology: Discovery Through Fieldwork*. Cham, Switzerland: Springer.

Rock, P. (2001) 'Symbolic interactionism and ethnography', in P. Atkinson, A. Coffey, S. Delamont, J. Lofland and L. Lofland (eds), *Handbook of Ethnography*. London: Sage, pp. 26–38.

Ronai, C. R. (1995) 'Multiple reflections of child sex abuse: an argument for a layered account', *Journal of Contemporary Ethnography*, 23 (4): 395–426.

Salinas Edwards, M. (2013) 'Men at work: an ethnography of drug markets and youth transitions at times of austerity', unpublished PhD Thesis, University of Manchester. Available at www.escholar.manchester.ac.uk/api/datastream?publicationPid=uk-ac-man-scw:220811&datastreamId=FULL-TEXT.PDF (accessed 20 March 2019).

Salinas Edwards, M. (2014) *Men at Work: An Ethnography of Drug Markets and Youth Transitions in Times of Austerity*. Manchester: Manchester University. Available online: https://www.escholar.manchester.ac.uk/uk-ac-man-scw:220811 (accessed 10 September 2019).

Sampson, H. (2014) *International Seafarers and Transnationalism in the Twenty-First Century*. Manchester: Manchester University Press.

Savin-Baden, M. and Howell Major, C. (2013) *Qualitative Research*. Routledge: London.

Scheper-Hughes, N. (2004) 'Parts unknown: undercover ethnography of the organs-trafficking underworld', *Ethnography*, 5 (1): 29–73.

Scheffer, T. (2010) *Adversarial Case-Making: An ethnography of English Crown Court Procedure*. Leiden, Boston: Brill.

Shaw, C. R. (1930) *The Jack-Roller: A Delinquent Boy's Own Story* Chicago: University of Chicago Press.

Silverman, D. (2017) *Doing Qualitative Research* (5th edn). London: Sage.

Singal, J. (2015) 'The internet accused Alice Goffman of faking details in her study of a black neighborhood. I went to Philadelphia to check', *The Cut*, 18 June. Available at www.thecut.com/2015/06/i-fact-checked-alice-goffman-with-her-subjects.html (accessed 17 June 2019).

Sloan, J. (2016) *Masculinities and the Adult Male Prison Experience*. London; Palgrave Macmillan

Smith, D. (2005) *Institutional Ethnography: A Sociology for People*. New York: Altamira Press.

Smith, O. (2014) *Contemporary Adulthood and the Night Time Economy*. London: Palgrave Macmillan.

Smith, O. and Raymen, T. (2017) 'Shopping with violence: Black Friday sales in the British context', *Journal of Consumer Culture*, 17 (3): 677–694.

Snodgrass, J. (1982) *The Jack-Roller at Seventy: A Fifty-Year Follow-Up*. Lexington MA. Lexington Books.

Snyder, G. (2011) *Graffiti Lives: Beyond the Tag in New York's Urban Underground*. New York: New York University Press.

Sollund, R. (2017) 'Doing green, critical criminology with an auto-ethnographic, feminist approach', *Critical Criminology*, 25 (2): 245–260.

Soyini Madison, D. (2012) *Critical Ethnography*. London: Sage.

Sparks, R., Bottoms, A. and Hay, W. (1996) *Prisons and the Problem of Order*. Oxford: Clarendon Press.

Spradley, J. P. (1980) *Participant Observation*. Orlando, FL: Harcourt Brace Jovanovich.

Stacey, J. (1988) 'Can there be a feminist ethnography?', *Women's Studies International Forum*, 11 (1): 21–27.

Stuart, F. (2016) *Down, Out, and Under Arrest: Policing and Everyday Life in Skid Row*. Chicago: University of Chicago Press.

Sullivan, M. L. (1989) 'Getting Paid', *Youth Crime and Work in the Inner City*. Ithica: Cornell University Press.

Sutherland, E. H. (1939) *Principles of Criminology*. New York: J. B. Lippincott Company.

Sykes, G. (1958) *The Society of Captives: A Study of a Maximum-Security Prison*. Princeton, NJ: Princeton University Press.

Tewksbury, R. (2009) 'Edge ethnography', in M. Miller (ed.), *In 21st Century Criminology: A Reference Handbook*, Thousand Oaks: Sage.

Tewksbury, R., Dabney, D.A. and Copes, H. (2010) 'The prominence of qualitative research in criminology and criminal justice scholarship', *Journal of Criminal Justice Education*, 21: 391–411.

Thompson, H. S. (1967) *Hells Angels*. London: Penguin.

Thrasher, F. (1927) *The Gang: A Study of 1,313 Gangs in Chicago*. Chicago: University of Chicago Press.

Treadwell, J. (2012) 'From the car boot to booting it up? eBay, online counterfeit crime and the transformation of the criminal marketplace', *Criminology and Criminal Justice: An International Journal*, 12 (2): 175–191.

Treadwell, J. (2013) *Criminology: The Essentials*. London: Sage.

Treadwell, J. (2018) 'Doing ultrarealist ethnography: romanticism and running with the riotous (while buying your round)', in S. Rice and M. Maltz (eds), *Doing Ethnography in Criminology: Discovery Through Fieldwork*. Cham, Switzerland: Springer, pp. 289–302.

Treadwell, J., Briggs, D., Winlow, S. and Hall, S. (2013) 'Shopocalypse now: consumer culture and the English Riots of 2011', *British Journal of Criminology*, 53 (1): 1–17.

Treadwell, J. and Garland, J. (2011) 'Masculinity, marginalisation and violence: a case study of the English Defence League', *British Journal of Criminology*, 51 (4): 621–634.

Ugelvik, T. (2014) *Power and Resistance in Prison: Doing Time, Doing Freedom*. London: Palgrave Macmillan.

Vanderstaay, S. (2005) 'One hundred dollars and a dead man: ethical decision making in ethnographic fieldwork', *Journal of Contemporary Ethnography*, 34: 371–409.

van Gemert, F. H. M. (2015) 'Life history and biographies in criminology', in H. Copes and M. Miller (eds), *Routledge Handbook of Qualitative Criminology*. Abingdon and New York: Routledge, pp. 72–87.

Van Maanen, J. (1978) 'The asshole', in P. Manning and J. Van Maanen (eds), *Policing: A View from the Streets*. New York: Random House, pp. 221–238.

Van Maanen, J. (2011) *Tales of the Field: On Writing Ethnography* (2nd edn). Chicago: Chicago University Press.

Venkatesh, S. (2009) *Gang Leader for a Day*. London: Penguin.

Wacquant, L. (2002) 'The curious eclipse of prison ethnography in the age of mass incarceration', *Ethnography*, 3 (4): 371–397.

Wakeman, S. (2018) 'Doing Criminological Autoethnography: Learning from Conversations with Ourselves', in S. Rice and M. Maltz (eds) *Doing Ethnography in Criminology: Discovery through Fieldwork,* Cham, Switzerland: Springer.

Wakeman, S. (2014) 'Fieldwork, biography and emotion: doing criminological autoethnography', *The British Journal of Criminology*, 54 (5): 705–721.

Ward, T. (2013) *Gangsters Without Borders: An Ethnography of a Salvadoran Street Gang*. Oxford: Oxford University.

Webber, C. and Yip, M. (2013) *'Drifting on and off-line: humanising the cybercriminal'*, in S. Winlow and R. Atkinson (eds), *Future Directions in Crime and Deviancy: Proceedings of the York Deviancy Conference*. Abington: Routledge, pp. 191–205.

Weisheit, R. A. (1998) 'Marijuana subcultures: studying crime in rural America', in J. Ferrell and M. Hamm (eds), *Ethnography at the Edge: Crime, Deviance and Field Research*. Boston, MA: Northeastern University Press, pp. 178–203.

Welsh, M. and Rajah V. (2014) 'Rendering invisible punishments visible: using institutional ethnography in feminist criminology', *Feminist Criminology*, 9 (4): 323–343.

Westmarland, L. (2001) 'Blowing the whistle on police violence: gender, ethnography and ethics,' *British Journal of Criminology*, 41 (3): 523–535.

Westmarland, L. (2011) *Researching Crime and Justice: Tales from the Field*. London: Routledge.

Whyte, W. (1943) *Street Corner Society*. Chicago: University of Chicago Press.

Williams, K. and Treadwell, J. (2008) 'Similarity and difference: the ethnographer, the subject, and objectivity', *Methodological Innovations Online*, 3 (1): 56–68.

Williamson, H. (2004) *The Milltown Boys Revisited*. Oxford: Berg.

Williamson, H. and Williamson, P. (1981) *Five Years*, Leicester: National Youth Bureau.

Willis, P. (1978) *Learning to Labour: How Working Class Kids Get Working Class Jobs*. Farnborough: Saxon House.

Willis, P. (2000) *The Ethnographic Imagination*. Cambridge, Polity Press.

Wilson, A. (2007) *Northern Soul: Music, Drugs and Subcultural Identity*. Cullompton: Willan.

Wilson, D. (2006) 'Some reflections on researching with young black people and the youth justice system', *Youth Justice*, 6 (3): 181–193.

Wilson, D. (2009) 'Testing a civilisation: Charles Dickens on the American penitentiary system', *The Howard Journal of Criminal Justice*, 48 (3): 280–296.

Wincup, E. (2017) *Criminological Research: Understanding Qualitative Methods*. London: Sage.

Winlow, S. (2001) *Badfellas: Crime Traditions and New Masculinities*. Oxford: Berg.

Winlow, S. (2014) 'Trauma, guilt and the unconscious: some theoretical notes on violent subjectivity', *Sociological Review*, 62 (1): 32–49.

Winlow, S. and Hall, S. (2012) 'What is an 'Ethics Committee'? Academic governance in an epoch of belief and incredulity', *The British Journal of Criminology*, 52 (2): 400–416.

Winlow, S., Hall, S. and Treadwell, J. (2017) *Rise of the Right: English Nationalism and the Transformation of Working-Class Politics*. Bristol: Policy Press.

Winlow, S., Hall, S., Treadwell, J. and Briggs, D. (2015) *Riots and Political Protest: Notes from the Post-Political Present*. London: Routledge.

Winlow, S., Hobbs, D., Lister, S. and Hadfield, P. (2001) 'Get ready to duck: bouncers and the realities of ethnographic research on violent groups', *British Journal of Criminology*, 41 (3): 536–548.

Wolcott, H. (1999) *Ethnography: A Way of Seeing*. London: AltaMira Press.

Wolf, D. (1991) *The Rebels: A Brotherhood of Outlaw Bikers*. Toronto: University of Toronto Press.

Xu, J., Laidler, K. J. and Lee, M. (2013) 'Doing criminological ethnography in China: opportunities and challenges', *Theoretical Criminology*, 17 (2): 271–279.

Yates, J. (2004) 'Criminological ethnography: risks, dilemmas and their negotiation', *British Journal of Community Justice*, 3: 19–33.

Young, J. (1971) The Drugtakers: *The Social Meaning of Drug Use*. London: McGibbon and Kee.

Young, J. (2003) 'In praise of dangerous thoughts', *Punishment & Society*, 5 (1): 97–107.

Young, J. (2011) *The Criminological Imagination*. Cambridge: Polity Press.

Yuen Thompson, B. (2015) *Covered in Ink: Tattoos, Women and the Politics of the Body*. New York: New York University Press.

INDEX